United and Divided

United and Divided

Germany since 1990

Edited by
Mike Dennis and Eva Kolinsky

Berghahn Books
New York • Oxford

First published in 2004 by

Berghahn Books

www.berghahnbooks.com

© 2004 Mike Dennis and Eva Kolinsky

Library of Congress Cataloging-in-Publication Data

United and divided: Germany since 1990 / edited by Mike Dennis
    and Eva Kolinsky.
    p. cm.
    ISBN 1-57181-513-9 (alk. paper)
    1. Germany (East)--History--Historiography. 2. Germany (East)--Social conditions.
    3. Political culture--Germany (East). 4. Germany--Politics and government--1990.
    I. Dennis, Mike, 1940- II. Kolinsky, Eva.

DD289.5.U55 2003
943'.10879--dc22   2003057830

British Library Cataloguing in Publication Data

A catalogue record for this book is available from the British Library.

Printed in the United States on acid-free paper

ISBN 1–57181–513-9 (hardback)

Contents

List of Figures

List of Tables

List of Contributors

Peter Barker is Lecturer in German Studies at the University of Reading

Mike Dennis is Professor of German History at the University of Wolverhampton

Christopher Flockton is Professor of European Economic Studies at the University of Surrey

Anthony Glees is Professor in Government at Brunel University

Eva Kolinsky is Professorial Research Fellow in German History at the University of Wolverhampton, and Emeritus Professor of German at Keele University

Marianne Kriszio teaches Sociology at the Humboldt University, Berlin, where she is also *Frauenbeauftragte* (Equal Opportunities Officer)

Rosalind Pritchard is Professor of Education at the University of Ulster in Coleraine

Karin Weiss is Professor of Applied Social Studies at the *Fachhochschule* Potsdam.

United and Divided: Germany since 1990. An Introduction

Mike Dennis and Eva Kolinsky

Unification after Division

The German Democratic Republic (GDR) existed as a separate state between 17 October 1949 and 3 October 1990 when it opted to join the Federal Republic of Germany (FRG) and subscribe to its constitutional order, the Basic Law. The formal act of unification put an end to a postwar history of political division that commenced in 1945 with the occupation of Germany by the victorious Allies after the Second World War. Since then, the Cold War and its competition for political control and military dominance between East and West, placed Germany at the hub of these rivalries, not as a major actor but as a testing ground and showcase. The creation of the two German states in 1949 – the FRG in May, the GDR five months later – was closely linked to the policy aims of the rival blocs and their determination to document their strength inside Germany. The West German and the East German states, therefore, became outposts for conflicting systems, each of them aiming at reinventing its part of Germany in its own way. Although Cold War rivalries had largely subsided at the time of German unification, the political, economic and social divides between the two Germanies were slower to fade, or refused to do so altogether.

In reinventing their part of occupied Germany, each of the Western Allies initially sought to recast the political order in their respective zone of influence in accordance with the democratic processes and institutions of their own country. As zones were merged from 1947 onwards, national differences were superseded by a concept of democracy which owed more to the Weimar Republic and the experiences gained there by the German political leaders of the first hour than to American, British or French assumptions as to how democracy should operate. As the Basic Law took shape, it defined the Federal Republic of Germany as a democratic polity and society, stipulating institutional parameters that proved, over time, successful in facilitating the emergence of a stable parliamentary government and a democratic political culture

(Almond and Verba, 1963; Smith, 1986). In the mid-1950s, this remade Germany 'rejoined the powers' as a sovereign state and established itself as a leading political force at a European and international level (Conradt, 1980; Edinger, 1986).

Inside Western Germany, the spectre of a National Socialist revival disappeared in the wake of rapid economic reconstruction, unprecedented growth rates and an increase in living standards across all social strata (Dahrendorf, 1965). Initially, Germany's new democracy may have been a fair-weather product based on economic performance and policy output rather than a liking for party pluralism, parliamentary decision-making and other hallmarks of democracy. In time, however, material output ceased to be a precondition for democratic orientations as Germans stopped asking whether they needed more than one political party, took party pluralism for granted and began to ask more searchingly about how each party served the citizens and their personal interests (Röhrig, 1983; Kolinsky, 1991). West Germany's affluent society offered multiple opportunities of education, training, advancement and social mobility that exceeded those enjoyed by previous generations. While this remade society entailed risks, such as unemployment, income poverty or experiences of social exclusion, it also held the promise, and even the chance, of realising personal life goals and reaping the rewards for individual efforts and achievements (Hradil, 1993; Beck, 1986).

In the Soviet zone, recasting occupied Germany took a different turn. While the Soviet Union was interested in extending its sphere of influence by adding a buffer state modelled on its own political and economic order, it was concerned, above all, to recoup some of the losses incurred during the Second World War by extracting reparations from the German territory under its control and by securing long-term trading advantages (Naimark, 1995). On the one hand, the Soviet Union directed German Communists, who had fled there from Nazi Germany and had been groomed as a future elite, to implement a socialist order and a centrally planned economic system in Eastern Germany, on the other hand it syphoned resources from the country and impeded postwar recovery. The project of reinventing Eastern Germany was, in any case, much more ambitious than that in the West, and involved the abolition of private enterprises, the collectivisation of agriculture, the creation from scratch of steel production in the region, and the mining and exploitation of lignite on a massive scale to meet energy needs. A system of state control and central planning was to determine all aspects of economic and social life (Schröder 1998). In the 1950s, state policy was aimed at excluding the former middle classes from leading positions and at giving an advantage to the working class in education, employment and political or economic leadership. Ten years on, the new elite contrived to retain their positions and secure similar privileges for their descendants (Dennis, 2000a). Increasingly, conformity with state ideology mattered in gaining access to education, advancement and social status (Geissler, 1996). Despite its self-proclaimed status as a Workers' and Peasants'

State, functionaries and officials operated the system that had developed in the GDR and also benefited from it.

East Looking West

At the heart of the GDR's collapse was a sense of injustice felt by its citizens that their own state had failed to offer them adequate rewards for their commitment and hard work (Jarausch, 1994). The urgency of this sense of injustice is borne out by the fact that migration from the GDR to the FRG could not be halted despite closed and guarded borders, and despite the construction of the Berlin Wall in 1961 to plug the loophole of those fleeing to the West by travelling from one side of Berlin to the other. While its borders were sealed or virtually sealed, the GDR lost some four million inhabitants who fled to the West (Zwahr, 1994: 438–447). After the Berlin Wall was declared open on 9 November 1989, about 300,000 left within a year, while a further 500,000 have moved from the former GDR to the former West since unification.

Several experiences contributed to a sense of injustice among East Germans. One such experience relates to the proximity of the Federal Republic. While the GDR leadership applied its most ardent rhetoric to rubbish the Western state and vilify it as a hotbed of National Socialist and reactionary politics, East Germans noted the rise in living standards and income, the freedom of West Germans to travel, and envied them their liberty and, even more fervently, their affluence. Of course, the GDR made progress and achieved successes in rebuilding the economy and in guaranteeing life without poverty for most. However, persistent shortages and a political pricing policy, which rendered consumer goods, such as television sets and cars, extremely expensive relative to family incomes, made East Germans resentful of their deprivation and of a government unable or unwilling to improve matters. Once Western television programmes could be viewed in the GDR, East Germans constructed their image of the West on the basis of advertisements, and developed a keen sense of quality brands and modern lifestyles, accessible in the GDR only in special outlets called 'intershop' and with payment in foreign currency, which most East Germans, of course, did not possess (Faulenbach *et. al.*, 2000). Blue collar workers in particular, whose status and rewards fell far short of those proclaimed in state ideology, lost confidence in the socialist project and grew increasingly detached from its aims and disillusioned with its functionaries (Vester *et. al.*, 1995). When East Germans took to the streets in 1989 with the chant 'we are the people', to admonish the government for having become too detached from ordinary citizens, the critical intent changed as soon as the students and intellectuals of the first demonstrations were outnumbered by blue collar workers and rank-and-file East Germans. To voice their sense of injustice, they coined the slogan that was to dislodge the regime: 'we are one people'.

East Joins West

Unification was intended to remove the differences that had accumulated over forty years between Eastern and Western Germany. Decisive in achieving this new equilibrium was the resolve to extend to the former GDR the institutional planks that had generated stability and prosperity in the West and had made the FRG into the more successful of the two Germanies (Grosser, 1998). The first of these planks consisted of the social market economy, its commitment to capitalism and free enterprise, and its use of a convertible currency as a measure of economic strength and an entry point to world markets. Prior to unification, therefore, economic and currency union introduced the Deutschmark to the GDR and placed its economy on a market footing, even before the formal process had started. This entailed abolishing state control, dismantling the fifteen vast cartel-like *Kombinate* (combines) that dominated all industrial sectors, and creating in Eastern Germany an economic structure based on private ownership. The second of these planks, intended to guarantee a successful transformation to the Western German model, consisted of extending the scope of the Basic Law to apply in Eastern Germany. This was accomplished by reconstituting five *Länder* in the GDR in place of the fifteen administrative districts (*Bezirke*) that had operated there since 1952, and by activating clause 23, whereby any East German *Land* was entitled to adopt the Basic Law and effectively become part of the Federal Republic. The Basic Law had been drafted in the 1940s when *Länder* existed in Eastern Germany, while the chance of unification arose after their abolition. For this reason, recreating *Länder* was a requirement if unification was to take place without formulating a new, tailor-made constitution for the united country. Given the perceived strength and success of the Basic Law, its ascribed status as the backbone of democratic stability, and also a reluctance of West German political decision makers to give East Germans an equal voice in shaping post-unification developments, unification followed the administrative route of transferring Western institutions, structures, intentions and policies to the East in order to adapt it, instead of initiating a process of mutual adjustment.

Some East Germans, notably intellectuals and stalwart supporters of the discredited Socialist Unity Party, SED, condemned the one-directional process of unification as a take-over and as humiliating and destructive in its effects as colonialism had been in Third World countries (Jarausch and Gransow, 1994). Most East Germans, however, were too distrustful of their own leaders, politicians or institutions to doubt that anything Western would be better than the quagmire of inefficiency and double-speak it was to replace. Above all, they were persuaded by the promise that the material gap to the West would be closed. After the opening of the Berlin Wall, consumer goods began to fill East German shops, and after the currency union in July 1990, the consumer society appeared to have arrived for good (Segert and Zierke, 1997). East Germans, who had been waiting to purchase a car for ten years or so and had only been able to keep their place on the waiting list if they complied with the ideological norms laid down by the ruling party and interpreted by local functionaries, could now enter a showroom and acquire the car of their choice. The same liberating experience applied to television sets, automatic washing machines, furniture and all the other items defined as luxury goods by the GDR government and priced out of reach for most East Germans. Longer standing injustices also seemed set to disappear. In the mid-1950s, wages in both parts of Germany had been at about the same level. In 1990, average earnings in Western Germany were about three times higher than in the East (Winkler, 1990). Unification promised to close the gap and raise earned incomes of East Germans to 'normal' German levels. Moreover, in Western Germany, the working week had been reduced to thirty-five hours without loss of income. In the GDR, it had remained above forty-three hours, a discrepancy exacerbated in a comparative perspective by the lower income levels. At the macro level, unification seemed to pave the way for private and public investment to flow into the region and invigorate what East Germans continued to perceive as a sound economy. Their personal sense of disadvantage compared to Western conditions did not lead to the conclusion that the East German economy had failed and could not be sustained. Although East Germans were widely aware of constant shortages of raw materials and the disruption they caused to all processes of production, distribution and administration, official figures had always projected a positive picture to the country and to the world at large. Moreover, planning procedures tended to obfuscate weaknesses rather than illuminate or remedy them. Only a small inner circle of top functionaries, possibly confined to the *Politburo*, knew that the GDR was virtually bankrupt before its leadership succumbed to the popular pressures for change, helped by the refusal of the Soviet Union, under Michael Gorbachev, to keep the GDR afloat by providing military backing.

Expectations after Unification

Unification, therefore, occurred in a unique and problem-laden setting of expectations and assumptions. East Germans anticipated that material conditions would improve rapidly to match Western German levels. They also believed that their home-grown economy could flourish with new investment and could close the modernisation gap with the West (Dennis, 1993). Joining forces with the West would underpin the productive strength of the region and complement the expected rise in living standards after unification. At no point did East Germans regard their economy and its enterprises beyond salvation or connect restructuring with plant closures, unemployment and extensive de-industrialisation.

Expectations about the kind of changes that would impact on everyday lives after unification incorporated assumptions about the permanency of GDR institutions and practices. They also included pockets of personal dissatisfaction and models of Western living (Kolinsky, 1995). The East German vision of life after the GDR did not include the risks and uncertainties at the heart of the competitive and individualised culture of the West. When such risks and uncertainties penetrated their personal space, East Germans were disorientated and frequently responded by glorifying the GDR in retrospect as a more secure and humane living environment (Schmitt and Montada, 1999). For example, unemployment as a structural risk of a market economy had been virtually ignored in the run-up to unification. In their attempt to gain favour with an East German public impatient to partake in the successes of the West, most media and political parties painted a vibrant picture of future gains. Chancellor Kohl promised 'blooming landscapes' for Eastern Germany.

At the time, many leaders believed that the economic miracle of the postwar years could be replicated and even improved upon after unification; some surmised that the concerted effort of rebuilding and upgrading the East would soon make it the most modern, most advanced and most successful region in Germany, turning the old FRG into a backwater by comparison (Dennis, 2000a). Of the established political forces, only the Social Democratic Party remained sceptical and warned, in its policy statements and its election campaigns of 1990, that the cost of unification might threaten Western German prosperity, and that the East was destined for a massive economic decline and a rise in unemployment. Few voters in East Germany believed these warnings (Padgett and Poguntke, 2001). Even the Party of Democratic Socialism, PDS, which had replaced the Socialist Unity Party in the GDR when one-party government finally collapsed in December 1989, could not turn its disdain for unification into electoral gains beyond a hard-core of staunch SED supporters determined to warn of impending disasters. Since the East German public had learned to dismiss proclamations by their ruling party as untruthful, they were unwilling to listen to its successor, not least since the public mood in 1990 had swung emotively and fervently against a continuation of the GDR and in favour of unification as a new beginning.

New Divisions and Opportunities

The unexpected outcomes of unification have been too numerous to list here (see Reissig, 1993). After all, a whole system was replaced, its economic structure, its political organisation and processes, its social fabrics and patterns of opportunities remodelled, abolished, reinvented. At its core, unification was lopsided, intended to change the East while the West would emerge unaltered and even confirmed as superior in all aspects of its political, economic and social system. These parameters of system transfer ignored the fact that most East Germans had never questioned the key institutions of the GDR and liked many (although not all) manifestations of state policy in their lives. Thus, stable employment biographies were taken for granted in Eastern Germany when West Germans had already learned to live with unemployment and endure periods of income poverty and social exclusion (Kolinsky, 1998a). Employment for women and the provision of state-funded child care were taken for granted in Eastern Germany, but not in the West. A flat wage structure with modest differences between income groups in Eastern Germany was taken to signify equal treatment of all working people; the wage differentiation after unification, based on educational and professional qualifications, occupational groups and levels of seniority, created winners and losers and defined new risks of income poverty (Hanesch *et al.*, 1994).

These risks were exacerbated by the unexpected fundamental significance of money (Starke, 1995). In the GDR, the cost of housing, energy, essential foodstuffs and child rearing, for instance, had been heavily subsidised. After unification, market principles applied while state support was phased out, leaving east German families and individuals to face newly significant costs and unfamiliar demands on household budgets. The increase of rental charges in particular created a new dependency on state benefit and heightened risks of homelessness (Flockton, 1999). At the same time, the dismemberment of the socialist order reversed decades of social demotion. House owners, whose property had been taken into state administration or was left to decay for lack of building materials and access to repair work, found themselves reinstated as landlords or owner-occupiers, able to improve, dispose of and profit from their inherited assets in a manner that had been impossible in the GDR. Of course, owners from outside eastern Germany could also reclaim their rights and were resented for doing so. Among east Germans, however, home ownership through inheritance became more meaningful than it had been for decades, while high earners utilised their new purchasing power to acquire property and, above all, buy their own homes (Kolinsky, 1998b: 107). Moreover, a significant number of fledgling entrepreneurs used their own premises to open a business. While the location of such business premises was not always suitable for attracting customers and building success, property ownership opened opportunities for income generation and constituted a potential entry route to an emerging middle class.

East Still Looking West

The state-administered levelling of GDR society fractured when unification unleashed the multiple forces of social mobility, income differentiation, class difference, personal opportunity and unexpected exclusion that had characterised western German society for decades. The recasting of eastern Germany left no marks in the west beyond a policy commitment to curtail social dislocation and stifle discontent by transferring substantial funds into the region to provide a borrowed affluence and sustain social peace. In responding to their altered environment, east Germans engaged with the new opportunities but in doing so relied on values, orientations and assumptions that were familiar to them from the GDR era. This blend of GDR-legacies with the system parameters and social conventions that had been extended to the east from the west had not been expected by the architects of unification. They had been confident that abolishing the GDR would free east Germans to emulate west German models of organisation and behaviour. They had not expected to find east Germans more firmly conditioned by their history and past and had not anticipated that the transformation unleashed by unification would be experienced negatively as uncertainty and serve to reconstruct a positive image of the GDR as a stable, caring and secure setting. At the time of unification, only a handful of east Germans found anything to recommend the GDR. More than a decade on, few wish to reinstate it, but a majority claim that the wholesale abolition of its institutions and practices had been rash, and to the detriment of ordinary people (Dennis, 2000b). Even the young generation, who grew up in eastern Germany after unification, believe that unification exacerbated inequalities and would have yielded better results if more had been preserved of the GDR and its defined pathways through life.

In evaluating their own circumstances and socio-economic prospects, east Germans tend to look back to the GDR and sideways to the old FRG. Conclusions rely to some extent on perceived advantages and disadvantages, on personal memories or second-hand images, notably of life in western Germany. Increasingly, however, conclusions can draw on information in the public domain and define their own evidence. While public authorities in the GDR had controlled virtually all information flows and muzzled the media in an attempt to institutionalise consensus and suppress critical comment, unification ended these restrictions. Of course, East Germans had learned to read between the lines and detect the spin, but the policy of non-information or mis-information left them short of hard facts, data and reliable insights into their own situation and that of others. Unification changed all this. Now, the media, politicians, political parties, members of the elite or celebrities were free to report, comment and voice opinions, leaving east Germans, for the first time since the early 1930s, free to assemble information from a variety of sources with different slants, and to make up their own mind.

The outcome has been a dual perspective on post-unification developments. At the personal level of material circumstances, income change and long-term prospects, a majority of east Germans hold that matters have improved for them. At the collective level, negative conclusions prevail. Thus, most east Germans think that they are treated as second class citizens in unified Germany and that their region remains disadvantaged (Reissig, 2000; Schmitt and Montada, 1999). These perceptions are borne out, for example, by the federal government's report on poverty and wealth, the first of its kind in post-war German history. Published in April 2001, the report showed that in 1998, west German households remained, on average, three times as wealthy as households in the east. Here, the division of Germany casts a shadow, since West Germans had been able to accumulate wealth in addition to earned income while East Germans had not. The east/west gap was at its widest among the over sixty-fives for whom unification offered few chances, since it occurred near the end of their working lives or limited their earnings potential through early retirement or unemployment. Best placed, by comparison, were east Germans under the age of thirty-five whose assets amounted to 52 per cent of their west German peers and who were able to benefit from the new opportunities in a market environment. The wealth gap between west and east remains considerable (Preller, 2001: 5). The same survey showed that in the late 1990s, the richest 10 per cent in western Germany controlled, on average, assets worth 1.1 million Deutschmark, the richest 10 per cent in eastern Germany just 422,000. At the bottom end of the spectrum, a similar discrepancy prevailed: the poorest half of the population owned assets worth 22,000 Deutschmark in the west and just 8,000 Deutschmark in the east (ibid.: 6).

Discrepancies of this kind are no longer camouflaged by socialist state ideology nor hidden from public view. Although wage adjustments have narrowed the east/west gap to 25 per cent and public policy is committed to its disappearance, east Germans understand the difference between reliance on earned income and wages on the one hand, and on the other the accumulation of wealth in the shape of property, investments or savings. In basing their sense of injustice on these discrepancies, they do not point the finger at the GDR and the after-effects of curtailing private ownership and imposing state administration. Their comparative perspective is confined to the period between German unification and the present time because they expect the state to intervene with special measures in order to remove the perceived material disadvantages. Meeting these expectations of equality with the west is all the more difficult since many east Germans continue to view the GDR as a polity and society that had been committed to the equality of its citizens, and was successful in instituting it (Kolinsky, 2002). While previously unpublished information has shown that discrimination and unequal treatment had been practised in the GDR, few east Germans adjusted their GDR-image to reflect its shortcomings.

Regardless of the changed parameters since unification, east Germans do what they have always done: look west to compare lifestyles, and define their expectations of the future. For those who remain in eastern Germany, the comparative focus on the west translates into a sense of being disadvantaged, treated unjustly and shortchanged by unification. This distrust of transformation and its effects in eastern Germany continues to persuade significant numbers to leave for the west. The migratory pressures that had prevailed in, and finally dislodged, the GDR continue to manifest themselves more than a decade after its demise.

United and Divided: Eastern Germany since 1990

In applying the west German model to recast the east, unification initiated a transfer of institutions, structures, policies and personnel that closed the west-east divide that had opened in the post-war era, but it did so in a one-sided way. It confirmed the processes and practices that had emerged in the west as a blueprint for successful development in the east. In so doing, unification obfuscated shortcomings pertaining to the west and approached eastern Germany as if it contained nothing but shortcomings. Unification could have been an opportunity to embrace reform by transferring policies and structures only after faults, that had been evident before 1990 in western Germany, had been ironed out. Instead, unification served as a protective shield against pressures for change and allowed west German policy makers to upgrade to the status of a model in terms of whatever happened to be current practice. Flaws that had inspired political debate and a search for improvements in West Germany when the division was still in force, were condoned and implemented in the East in the course of system transfer.

The one-directional thrust of unification created its own imbalances. The architects of unification were right to expect that system transfer would aid stability and curtail many of the uncertainties that plagued other post-communist countries in their bid for a new beginning. They were too confident in assuming, however, that the east would replicate the west once the system was in place. Rather than replicating the west, the east produced its own divided history after unification. This divided history is the theme of this book.

In the opening chapter, Mike Dennis reviews the writing of GDR history since unification. Generally speaking, research on the GDR has been buoyed by access to new archival materials, the availability of personal testimony by former functionaries as well as by standard-bearers of opposition, and has been freed from the ideological pressures of matching historical interpretation to political assumptions about the nature of East Germany which were present in the era of division. Dennis argues that the GDR was a paradigm of a modern dictatorship in its practice of political control and its agendas of economic and social modernisation. Some studies have highlighted the multiple injustices perpetrated by the state, its Ministry of State Security (Stasi) or major leaders and minor functionaries against ordinary citizens, dissidents and others deemed to violate the prescribed consensus with state policy. Yet, the GDR was more complex than the notion of an unjust state, an *Unrechtsstaat*, suggests. Former members of the elite have not only tried to use autobiographical accounts to document their hidden motivations and personal sensitivities. More important has been a new emphasis for historical research on everyday history and assumptions of normality in the GDR. These accounts have unearthed a wealth of detail on the lifestyles, expectations and values of East Germans before unification and their lasting impact as east/west differences since then.

The main body of the book explores some of the changes triggered by unification inside eastern Germany and evaluates their impact on the proximity or distance between west and east. In chapter two, Chris Flockton reviews the massive financial support provided by west Germany to the east as soon as unification got under way. The story he tells is one of ambitious intent to achieve system innovation by means of monetary transfers, and also one of repeated shortfalls, revisions, and new initiatives. Transforming the east has been much more complex and demanding of additional resources, requiring west Germans to make much larger contributions via taxation and special aid programmes than anyone had anticipated. In the second decade after unification, confidence is wearing thin that funding can close the east/west gap and inject the same momentum and formula of success into the east German economy that had lifted its west German counterpart from post-war gloom to post-war miracle.

On the face of it, political transformation to the west German model should have been more straight forward. The transfer of electoral and party legislation replicated the framework for political participation, while the west German parties themselves sought east German partners and extended their organisations, machinery and policies to apply in the new *Länder*. A hidden assumption underlying this aspect of system transfer was that the Socialist Unity Party (SED) had been so discredited that its successor, the Party of Democratic Socialism (PDS), stood no chance of revival. Peter Barker shows in chapter three that after a slow start, the PDS gained ground from the mid-1990s onwards inside east Germany as a potential coalition partner, and at a national level as the trusted voice of east Germany in the parliamentary and political arena. While the political system has been united, the German party landscape has displayed new diversity and divides.

From a system perspective, the GDR and the FRG occupied opposite poles of the political spectrum. The state socialist order in the East may have linked its organisation as a dictatorship with extensive welfare provisions and an agenda of modernisation, but it had no place for personal liberties, social or political diversity and unconditional human rights. In this perspective, the better Germany was situated in the West. Yet, as Anthony Glees argues in chapter four, the Federal Republic did not live up to its constitutional promise of equal rights and political accountability but allowed infringements to be perpetrated that undermined its credibility and credentials. Glees interprets the financial scandal surrounding Helmut Kohl, the former German Chancellor, as a violation of democratic principles, perpetrated at the very heart of democracy and contrasts this case with the human rights violations perpetrated on behalf of the state by the Stasi in the GDR era. The chapter challenges the complacent view that democracy has been well served by the west German model without minimising the scale of injustices it replaced in the east.

Economic renewal of the east also revealed the absence of a transferrable model. Of course, the dismemberment of state enterprises and a massive programme of privatisation were prerequisites of implementing social market principles. As Chris Flockton shows in chapter five, eastern renewal was designed with small and medium-sized businesses at its centre, a formula that had stood West Germany in good stead in the post-war era and placed regions such as Bavaria and Baden-Württemberg in pole position with regard to economic success. In eastern Germany, however, small and medium-sized business proved unstable, inadequately financed and badly served by product development with limited export potential and without an innovative edge. Moreover, a plethora of new funding programmes at regional, national and European levels have failed to promote growth and successful performance in the sector. Developments since 1990 have disproved the assumption that the eastern German economy could best be rebuilt from below. Here, as in the political arena, the west German model lacked the strength ascribed to it and failed to produce the expected results.

As a trajectory of social mobility and enhanced opportunities, education occupies a central position in modern society. In chapter six, Rosalind Pritchard compares the higher education cultures in the GDR and the FRG and evaluates the advantages and disadvantages of system transfer. The GDR had utilised higher education to institutionalise political consensus and produce skilled personnel who were loyal to the state and able to fill positions in the professions, the economy, the political apparatus, the arts and sports. Their number, focus and seniority were pre-determined and their holders had to perform to the satisfaction of the state authorities and their functionaries. While access was restricted, well structured courses, small seminar groups, extensive tutorial and social support, and a strong vocational orientation shortened study times and optimised students' chances of obtaining a degree. The West German system of higher education, by contrast, had already been plagued by exorbitant study times and legacies of Humboldt's educational philosophy that were ill-suited to the demands of a modern economy, while overcrowding and fuzzy objectives that oscillated between research training and vocational purposes resulted in high drop-out rates and irrelevant qualifications. Despite the transfer of a flawed system to the east, students there have retained a vocational focus and a determination to shorten study times, reminiscent of the GDR era.

Drawing on her first-hand knowledge of east German universities, Marianne Kriszio, who has been Equal Opportunities Officer at the Humboldt University in (east) Berlin since 1993, examines in chapter seven how the imposition of west German staffing levels and appointment criteria affected women. At each institution of higher education, individuals had their track record, the quality of their research and their suitability for appointment evaluated by a special committee. Since the criteria applied had been derived from west German practices, many east Germans were judged wanting. Academic staff in the humanities and those of middle rank were particularly at risk of losing their employment. Even those who were judged to meet the new quality standards might still have lost their tenure. Women were strongly represented in both categories. By 1993, it appeared as if east Germans generally, and women in particular, would be squeezed out of higher education in the region. As the cleansing of the first hour gave way to new developments and as young east Germans intensified their participation rate and qualified for academic appointment by gaining higher degrees, these fears proved unfounded. As with the educational system generally, the transfer of staffing policy imported flawed practices with limited opportunities for women. The decade after unification, however, saw gradual improvements in women's academic opportunities in the west, and a consolidation of appointment practices in the east. At the top level of professor, women were better represented in east Germany than in the west, and also more visible than they had been in the GDR. At the lower level of academic assistant, special programmes to support women's appointments helped to redress the gender imbalance that had opened up after 1990, while the freedom of research, teaching and decision-making resulted in the creation of several centres for Women's Studies, new undergraduate programmes and a new network of Equal Opportunities Officers to address and help to remedy disadvantages based on gender.

In chapter eight, Eva Kolinsky traces one of the most unexpected consequences of unification: the onset of migration in a region that had kept its borders closed for more than forty years in both directions. East Germans were forbidden to leave, while the entry and residency of others, notably labour migrants, refugees and asylum seekers was strictly controlled by the state or banned altogether. How can a society where migration had not been embedded reinvent itself to accommodate, as east Germany was required to do after unification, a certain proportion of asylum seekers in accordance with population figures, and how did it interpret the civil rights of these newcomers and process their applications to settle? The chapter argues that the GDR's treatment of foreign workers (*Vertragsarbeiter*) and other migrants was designed to prevent residency and ensure segregation. It amounted to institutionalised exclusion. From 1990 onwards, Foreigners' Commissioners began to operate at local and regional levels. Initially set up to co-ordinate the departure of unwanted migrants, they soon emerged as key agencies of support and advice to would-be residents, although hostilities and negative views about cultural differences continue to exist among officials who deal with non-Germans and among east Germans who tend to eye migrants with suspicion and appear to have replaced the institutionalised exclusion of the GDR era with personal expressions of dislike.

In the concluding chapter, Karin Weiss surveys a transformation that affected both west and east, albeit it not to the same extent: the migration and settlement of Jewish refugees from the former Soviet Union. Originally agreed by the last GDR *Volkskammer* in 1990, and limited to a maximum of 2,000 individuals, German legislation was amended in 1991 and removed the numerical restrictions. A decade later, Jewish migration into Germany had reached nearly

100,000. While the German government celebrated the restoration of Jewish communities and Jewish life after the devastation inflicted by the Holocaust, the scope of Jewish migration and its composition posed major problems for the communities charged with integrating newcomers. In west Germany, existing communities more than doubled in size, often leaving Russian Jews in a majority. In east Germany, where the number of Jewish community members had dwindled to below 500 by 1990, the influx and the policy of dispersion across the region meant that new Russian-only communities were founded in Potsdam, Schwerin and elsewhere. What, at first glance, might appear as revitalisation and enrichment amounted in reality to massive financial burdens on existing communities and divisive cultural pressures. Most of the newcomers are without earned income, unable to secure employment and look to community organisations for support. These, in turn, cannot collect membership dues from these impoverished newcomers. Yet, they are challenged to provide social care and avenues of cultural integration. Few Russian Jews have any knowledge of the German language, and continue to communicate in Russian, even years after their arrival; few have any knowledge of Jewish religious or cultural traditions since these were criminalised in the Soviet Union. Moreover, many of the newcomers are non-Jewish family members, or do not have a Jewish mother and are, therefore, not deemed to be Jewish by the religious authorities and the community leadership. In eastern Germany at least, the 4,000 or so Jewish newcomers are too few in number to restore Jewish life as a visible and vibrant social or cultural force.

Outlook

Unification in 1990 united East and West Germany. It confined to history the existence on German soil of two separate states with their own governments, flags, anthems, borders and other symbols of nationhood. As shown in this volume, unification celebrated the western model and denigrated what had developed in the east. It institutionalised an east/west imbalance. Of course, when socialist control collapsed in the GDR in 1989, a majority of East Germans had already lost confidence in their system and wanted it abolished. In the west, by contrast, the disintegration of the GDR buoyed the belief that the FRG had been the better Germany all along.

Uniting Germany always meant doing so along West German lines. Underpinning this approach were assumptions about common German priorities and values that had survived the GDR unaltered, and would result (again) in shared orientations and attitudes after its abolition. Unexpectedly, east Germans were willing enough to discard their discredited system but clung to different interpretations of their own past and how it compared with the present. Conditioned more substantially by GDR policies and practices than anyone had thought possible, east Germans have responded differently to the system and its mixture of gains and losses. Far from bringing the east in line with the west, unification encouraged the east to articulate its sense of difference, and added a new diversity to the meaning of Germany. Rooted in a sense of past and present injustice perpetrated in the east and imposed on its allegedly luckless residents, eastern distinctiveness has tended to doubt the ubiquitous supremacy of the democratic model and looked to the GDR as a corrective. Unification relocated east/west division from the state level of borders, governments and national symbols to the societal level of living conditions and expectations. After the first flush of system change, eastern needs and misgivings about the validity of the western model proliferate.

Bibliography

Almond, Gabriel A. and Verba, Sydney (eds.) (1963) *The Civic Culture.* (Boston: Little, Brown & Co)

Beck, Ulrich (1986) *Risikogesellschaft. Auf dem Weg in eine andere Moderne.* (Frankfurt/Main: Suhrkamp)

Conradt, David P. (1980) 'Changing Political Culture in Germany' in Almond, Gabriel A. and Verba, Sydney (eds.), *The Civic Culture Revisited.* (Boston: Little, Brown & Co), pp. 212–272

Dennis, Mike (1993) *Economic and Social Modernization in Eastern Germany from Honecker to Kohl.* (Basingstoke: Macmillan)

Dennis, Mike (2000a) *The Rise and Fall of the German Democratic Republic 1945–1990.* (London: Longman)

Dennis, Mike (2000b) 'Perceptions of GDR Society and its Transformation: East German Identity Ten Years after Unity' in Flockton, Chris, Kolinsky, Eva and Pritchard, Rosalind (eds.), *The New Germany in the East. Policy Agendas and Social Developments since Unification.* (London: Cass), pp. 87–105

Edinger, Lewis (1986) *Germany.* (Boston: Little, Brown & Co), 2nd revised edition

Faulenbach, Bernd, Leo, Annette and Weberskrich, Klaus (2000) *Zweierlei Geschichte. Lebensgeschichte und Geschichtsbewusstsein von Arbeitnehmern in West- und Ostdeutschland.* (Essen: Klartext)

Flockton, Chris (1999) 'Housing Situation and Housing Policy in East Germany' in Flockton, Chris and Kolinsky, Eva (eds.), *Recasting East Germany. Social Transformation after the GDR.* (London: Cass), pp. 69–82

Geissler, Rainer (1996) *Die Sozialstruktur Deutschlands.* (Opladen: Westdeutscher Verlag), 2nd edition

Grosser, Dieter (1998) *Das Wagnis der Währungs-, Wirtschafts- und Sozialunion. Politische Zwänge im Konflikt mit ökonomischen Regeln.* (Stuttgart: Deutsche Verlagsanstalt)

Hanesch, Walter *et al.* (1994) *Armut in Deutschland.* (Reinbek: Rowohlt)

Hradil, Stefan (1993) *Sozialstrukturanalyse in einer fortgeschrittenen Gesellschaft.* (Opladen: Leske+Budrich)

Jarausch, Konrad H. (1994) *The Rush to German Unity.* (Oxford and New York: Oxford University Press)

Jarausch, Konrad H. and Gransow, Volker (eds.) (1997) *Uniting Germany. Documents and Debates, 1944–1993.* (Oxford and New York: Berghahn)

Kolinsky, Eva (1991) 'Socio-Economic Change and Political Culture in West Germany' in Gaffney, John and Kolinsky, Eva (eds.), *Political Culture in France and Germany.* (London: Routledge), pp. 34–65

Kolinsky, Eva (1995) (ed.) *Between Hope and Fear. Everyday Life in Post-Unification East Germany.* (Keele: Keele University Press)

Kolinsky, Eva (1998a) 'Recasting Biographies: Women and the Family' in Kolinsky, Eva (ed.), *Social Transformation and the Family in Post-Communist Germany.* (Basingstoke: Macmillan), pp. 118–140

Kolinsky, Eva (1998b) 'In Search of a Future: Leipzig since the "Wende"', *German Politics and Society*, vol. 16, no. 4, pp. 103–121

Kolinsky, Eva (2002) 'The Limits of Equality' in Kolinsky, Eva and Nickel, Hildegard Maria (eds.), *Reinventing Gender. Women in East Germany since Unification.* (London: Cass), pp. 100–127

Naimark, Norman M. (1995) *The Russians in Germany. A History of the Soviet Zone of Occupation 1945–1949.* (Cambridge, Massachusetts: Harvard University Press)

Padgett, Stephen and Poguntke, Thomas (2001) *Party Government and Political Culture in Germany.* (London: Cass)

Preller, Sabine (2001) *Arm und Reich in Deutschland. Der erste Armuts- und Reichtumsbericht der Bundesregierung.* (Bonn: Internationes)

Reissig, Rolf (ed.) (1993) *Rückweg in die Zukunft. Über den schwierigen Transformationprozess in Ostdeutschland.* (Frankfurt/Main: Campus)

Reissig, Rolf (2000) *Die gespaltende Vereinigungsgesellschaft. Bilanz und Perspektiven der Transformation in Ostdeutschland und der deutschen Vereinigung.* (Berlin: Karl Dietz)

Röhrig, Wolfgang (1983) *Die verspätete Demokratie. Zur politischen Kultur der Bundesrepublik Deutschland.* (Cologne: Diederichs)

Schmitt, Manfred and Montada, Leo (1999) *Gerechtigkeitserleben im wiedervereinigten Deutschland.* (Opladen: Leske+Budrich)

Schröder, Klaus (1998) *Der SED Staat. Partei, Staat und Gesellschaft 1949–1990.* (Munich: Carl Hanser)

Segert, Astrid and Zierke, Irene (1997) *Sozialstruktur und Milieuerfahrungen. Aspekte des alltagskulturellen Wandels in Ostdeutschland.* (Opladen: Westdeutscher Verlag)

Smith, Gordon (1986) *Democracy in Western Germany. Parties and Politics in the Federal Republic.* (Aldershot: Gower) 3rd edition

Starke, Uta (1995) 'Young People: Lifestyles, Experiences and Value Orientations since the "Wende"' in Kolinsky, Eva (ed.), *Between Hope and Fear. Everyday Life in Post-Unification East Germany.* (Keele: Keele University Press), pp. 155–176

Vester, Michael, Hofmann, Michael and Zierke, Irene (1995) (eds.) *Soziale Milieus in Ostdeutschland. Gesellschaftliche Strukturen zwischen Zerfall und Neubeginn.* (Cologne: Bund Verlag)

Winkler, Gunnar (1990) *Sozialreport.* (Berlin: Die Wirtschaft)

Zwahr, Hartmut (1994) 'Umbruch durch Ausbruch und Aufbruch: Die DDR auf dem Höhepunkt der Staatskrise 1989' in Kaelble, Hartmut, Kocka, Jürgen and Zwahr, Hartmut (eds.) *Sozialgeschichte der DDR.* (Stuttgart: Klett-Cotta), pp. 426–465

Chapter One

Constructing East Germany: Interpretations of GDR History since Unification

Mike Dennis

Introduction

Although many of the heated historical controversies over East Germans' collaboration with the state and the equation of the GDR with the Third Reich as totalitarian regimes have lost some of their original intensity, GDR history continues to divide rather than heal. This is not surprising as perceptions of its history are embedded in the contentious reconfiguration of German identities since 1990 and of various attempts 'to work through history' (*Geschichtsaufarbeitung*) and perhaps 'to overcome a problematic past' (*Vergangenheitsbewälti-gung*). The very fact that there is no clear definition of what constitutes an overcoming of the past and that several key words in German are translated into English in different ways is symptomatic of the complexity of the transition from the SED dictatorship (Garton Ash, 1999: 294–5). Furthermore, the term 'overcoming the past' is deceptively simple, as it suggests a finite rather than a fractured process with different implications for individuals, groups and society as a whole. Germany is, of course, not alone in having to adjust to a difficult past, but it is unique in that it has gone through the process twice in the second half of the twentieth century. This is often referred to as Germany's double overcoming of the past.

This chapter will first examine some of the problems inherent in a judicial reckoning with the SED dictatorship before focusing on the political, ideological and methodological issues associated with the search for appropriate models for the interpretation of the history of the GDR. The perils of overarching concepts with a heavy ideological baggage, such as totalitarianism and modernisation, combined with access to the archival treasure-trove of the former GDR have shifted research towards the history of everyday life which is shedding fresh light on the intricacies of the interaction between rulers and ruled. As long as sight is not lost of the coercive and repressive components of the dictatorship, then the delineation of the economic, cultural, social and personal contours of the East German past may assist in the understanding of some of the difficulties faced by both easterners and westerners in reconstructing their personal identities and political cultures.

Dealing with a Difficult Past

The experiences of other post-dictatorship countries, whether the former communist states, or post-authoritarian Portugal, Greece and Spain, or South Africa after apartheid, differ considerably from those of Germany, as well as from each other, as regards scope and aims. How such societies proceed is related to a series of difficult – sometimes unanswerable – questions regarding the purpose and methods of dealing with the past (König, 1998: 371–2, 376–80). Should perpetrators be prosecuted and victims compensated, and how should the political culture be reconfigured? Or would it not be preferable to draw a judicial line under the past as the veteran SPD politician Egon Bahr has advocated, a view which accords with the wishes of many easterners'.[1] One objection to Bahr's argument is the oft-quoted warning from historians that those who forget the past are in danger of repeating it.

If the former course is implemented, what kind of balance can be struck between judicial trials, commissions of enquiry, public education programmes and the dismissal from office of active collaborators and senior officials? The answers are complex and varied, depending in part on the nature of the preceding regime as well as on the durability of the old elites. For example, reconciliation and reconstruction might be prejudiced by punitive measures based on unreliable sources and witnesses and by the ensuing poisoning of the political atmosphere. On the other hand, suppressing a confrontation with the past runs the danger of storing up trouble later, as happened in post-communist Poland where, in the early 1990s, accusations of working for the secret police brought down members of the government. This prompted one contemporary historian, Timothy Garton Ash, to reflect that: 'Dirty fragments of the past constantly resurface and are used, often dirtily, in current political disputes' (Garton Ash, 1999: 298). Finally, sight must not be lost of the moral dimension which is encapsulated in Angelika Barbe's phrase: 'Before forgiveness comes the recognition of guilt'.[2]

If Germany has dealt with its communist past in a more systematic manner than have the post-communist countries of eastern and central Europe, this is influenced by a determination not to repeat the many shortcomings in West Germany's dealing with the legacy of the Third Reich. Border guards have been brought to trial; many functionaries of the old regime have lost their positions; and ex-SED *Politbüro* members, such as Krenz and Schabowski, have received prison sentences of six and three years respectively for indirect participation in manslaughter. The latter refers to their role in the death of people trying to flee the GDR.

Criticism of this punitive kind of reckoning with the SED past is widespread. Despite the sentences imposed on SED leaders and the high turnover of the old elites in government and industry, many critics contend that the punishment does not fit the crime and that too few cases are pursued. While most of the border guards who have been brought to trial have been sentenced, only a small number have been jailed. In what was probably the last trial of former SED *Politbüro* members, Herbert Häber, Siegfried Lorenz and Hans-Joachim Böhme were all acquitted of the charge of manslaughter by omission. This charge, which was less serious than that levelled against Krenz and Schabowski, concerned their alleged failure to pursue measures which would have helped to humanise the border regime. Their acquittal, which was justified in the case of Häber, the head of the SED Central Committee's department for relations with West Germany, triggered off both criticism and astonishment among civil rights activists and victims of the communist system.[3] The trial highlighted the intractability of the problems inherent in a judicial reckoning with a complex past. The prosecution had hoped that the charge of manslaughter by omission would bring to account those individuals who, while not directly involved in the initial implementation and the subsequent elaboration of the border regulations, had nevertheless neglected to use their position to humanise the murderous system. Although neither Lorenz nor Böhme expressed regret, they were acquitted, partly because, unlike Krenz, they had not been members when the *Politbüro* addressed the border regulations for the final time, in March 1986, and because it was anyhow difficult to assess objectively whether their actions could have helped save lives (Winters, 2000: 525–8).

Another frequent criticism of the official reckoning with the past is that personnel changes have been insufficient in many crucial areas of society. Siegfried Suckut of the BStU (the Federal Authority for the Records of the State Security Service of the Former GDR) has estimated that 75 per cent of teachers who once worked for the Stasi remain in the profession (Raue, 1998: 147). The whole process is complicated by a further factor: while many east Germans have called for a thorough reckoning with the old regime, west Germans are so intimately, even decisively, involved in the judicial and administrative aspects of the process that accusations of 'victors' justice' fly thick and fast. The lament of the prominent GDR dissident Bärbel Bohley that they expected justice but instead got the rule of law (*Rechtsstaat*) homes in on the dilemma of obtaining justice through complex and slow legal procedures which demand incontrovertible proof of guilt. The problems are compounded by the question of whether legislation can be applied retrospectively to crimes and abuses perpetrated by the leaders and functionaries of the SED regime. This revolves around whether an act is punishable only if it was an offence against the law before it was committed (*nulla poena sine lege*) or whether the prohibition against retroactivity, which was incorporated into the Basic Law and the Unification Treaty in 1990, can be modified. At times, the German courts have justified a measure of retroactivity on the basis of the principle enunciated by the West German legal philosopher Gustav Radbach that a statute is 'incorrect law' if the contradiction between a dictatorial statute and justice becomes 'unbearable' (Quint, 1999: 310–15). Although this principle was applied by the presiding judge in the first border guard trial in 1991, unease over *ex-post-facto* law-making against a regime whose crimes were of a different order from those of Nazi Germany soon resulted in the emphasis shifting towards convictions based primarily within the framework of a reinterpretation of GDR law. Yet while the courts have found criminal guilt in most of the cases brought against the border guards, suspended sentences, not jail terms, have been the norm because of what are judged extenuating circumstances. Among the latter are the division of Germany during the Cold War and the so-called 'special conditions' prevailing in the GDR.

Whereas Bohley was, not without good reason, critical of the inadequacies of the legal and political treatment of SED functionaries – a reflection of what some commentators regard as the impossibility of achieving justice in any absolute sense of the word (McAdams, 1996: 79–80) – members of the old regime tend to put a different gloss on matters. Egon Krenz, Honecker's short-lived successor as head of party and state, attacked his own sentence as one further example of victors' justice. Yet although the PDS's official position on the court's judgement was highly critical, an investigation of party members revealed that 74 per cent disagreed with Krenz's interpretation of the verdict and that 20 per cent favoured an even higher penalty (Krisch, 1998: 43–4).

The long-running controversy over the Stasi contacts of Manfred Stolpe, the current SPD Minister President of the federal state of Brandenburg, was resonant of an earlier contentious debate in West Germany over the merits of *Ost-politik* and rapprochement with the GDR. It also concerned the issue of an individual's room for manoeuvre and strategic choices under a dictatorship, as well as the question of complicity and responsibility in East German society as a whole. In the early stages of unification, the latter was an emotionally-charged issue which prompted statements like that of Arno Widmann in the daily newspaper *taz* in April 1990: 'The whole system worked only because everyone – or at least almost everyone – helped. The neighbours, for example, who no longer greeted the young couple that had applied for exit visas [...] or the decent citizens who reported their neighbours' Western contacts' (cited in Sa'adah, 1998: 109). Stolpe, as the top lay official of the Protestant Churches, necessarily had frequent contacts with Stasi and SED functionaries but he was also involved in conspiratorial meetings with MfS personnel for almost three decades. Although he was registered by the Stasi as an unofficial collaborator (IM '*Sekretär*'), there is no evidence that Stolpe entered into a contractual relationship with the ministry.[4]

Stolpe defends his *modus operandi* on the grounds that as the system showed so few signs of disintegration, it was necessary to safeguard Church interests through dialogue. After the collapse of the GDR, he claimed that the

GDR 'was a dictatorship, but one which wore velvet gloves, and despite every-thing, it was possible to do a great deal' (cited in ibid.: 191).

The *Ostpolitik* launched by the SPD Chancellor, Willy Brandt, – and contin-ued in essence by Helmut Kohl after 1982 – was designed to change the com-munist system through a gradual rapprochement with the West. For many East German dissidents, this policy, together with the relatively cordial rela-tions between Bonn and East Berlin, was erected on false premises as it helped to prop up the SED dictatorship. A similar controversy erupted in the academic world of GDR studies over the system immanent approach of West German research on the GDR pioneered by scholars such as Ludz, Zimmermann and Glaessner of the Free University of Berlin. They stood accused, with Jens Hacker leading the attack (Hacker, 1992: 422–6), of failing to expose the inherently coercive nature of the SED totalitarian regime and of locating their research within the context of the goals and norms of SED policy. In 1994, the exposure as a Stasi informer of one of the leading GDR experts in the West, Dietrich Staritz of the University of Mannheim, was grist to the conservatives' mill (Knabe, 1999: 197–201, 213–16, 344–8).

Finally, it is frequently argued by liberals and socialists that the rapidity of unification, the full-scale dismantling of the GDR's socio-economic and cul-tural assets, and the demonisation of the GDR as an *Unrechtsstaat* – that is, a state not based on the rule of law – have impeded the much-needed reform of the West German model. This kind of argument underpins calls for an evalua-tion of the 'double biography' of contemporary Germany which is not fixated on the negative aspects of the GDR past, but embraces a critical assessment of the history of both the FRG and the GDR. The PDS, the reformed successor to the SED, draws attention to the suppression of protest movements in both Ger-man states, which were partly the result of the friend-foe dichotomy of the Cold War era. Furthermore, the party claims that *Unrecht* was not the sole preserve of the GDR as, for example, drugs were administered illegally to West German athletes, albeit not as part of a state-run programme (Keller and Mocek, 1998: 26).

The Broader Historical Framework

The doyen of historians of the GDR, Hermann Weber, has stressed that: 'The first prerequisite of any political working through of the past is the scientific study of GDR history', a task which, in his opinion, must not degenerate into a mere instrument of politics (Weber, 1997: 3). The solid research of the empiri-cist advocated by Weber should, however, be placed within explanatory and classificatory frameworks which have been developed by historians and social scientists. Before examining these frameworks, a comment is required on which persons are qualified to interpret GDR history. In 1995, 97 per cent of an Emnid sample of east Germans concurred with the statement that: 'The only people who can talk about the GDR are those who lived there' (*Der Spiegel*, 3 July 1995, p. 49). Whatever the merits of this argument, the opportunity has been denied to the vast majority of historians who worked in the former GDR. Since 1990, the structures of GDR historical studies have been swept away and attempts at renewal thwarted. It is estimated that only 25 per cent of historians of the former Academy of Sciences and the SED Central Committee's Academy of Social Sciences, and about ten per cent of university professors managed to survive the destruction of their profession (Berger, 1997: 159, 162–63).

Not only have GDR institutes been swept away, but many West German bodies which specialised in GDR studies have also disappeared. One notable victim was the Federal Office for All-German Affairs. Others have had their funding cut off or drastically reduced. However, the new opportunities for studying the history of the GDR, in particular scholars' access to witnesses and to the mountain of documentation accumulated by the SED and the Ministry for State Security, have spawned many fresh research groups. Among the most prominent of the new foundations are the Hannah Arendt Institute for the Study of Totalitarianism in Dresden, the Centre for Contemporary Historical Research in Potsdam, the Department of Education and Research of the Federal Commissioner for the Documents of the State Security Service of the former GDR, and the Centre for Research on the SED State at the Free University of Berlin.

The Centre for Contemporary History is of particular interest as it has consciously utilised ex-GDR scholars who have met the stringent criteria set by the Council on Scholarship (*Wissenschaftsrat*). Central to its mission is the development of comparative studies which delve into social and cultural history and everday life in the 'thoroughly dominated society' of the GDR. The Association of Independent Historians, a small but vocal group of younger ex-GDR historians whose careers had been impeded by the SED authorities, took exception to the employment of historians who were reckoned to have been close to the SED regime, and many conservative critics, especially from within the ranks of the CDU and in the columns of the daily *Frankfurter Allgemeine Zeitung*, objected to the Centre's abandonment of the totalitarian paradigm. Armin Mitter and Stefan Wolle, two historians who had once occupied minor positions at the Academy of Sciences of the GDR, launched fierce attacks on Potsdam, accusing it of 'teeming' with functionaries and water-carriers of the SED regime whose pre-1989 writings should have disqualifed them from research into the history of the GDR (Mitter and Wolle, 1994: 264). Jürgen Kocka, Potsdam's first acting head, countered that the Centre employed mainly young East German historians as well as a smaller number of older historians who had practised their trade with considerable success in the GDR. In the latter case, not only had they met the requisite academic criteria but had undertaken a self-critical and open analysis of their past. Reminding his critics that 'academics can also learn', he pointed out that these ex-GDR historians had produced solid historical studies since the collapse of the communist system.

While they had not been undamaged by life under a dictatorship, they were, he insisted, not compromised in any major way and were playing an important role in unravelling their country's past (Kocka in Eckert, Küttler, Kowalczuk and Stark, 1994: 168–9, 296). Kocka's remarks can be interpreted as a timely plea for reconciliation and trust in the newly emerging political culture of the east, not only between 'Ossis' and 'Wessis' but also between easterners.

The Association of Independent Historians, which was founded in 1990, triggered off an east German historians' controversy (*Historikerstreit*) over the allocation of resources and academic posts. The dispute echoed the even more fractious writers' controversy (*Literaturstreit*) which erupted over the ambiguous political past of writers such as Christa Wolf. In the Association's founding call, humanities subjects in the GDR, including history, were dismissed as 'an inedible mash of lies and half-truths' which 'stifled intellectual impulses'. 'Scholastic nonsense' and 'stale platitudes' were inflated to the status of a scientific *Weltanschauung* and pseudo-academics presided over their disciplines (see the document in ibid.: 32). Representative voices of the Association, such as those of Mitter and Wolle, did not restrict themselves to criticism of former luminaries of GDR historical sciences, but objected strongly to what they saw as western colonisation of the new historical landscape and the marginalisation of able east German historians who had not belonged to the former GDR establishment.

The ideological, political and epistemological battles over the depiction and interpretation of the past have raged most fiercely over the value of the totalitarian paradigm for the study of communist and fascist systems. Among the many variants of totalitarianism, the six-point syndrome of Friedrich and Brzezinski came to dominate Western interpretations of the Soviet Union and its East European satellites during the first half of the Cold War. Insisting on a generic similarity between communist and fascist totalitarian dictatorships, it highlighted rule by a single party, a totalistic ideology, a system of terror, a centrally directed economy and a monopoly over mass communications and weapons. The goal – which Friedrich recognised had not been achieved – was total control and the elimination of genuine subjectivity. The paradigm went into decline from about the late 1960s, with the amelioration of relations between the two power blocs and a growing awareness of the model's inherent methodological flaws. It no longer appeared to do justice to the communist states' economic modernisation programmes and to the relaxation, but not the abandonment, of coercive methods of control. New concepts such as consultative authoritarianism and administered society were elaborated to encapsulate these new developments. Widely condemned as an ideological instrument of the West, the totalitarian model had, by the later 1970s, fallen into such disfavour that one leading West German expert on communism, Gert Meyer, argued that it was time to pension it off. While this may have been the majority view, the approach had staunch advocates among academics like Siegfried Mampel and Jens Hacker who were clustered around the Society for

Research on Germany (*Gesellschaft für Deutschlandforschung*), which was founded in 1978. Ironically, as the model lost support in the West, the crushing of the Prague Spring in 1968 contributed to its renaissance among East European dissidents like Adam Michnik, Jacek Kuron and Václav Havel, as part of their strategy to liberate society from communist rule (Rupnik, 1988: 224–6).

With the fall of the Berlin Wall and the uncovering of the comprehensive surveillance of society by the Stasi, the totalitarian perspective received so powerful a boost that one historian, Christoph Klessmann, was persuaded that George Orwell's negative utopia was realised to a greater extent in the GDR than was ever the case in the Third Reich (Klessmann, 1998: 43). Even fierce critics of the totalitarian model during the Cold War, such as the political scientist Klaus von Beyme of the University of Heidelberg and Gerhard Lozek (Lozek, 1994: 113, 117–18),[5] a historian at the SED Central Committee's Academy of Social Sciences, have modified their earlier views. Von Beyme, once an advocate of consultative authoritarianism, an alternative paradigm to totalitarianism, now accepts, as a self-styled 'pragmatist', the value of the concept of totalitarianism for the study of a past type of rule (von Beyme, 1998: 44, 53).

The resurrection of the totalitarian paradigm, or what Wolfgang Wippermann, among others, has referred to as its 'quiet victory' (Wippermann, 1997: 103), was welcomed by many former GDR civil rights activists, as well as by those victims of communism who had long insisted on the intrinsically repressive nature of the GDR. Among the latter is the *Union der Opferverbände kommunistischer Gewalt*, whose chair is Gerhard Finn. In support of their case, they can point to the thorough politicisation of justice in the GDR, the shootings at the Wall, and the brutal treatment of political prisoners in Bautzen, Berlin-Hohenschönhausen and other prisons (Finn, 1996). Recent estimates indicate that over 900 people may have been killed on the GDR's borders with the Federal Republic and its other neighbours and that 200,000 to 250,000 East Germans suffered imprisonment for political reasons between 1949 and 1989 (Dennis, 2000: 99–100, 229). The verdict of Hans-Peter Schwarz, the political scientist and a former head of the CDU's Konrad-Adenauer-Foundation, is that the communists of the GDR can be likened to an 'association of slave-drivers' who fostered a 'camp mentality' within the 'mega concentration camp' GDR (cited in Berger, 1997: 153). From this perspective, the GDR was an *Unrechtsstaat* without popular legitimacy, whose servants should be prosecuted in the courts of law, and whose very existence serves as a warning against Left as well as Right extremism.

A kind of semi-official blessing for totalitarianism arrived in 1994 when the German Parliament's first *Enquete-Kommission* endorsed the validity of the model for both the Third Reich and the GDR. The Commission was by no means a west German creation. It was set up in 1992 on the basis of a proposal by Markus Meckel, a founder member of the East German SPD and the Foreign Minister in the de Mazière coalition government of 1990. Its chair, the CDU *Bundestag* deputy, Rainer Eppelmann, had been a constant thorn in the side of the SED and the Stasi as a dissident Protestant pastor in East Berlin. The Commission sat for over two years and took evidence from historians, east and west German politicians, victims of the system and legislators. It also received specialists' briefs, held open debates on key issues, and its proceedings were televised. The final report of over 15,000 pages provides a wealth of material on the GDR – its power structures, the role of ideology, the judiciary, the state security services, the Churches, opposition and German-German relations.

Many of the west German participants in the Commission's sessions – Hacker, Manfred Wilke and Horst Möller, the director of Munich's Institute for Contemporary History – were proponents of the totalitarian approach. There was no clear east-west divide, as former GDR dissidents such as Jürgen Fuchs, Roland Jahn and Wolfgang Templin provided personal insights into the repressive nature of the system. The Commission's concluding report, which adopted Möller's analogy between the Third Reich and the GDR, stressed the similarities between the two totalitarian dictatorships as regards the systematic infringement of human rights, the persecution of opposition, rule by a single party, an exclusive ideology, modern methods of surveillance and propaganda, and a radical restructuring of society (Deutscher Bundestag IX, 1995: 577–87). This accorded with the Commission's mission to underpin the 'anti-totalitarian consensus' of the Federal Republic (Deutscher Bundestag I, 1995: 745).

The 'anti-totalitarian consensus', which the *Bundestag* proclaimed as one of the 'spiritual props' of a stable democracy (ibid.: 783), came under fire from various sources (see Roth, 1998: 135). In the opinion of many critics, such as Wolfgang Kraushaar of the Hamburg Institute for Social Research, the totalitarian approach, regardless of recent modifications, is plagued by the many defects which are inherent in its normative underpinnings and ideological functions: the *a priori* discrediting of all communist and socialist states, the demonisation of political opponents, the relativisation of the National Socialist past and the immunisation of the Western value system against criticism (Kraushaar, 1996: 457). The PDS, too, joined in the fray. The party sees itself as one of the main advocates of east German interests and identity, a task which includes combating any distortion of GDR history. Not only did the PDS refuse to add its signature to the Commission's final report, but it submitted its own minority statement. The latter only emerged after a heated internal debate between modernisers and traditionalists in the party. The PDS objected fiercely to the placing of the GDR and the Third Reich under the same totalitarian umbrella, as it failed to do justice to the fundamental differences between the two, such as the GDR's commitment to social equality in education, culture and the workplace, and also to the elimination of unemployment and homelessness, in contrast to the Third Reich's systematic deprivation of people's rights in the labour and social spheres (Deutscher Bundestag 1995, 1: 709–12). The party feared that equating the Third Reich and the GDR was yet one more device to justify the ruthless dismantling of the GDR's cultural, economic and other assets and the promotion of a conservative historical revisionism (Elm, 1998: 78).

On the basis of the SED's achievements in the social sphere and its commitment to anti-fascism and peace, the GDR, according to the PDS, was accepted by a clear majority of East Germans from the end of the 1950s to the beginning of the 1980s (Deutscher Bundestag, 1995, 1: 713–15). However, viewing the GDR through such rose-tinted spectacles not only overlooks the internal reasons for the construction of the Berlin Wall, but also fails to take into account the kind of balanced assessment put forward by Richard Schröder of the Humboldt University in Berlin. GDR citizens' awareness of the system's positive feature, he believes, can be encapsulated in the following phrase: 'Much was bad in the GDR, BUT we had no unemployed, no drug problems'. He stresses, however, that the advantages which appear after the 'BUT' are smaller in proportion to the disadvantages which stand in front of it (Schröder, 1993: 21). The PDS, which drew up a different balance sheet, acknowledged that the system was beset by contradictions and problems. In its view, the fundamental flaw was the suppression of the original democratic Marxist impulse by the rule of a minority. While careful to avoid any sweeping denigration of the GDR as a totalitarian dictatorship, the PDS minority statement nevertheless conceded that the system could be classified as a dictatorship of the SED leadership, essentially that of the *Politbüro*, with Stalinist underpinnings. In the course of time, it acquired authoritarian and dictatorial components intertwined with the democratic elements which were to be found in the workplace, in residential areas and on the middle rungs of the societal ladder (ibid.: 712).

The PDS statement to the Commission was shaped by the party programme and other authoritative documents, as well as by the deliberations of the Historical Commission attached to the party executive. PDS views on GDR history are also elaborated in journals such as *Utopie kreativ*, the party organ, *Neues Deutschland*, the memoirs of former SED functionaries, the volumes in the series *Ansichten zur Geschichte der DDR*, and by historians who are close to the party. The core elements of the PDS's historical picture – the GDR's commitment to peace and social equality – rest on the assumption that the socialist and anti-fascist features of the immediate post-war period offered a genuine alternative to the capitalist model of West Germany and that the GDR was not doomed from the start (see Eckert, 1995: 8–16). Such a depiction appeals to the many former SED functionaries among the party membership as well as to the belief of its east German constituency that life in the GDR had not been in vain. It is also integral to the socialist counter discourse which is pitted against the prevailing neo-liberalism of the FRG. However, it should be stressed that the PDS interpretation of the GDR's historical legacy is rejected by many easterners, especially former dissidents, and that the past arouses bitter disputes among the party faithful (Barker, 2000: 86–92). There is no uniform PDS historiography, partly because the PDS embraces such a wide variety of left-wing groupings and political persuasions. One such group, the Communist Platform, challenges the reform-oriented wing around people like Petra Pau, André Brie and Dietmar Keller. One of the Platform's spokespersons, Sarah Wagenkenecht, has even contended that the Stalinist model in the Soviet Union represents the only viable form of socialism (Segert, 1995: 2–3). The PDS cannot, however, afford to follow this line if it wishes to be a viable left-wing force in contemporary German politics. The apology by the party's new chair, Gabriele Zimmer, for the acts of repression used to bring about the merger of the KPD and the SPD in 1946 is indicative of the leadership's desire for some form of reconciliation with the SPD in order to make the PDS an acceptable coalition partner at the regional level. The response from Zimmer's critics was immediate: Wagenknecht, who is a member of the PDS executive, denounced the apology as an act of 'self-denial' (Der Spiegel, 23 April 2001: 36). This potentially explosive debate was set within the broader discussion on the draft of a new party programme which takes a more critical view than in the past of the repressive nature of the GDR's 'Soviet state socialist system' and of the structural deficits of an all-pervasive state control of the economy and society (Sozialist, 2001). The cleavages were also apparent during the negotiations which led to the formation of the SPD-PDS coalition in Berlin in January 2002, as discussed by Peter Barker in this volume.

Post-totalitarianism

The strength of the case against the totalitarian paradigm persuaded many historians and social scientists either to abandon the Friedrich-type model or to search for a more flexible variant. For example, the Honecker regime's efforts to establish a *modus vivendi* with the population through better housing, higher pensions, low rents and cheap basic foodstuffs has given rise to the notion of the GDR as a form of 'welfare authoritarianism' or a 'welfare dictatorship' (Staritz, 2000: 14–15). In this context, Norbert Kapferer, somewhat dismissively, likens Honecker's GDR to 'an extremely authoritarian old people's home' rather than a prison cell (Kapferer, 2000: 35). These indicators of more flexible and softer methods of political control in the late Honecker era, led Eckhard Jesse, an authority on extremism, to conflate the totalitarian and authoritarian elements in the ugly hybrid 'autolitarian dictatorship (Jesse, 1994: 23). A more promising approach is Juan Linz's categorisation of Honecker's GDR as a 'frozen' sub-type of post-totalitarianism located along a continuum extending from totalitarianism to democracy. Jürgen Kocka of the Free University of Berlin, and a former acting head of the Centre for Contemporary History in Potsdam, is sympathetic to this kind of approach as post-totalitarianism helps, in his opinion, to differentiate the GDR of the 1970s and 1980s from the terroristic and murderous Third Reich and the Stalinist USSR, as well as from the violent Stalinist phase of Soviet-type dictatorships in the Eastern European satellite states in the 1950s and early 1960s (Kocka, 1999: 24). Finally, mention should also be made of the efforts of some former GDR scholars to devise analytical alternatives to totalitarianism. These include

Artur Meier's feudalistic sounding 'society of socialist estates' and Wolfgang Engler's conception of the GDR as a 'negotiating society' in which rulers and ruled were engaged in a series of compromises and arrangements (see Jarausch, 1999: 54).

A Modern Dictatorship

While the preceding remarks testify to a broad consensus on the dictatorial nature of SED rule in that a monistic power centre enjoyed an extensive domination, opinions vary as to the ingredients of the dictatorship and an appropriate defining adjective. It is a common objection that simply to use the term 'dictatorship' runs the risk of trivialising the tyranny of a Hitler, a Stalin or an Ulbricht and of failing to distinguish sufficiently between communist dictatorships on the one hand, and autocracies such as those of Franco, Salazar, Napoleon and Cromwell on the other. The term 'modern dictatorship', as coined by Kocka, seeks to overcome the latter objection by highlighting so-called modern methods of mass mobilisation, surveillance, coercion, socialisation and enticement which both the NSDAP and the SED deployed. It also attempts to reintegrate the GDR into the framework of modernisation theory which, in the late 1960s and the 1970s, was the main theoretical alternative to totalitarianism. Ralf Dahrendorf, in his magisterial study of democracy and society in Germany, defined the GDR as 'the first modern society on German soil', albeit a modern form with 'totalitarian substance' (Dahrendorf, 1967: 424, 431). While this might be regarded as too positive an overall judgement, the GDR has recently been credited by the west German sociologist Rainer Geissler with a 'modernisation lead' over the FRG (Geissler, 1996: 363–4) in areas such as women's equality, protection from unemployment, liberal legislation on divorce and generous opportunities for vocational education.

The well-known historian of modern Germany, Hans-Ulrich Wehler, formerly of Bielefeld University, has pleaded for the development of a sophisticated theory of modernisation, but he offers little more than a sketch as to how the GDR might be placed within a comparative study of the challenges and crises of modernisation. Among the tasks performed by what he refers to as a modern polity are the articulation and aggregation of interests, elite recruitment and mobilisation. How these tasks are implemented can be assessed in the light of the recurrent crises of distribution, legitimation, identity and integration (Wehler, 1998: 349–52). Kocka has taken the modernisation approach a stage further through his application of the term 'modern dictatorship' to the GDR. Unlike some other scholars, he stresses that 'modern' should not be equated with 'democratic' or 'progressive' as the GDR and its socialist neighbours were characterised by the rule of a single party, with power restricted to a narrow circle of leaders, and by a lack of autonomous sub-systems (Kocka, 1999: 18–21). On the other hand, Kocka identifies modernisation developments in the form of technological innovation, industrial and urban expansion, land reform, social security and anti-traditionalist elements in everyday life, such as family planning, competitive sport and new forms of partnership between men and women. That this was a Janus-faced process is recognised by Kocka in that the destructive elements of the GDR's modernisation were more prominent and led to a modernisation deficit vis-à-vis the FRG. Among the barriers to modernisation were: the persecution and disempowerment of functional elites, especially from the middle class; the crushing of civil society; the stifling of innovation and creativity; and environmental damage in both rural and urban areas. The preliminary nature of much of this new work can be seen in Kocka's somewhat lame conclusion that the concept of 'modern dictatorship' 'cannot bear too much of an interpretive load' and that it represents little more than 'a preliminary sketch of the landscape' (ibid.: 22).

The east German sociologist, Detlef Pollack, prefers the term 'semi-modern mixed society' to Kocka's 'modern dictatorship' label as, in his view, the characteristics of modern societies were thwarted by over-centralisation (Cited in Jarausch, 1999: 56). Pollack argues that the modernisation of society, especially of the economy, was essential for the SED due to its lack of democratic legitimation. Economic success was intended to provide compensatory legitimation. Furthermore, the SED claimed to be on the side of progress in that it was building socialism, a system superior to all previous social formations (Pollack, 1999: 30–1, 35–6). As the SED prioritised the safeguarding of political power over a competitive economy, it was compelled to control all social areas, thereby blocking the very autonomy in the individual sub-systems, such as the economy, law, science, art and religion, which was essential to a society's modernisation (ibid.: 31). Here is a familiar re-iteration of the obstacles to modernisation inherent in the prioritisation of central steering instruments in the Soviet-type route to modernity.

Modernisation approaches like those of Dahrendorf and Wehler do have the undoubted merit of stimulating comparisons between the GDR and its capitalist and socialist contemporaries (see Kaeble, 1994: 560, 562) as well as locating the system within long-term socio-economic, cultural and political developments. However, modernisation theorising is no latter-day Holy Grail, as in the eyes of many critics it is too Western-centric. Even if the over optimistic predictions associated with modernisation theories in the 1960s and 1970s of the development towards a Western-type world of plenty and freedom have been replaced by a greater awareness of the pitfalls and risks associated with innovation, especially in the light of the leap into modernity of the new *Bundesländer* (Dennis, 1993: 1–3), confusion and eclecticism abound over the appropriate criteria for defining and operationalising the modernisation concept. This is apparent from the arguments over the question of a value-free modernisation theory which have erupted over the work of Rainer Zitelmann, one of the leading historians of the so-called New Right in Germany. In his *opus magnum* on Hitler, Zitelmann argues that Hitler's socio-economic programme had as its aim the revolutionary modernisation of Germany, including the abolition of class barriers, the dissolution of traditional regional ties and the comprehensive restructuring of the economy. The conquest of *Lebensraum* and racist policy were, contrary to the views of many other historians, not the primary goals, but rather a means to an end within a framework of conditions set by politics. Hitler, in Zitelmann's view, 'defined himself as a deliberate executor of that process of modernisation which is characterised by industrialisation, technicalisation and rationalisation' (Zitelmann, 1999: 336). That Hitler rejected pluralistic democracy did not rule him out as a moderniser as 'Democracy', to quote Zitelmann again, 'is one, but by no means the only, possible political form in which the process of modernization can take place' (ibid.: 337). This latter statement illustrates the general danger of relativising and normalising a dictatorial past, whether fascist or communist, which might serve a nationalist agenda as part of the recasting of German history (see Berger, 1997: 129–33, 141).

Domination as Social Practice

With neither totalitarianism nor modernisation theories providing a satisfactory understanding of the GDR, partly because of the problems inherent in any theory or model construction, a series of lower level concepts and alternative approaches have been utilised to shed light on the intricacies of life under a dictatorship and to capture the wide range of personal experiences (Engler, 1999: 9). The new concepts include a 'thoroughly penetrated dictatorship' (*durchherrschte Gesellschaft*), 'domination as social practice' (*Herrschaft als soziale Prazis*) and 'a sense of self-determination' (*Eigensinn*). Influenced by the history of everyday life (*Alltagsgeschichte*), by the insights of Foucault and Bourdieu, and by the critical historisation of the Third Reich as pioneered by Martin Broszat, many studies have examined the interaction of political and social history under the label of 'domination as social practice'. As used by Thomas Lindenberger and Alf Lüdtke, this approach is predicated on the view that domination is not exercised simply by *Diktat* from above but encompasses a series of bargains and even compromises with the dominated. While these historians accept that the autonomous sub-systems and democratic emancipatory potential were to a great extent eroded by the SED's totalitarian aspirations and authority, they deny the fact that society became moribund. The task is to explore, in what is recognised as a thoroughly penetrated society, the complex series of negotiations and adjustments between the agents of domination and individuals in the factory, the family, the neighbourhood, the Churches and in the leisure sphere (Lindenberger, 1996: 311–16). These patterns are gradually being identified through the study of the archival materials of the ruling party and its subsidiary organs, as well as from oral testimony, memoirs and literary texts. For example, the Stasi and FDGB archives are a rich seam for exploring popular opinion and labour problems, as is the Matthias-Domaschk archive in Berlin for the alternative political culture and the non-conformist youth sub-cultures of the 1980s.

The shift towards the new approaches was marked by the second *Enquete-Kommission*'s devotion of an entire volume to everyday life in the GDR and the five New *Länder*. Through micro-historical studies, it is possible to construct a differentiated picture of the complexities and contradictions of GDR society which substantiates the *cri de coeur* of the civil rights activist Gerd Poppe that the East Germans were 'not a people of oppositionalists, but even less one of denunciators' (Deutscher Bundestag, 1995, I: 53). *Alltagsgeschichte* has gathered momentum in recent years. Among the most significant contributions to the interface between high politics and everyday life are the investigations of the personal recollections of life in the GDR by workers in the state of Brandenburg (Faulenbach *et al.*, 2000) and Peter Hübner's monograph on workers and social policy (Hübner, 1995). To these can be added investigations into the social history of the June 1953 Uprising, studies of labour policy, agriculture, labour brigades and images of women workers in the early years of the GDR (in Hübner and Tenfelde, 1999), as well as work on doctors, abortion and professors (see Bessel and Jessen, 1996). Mention should also be made of pioneering investigations into xenophobia (Waibel, 1996) and of the Max-Planck-Institute's retrospective research into the life-courses of GDR citizens. The Institute's surveys, for example, of social equality, social mobility, partnership and marriage, and personal relationships provide an elaborate mosaic of East Germans' interactions with the state and the enterprise. They also shed light on the limits to the party-state's influence in areas such as the family and the work collective (Huinink, Meyer *et al.*, 1995: 42–3, 349–51, 354–7, 372–3). Wolfgang Engler has addressed this theme of the limitations of state power. The expansion of the Stasi in the Honecker era was, he argues, an expression of the inability of the rulers to mobilise social support and of the need to deploy ever more resources in order to control the different components of society. In particular, the work collective, though conceived from above as a transmission belt, served as a social buffer between the individual and the state. It helped to counter the pressures for improvements in labour productivity exerted by the authorities and to reduce an individual's feelings of isolation when confronted by the power of the state (Engler, 1999: 283, 289). The nature of this balance of forces is encapsulated in the phrase 'real socialist moratorium' which was applied by Lindenberger to the final two decades of SED rule (Lindenberger, 2000: 12). Without denying the value of the new research into the social history of the GDR, one has, however, to be wary of not losing sight of the wood for the trees – in this case, the communist bear lurking behind the trees – and of the possibility of the history of everyday life being used to 'relativise' the SED dictatorship. As Richard Schröder has observed, the much lauded solidarity and closeness of friendships in the GDR was the other side of the coin to the destruction of the public sphere (Schröder, 1993: 86).

Final Observations

Whatever the limitations of the new approaches, the insights and findings of social and everyday history have enabled historians to avoid a crude division of GDR history into one of heroes/heroines and perpetrators, and to help recover what Schröder calls the authentic remembrance of the 'normality' of life in the GDR (Schröder, 1993: 110). 'Ordinary people' adopted a variety of strategies ranging from external accommodation and conditional loyalty to a retreat into private niches and non-conformity. While coercion and repression were unquestionably endemic to the system, the GDR should not be reduced to little more than an *Unrechtsstaat*. Andreas Glaeser's interviews with former members of the German People's Police highlight the complexity of the motives behind IM collaboration with the Stasi, as well as of the danger to the inner unity of contemporary Germany arising from a sweeping demonisation of the GDR (Glaesser, 2000: 279–83). Furthermore, the exploration of daily life may help to combat what many east Germans regard as the devaluation and erasure of their personal biographies. For Reinhard Höppner, the east German SPD Minister President of the federal state of Saxony-Anhalt, while life in the GDR had its darker side, it could also be both full and happy (Höppner, 2000: 24, 67). These observations, as well as the discussion above of the totalitarian and modernisation paradigms, underline the need for caution when using history (or one binding model of interpretation) as an element in the construction of new German identities. A dismantling of the wall in people's heads remains a distant goal, given the differences in inherited mentalities and patterns of socialisation, the socio-economic gap between eastern and western Germany and the prevalence of mutual grievances and resentments (Fulbrook, 1999: 286–7, 290–1, 298). However, the new historical discourses and the conceptual variety may at least serve as a warning against treating inner unity as a monolith and assuming that easterners must somehow 'catch up' with the norms and values of their western counterparts.

Notes

1 At the end of 1992, in an investigation conducted by Emnid, 49 per cent of east Germans believed that a line should be drawn under the history of the GDR; by 1995, the figure had risen to 54 per cent. On the other hand, in 1995, only 25 per cent supported the destruction of the Stasi files. The results of the two surveys are in *Der Spiegel*, 18 January 1993, p. 56 and 3 July 1995, p. 49.
2 Cited in Sa'adah 1998: 99. Barbe also warns that forcing the question to rest represents a form of legal incapacitation of society and fosters the view that politics is a dirty game; see Barbe 1994: 133.
3 The trials of several *Politbüro* members, notably those of Honecker, Hager and Dohlus, were not concluded as the defendants were judged to be unfit. In the case of Honecker, this was

because he was fatally ill with liver cancer. Although outrage was provoked by Honecker's release, A James McAdams contends that the court's decision to dismiss the charges against Honecker for health reasons was in accordance with the Basic Law's promise in article 1 to recognise human dignity. See McAdams 1996: 68–69.
4 However, it should be noted that the MfS sometimes deliberately refrained from asking officials in sensitive positions, for example in the Churches, to enter into a formal contract. The decisive issue was the value, the conspiratorial nature and the regularity of the contact.
5 While accepting the value of the totalitarian concept for comparative analysis of fascist and state socialist systems of rule, Lozek insists that many qualitative differences existed between the National Socialist regime and the GDR, and that the latter consisted of a complex mix of totalitarian, authoritarian and democratic structures.

Bibliography

Barbe, Angelika (1994) 'Schlußstrich oder Auseinandersetzung' in Faulenbach, Bernd, Meckel, Markus and Weber, Hermann (eds.), *Die Partei hat immer Recht. Aufarbeitung von Geschichte und Folgen der SED-Diktatur.* (Essen: Klartext Verlag), pp. 127–135
Barker, Peter (2000) '"Geschichtsaufarbeitung" within the PDS and the Enquete-Kommission', *German Monitor*, no. 49, pp. 86–92
Berger, Stefan (1997) *The Search for Normality. National Identity and Historical Consciousness in Germany since 1800.* (New York and Oxford: Berghahn)
Bessel, Richard and Jessen, Ralph (eds.) (1996) *Die Grenzen der Diktatur. Staat und Gesellschaft in der DDR.* (Göttingen: Vandenhoeck and Ruprecht)
Dahrendorf, Ralf (1967) *Society and Democracy in Germany.* (New York: Doubleday)
Dennis, Mike (1993) *Social and Economic Modernization in Eastern Germany from Honecker to Kohl.* (London: Pinter, and New York: St. Martin's Press)
Dennis, Mike (2000a) *The Rise and Fall of the German Democratic Republic 1945–1990.* (Longman: Harlow)
Dennis, Mike (2000b) 'Perceptions of GDR Society and Its Transformation: East German Identity Ten Years after Unity' in Flockton, Chris, Kolinsky, Eva and Pritchard, Rosalind (eds.), *The New Germany in the East. Policy Agendas and Social Development since Unification.* (London: Cass), pp. 87–105
Deutscher Bundestag (ed.) (1995) *Materialien der Enquete-Kommission 'Aufarbeitung von Geschichte und Folgen der SED-Diktatur in Deutschland',* 9 volumes. (Baden-Baden: Nomos Verlag, and Frankfurt/Main: Suhrkamp Verlag)
Deutscher Bundestag (ed.) (1999) *Materialien der Enquete-Kommission 'Überwindung der Folgen der SED-Diktatur im Prozeß der deutschen Einheit',* 8 volumes. (Baden-Baden: Nomos Verlag, and Frankfurt/Main: Suhrkamp Verlag)
Eckert, Rainer (1995) 'Strukturen, Umfeldorganisationen und Geschichtsbild der PDS', *in Horch und Guck,* vol. 4, no. 2, pp. 1–16
Eckert, Rainer, Küttler, Wolfgang Kowulzcuk, Ilko-Sascha and Stark, Isolde (eds.) (1994) *Hure oder Muse' Klio in der DDR. Dokumente und Materialien des Unabhängigen Historiker-Verbandes.* (Berlin: Gesellschaft für sozialwissenschaftliche Forschung und Publizistik)
Elm, Ludwig (1998) 'Geschichte im Bundestag und Tendenzen des historisch politischen Selbstverständnisses der Bundesrepublik Deutschland' in Elm, Ludwig, Keller, Dietmar and Mozek, Reinhard (eds.), *Ansichten zur Geschichte der DDR,* vol. IX/X. (Eggersdorf: Verlag Matthias Kirchner), pp. 32–83
Engler, Wolfgang (1999) *Die Ostdeutschen. Kunde von einem verlorenen Land.* (Berlin: Aufbau-Verlag)

Faulenbach, Bernd, Leo, Annette and Weberskirch, Klaus (eds.) (2000) *Zweierlei Geschichte. Lebensgeschichte und Geschichtsbewußtsein von Arbeitsnehmern in West- und Ostdeutschland.* (Essen: Klartext Verlag)

Finn, Gerhard (1996) *Mauern – Gitter – Stacheldraht.* (Berlin and Bonn: Westkreuz Verlag)

Fulbrook, Mary (1999) 'Aufarbeitung der DDR-Vergangenheit und "innere Einheit" – Ein Widerspruch?' in Klessmann, Christoph, Misselwitz, Hans and Wichert, Günter (eds.), *Deutsche Vergangenheit eine gemeinsame Herausforderung. Der schwierige Umgang mit der doppelten Nachkriegsgeschichte.* (Berlin: Ch. Links Verlag), pp. 286–298

Garton Ash, Timothy (1999) *History of the Present. Essays, Sketches and Despatches from Europe in the 1990s.* (London: Allan Lane)

Geissler, Rainer (1996.) *Die Sozialstruktur Deutschlands. Ein Studienbuch zur Entwicklung im geteilten und vereinten Deutschland.* (Opladen: Westdeutscher Verlag) 2nd edition

Glaeser, Andreas (2000) *Divided in Unity. Identity, Germany and the Berlin Police.* (Chicago and London: University of Chicago Press)

Hacker, Jens (1992) *Deutsche Irrtümer. Schönfärber und Helfershilfer der SED-Diktatur im Westen.* (Berlin and Frankfurt/Main: Ullstein)

Höppner, Reinhard (2000) *Zukunft gibt es nur gemeinsam. Ein Solidaritätsbeitrag zur deutschen Einheit.* (Munich: Karl Blessing Verlag)

Hübner, Peter (1995) *Konsum, Konflikt und Kompromiß. Soziale Arbeiterinteressen und Sozialpolitik in der SBZ/DDR 1945–1970.* (Berlin: Akademie Verlag)

Hübner, Peter and Tenfelde, Klaus (eds.) (1999) *Arbeiter in der SBZ/DDR.* (Essen: Klartext Verlag)

Huinink, Johannes, Meyer, Karl Ulrich *et al.* (1995) *Kollektiv und Eigensinn. Lebensverläufe in der DDR und danach.* (Berlin: Akademie Verlag)

Jarausch, Konrad (1999) 'Beyond Uniformity: The Challenge of Historicizing the GDR' in Jarausch, Konrad (ed.), *Dictatorship as Experience. Towards a Socio-Cultural History of the GDR.* (New York and Oxford: Berghahn), pp. 3–14

Jesse, Eckhard (1994) 'War die DDR totalitär'? *Aus Politik und Zeitgeschichte*, no. 40, 7 October, pp. 12–23

Kaeble, Hartmut (1994) 'Die Gesellschaft der DDR im internationalen Vergleich' in Kaeble, Hartmut, Kocka, Jürgen and Zwahr, Hartmut (eds.), *Sozialgeschichte der DDR.* (Stuttgart: Klett Cotta), pp. 559–580

Kapferer, Norbert (2000) 'Nostalgia in Germany's New Federal States as a Political and Cultural Phenomenon of the Transformation Process' in Williams, Howard, Wright, Colin and Kapferer, Norbert (eds.), *Political Thought and German Unification. The New German Ideology?* (Basingstoke: Macmillan), pp. 28–49

Keller, Dietmar and Mozek, Reinhard (1998) 'Wir wollen die DDR nicht wiederhaben. Wir lassen sie uns auch nicht nehmen' in Elm, Ludwig, Keller, Dietmar and Mozek Reinhard (eds.), *Ansichten zur Geschichte der DDR*, vol. IX/X. (Eggersdorf: Verlag Matthias Kirchner), pp. 8–31

Klessmann, Christoph (1998) *Zeitgeschichte in Deutschland nach dem Ende des Ost-West Konflikts.* (Essen: Klartext Verlag)

Knabe, Hubertus (1999) *Die unterwanderte Republik. Stasi im Westen.* (Berlin: Propyläen)

Kocka, Jürgen (1999) 'The GDR: A Special Kind of Modern Dictatorship' in Jarausch, Konrad (ed.), *Dictatorship as Experience. Towards a Socio-Cultural History of the GDR.* (New York and Oxford: Berghahn), pp. 17–26

König, Helmut (1998) 'Von der Diktatur zur Demokratie oder Was ist Vergangenheitsbewältigung' in König, Helmut, Kohlstruck, Michael and Wolf, Andreas (eds.), *Vergangenheitsbewältigung am Ende des zwanzigsten Jahrhunderts.* (Opladen and Wiesbaden: Westdeutscher Verlag), pp. 371–392

Kraushaar, Wolfgang (1996) 'Sich aufs Eis wagen. Plädoyer für eine Auseinandersetzung mit der Totalitarismustheorie' in Jesse, Eckhard (ed.), *Totalitarismus im 20. Jahrhundert. Eine Bilanz der internationalen Forschung.* (Bonn: Bundeszentrale für politische Bildung), pp. 453–470

Krisch, Henry (1998) 'Searching for Voters: PDS Mobilisation Strategies, 1994–97', *German Monitor*, no. 42, pp. 38–53

Lindenberger, Thomas (1996) 'Alltagsgeschichte und ihr möglicher Beitrag zu einer Geschichte der DDR' in Bessel, Richard and Jessen, Ralph (eds.), *Die Grenzen der Diktatur. Staat und Gesellschaft in der DDR*. (Göttingen: Vandenhoeck and Ruprecht), pp. 298–325

Lindenberger, Thomas (2000) 'Herrschaft und Eigen-Sinn in der Diktatur. Das Alltagsleben der DDR und sein Platz in der Erinnerungskultur des vereinten Deutschlands', *Aus Politik und Zeitgeschichte*, no. 40, 29 September, pp. 5–12

Lozek, Gerhard (1994) 'Zum Diktaturvergleich von NS-Regime und SED-Staat' in Keller, Dietmar, Modrow, Hans and Wolf, Herbert (eds.), *Ansichten zur Geschichte der DDR*, vol. IV. (Eggersdorf: Verlag Matthias Kirchner), pp. 109–121

McAdams, A James (1996) 'The Honecker Trial: The East German Past and the German Future', *The Review of Politics*, vol. 58, no. 1, pp. 53–80

Mitter, Armin and Wolle, Stefan (1994) 'Der Bielefelder Weg' in Eckert, Rainer, Kowalczuk, Ilso-Sascha and Starke, Isolde (eds.), *Hure oder Muse? Klio in der DDR*. (Edition Berliner Debatte and Gesellschaft für sozialwissenschaftliche Forschung und Publizistik: Berlin), pp. 260–265

Pollack, Detlef (1999) 'Modernisation and Modernisation Blockages in GDR Society' in Jarausch, Konrad (ed.), *Dictatorship as Experience. Towards a Socio-Cultural History of the GDR*. (New York and Oxford: Berghahn), pp. 27–45

Quint, Peter (1999) 'Judging the Past: The Prosecution of East German Border Guards and the GDR Chain of Command', *The Review of Politics*, vol. 61, no. 2, pp. 310–315

Raue, Paul-Josef (1998) 'Demokratie und Diktatur in Deutschland. Rückblick auf ein Jahrhundert und einen viertägigen Kongreß in Bogensee', *Zeitschrift des Forschungsverbundes SED-Staat an der FU-Berlin*, no. 8, pp. 144–48

Roth, Karl-Heinz (1998) 'Der Einfluß der Totalitarismustheorie auf die Bundestag Enquete-Kommission 'Aufarbeitung von Geschichte und Folgen der SED-Diktatur in Deutschland' und die Auswirkungen auf die politische Kultur der Bundesrepublik' in Elm, Ludwig, Keller, Dietmar and Mozek, Reinhard (eds.), *Ansichten zur Geschichte der DDR*, vol. IX/X. (Eggersdorf: Verlag Matthias Kirchner), pp. 84–160

Rupnik, Jaques (1988) *The Other Europe*. (London: Weidenfeld and Nicolson)

Sa'adah, Anne (1998) *Germany's Second Chance. Trust, Justice and Democratization*. (Cambridge, Massachusetts, and London: Harvard University Press)

Schröder, Richard (1993) *Deutschland schwierig Vaterland. Für eine neue politische Kultur*. (Freiburg, Basel and Vienna: Herder)

Sozialist (2001) www.sozialistisen.de/programmentwurfg/kapitel4.htm

Staritz, Dietrich (2000) 'Das Ende der DDR. Erklärungsansätze', *Utopie kreativ*, Special Issue, October, pp. 11–20

Waibel, Harry (1996) *Rechtsextremismus in der DDR bis 1989*. (Cologne: PapyRossa Verlag)

Weber, Hermann (1997) '"Asymmetrie" bei der Erforschung des Kommunismus und der DDR Geschichte?' *Aus Politik und Zeitgeschichte*, no. 26, 20 June, pp. 3–14

Wehler, Hans-Ulrich (1998) 'Diktaturvergleich, Totalitarismustheorie und DDR-Geschichte', in Bauerkämper, Arnd Sabrow, Martin and Stöver, Bernd (eds.), *Doppelte Geschichte. Deutschdeutsche Beziehungen 1945–1990*. (Bonn: Verlag J. H. W. Dietz Nachfolger), pp. 346–352

Winters, Peter Jochen (2000) 'Zwiespältiges Urteil im letzten Politbüro-Prozeß', *Deutschland Archiv*, vol. 33, no. 4, pp. 525–528

Wippermann, Wolfgang (1997) *Totalitarismustheorien. Die Entwicklung der Diskussion von den Anfängen bis heute*. (Darmstadt: Primus Verlag)

Zitelmann, Rainer (.1999) *Hitler. The Politics of Seduction*. (London: London House)

Chapter Two

Financing German Unity: Challenges, Methods and Longer-term Consequences

Christopher Flockton

A Seriously Underestimated Challenge

The unification of Germany would inevitably have presented grave funding problems, given the development gap between east and west – there was the challenge posed by the inherited structures of central planning and also the obsolescence of productive capacity, infrastructures and a significant part of the housing stock. The income differences between the two regions would inevitably also pose adjustment problems when they were unified to form one large labour market and social welfare system. However, fateful decisions at economic union on 1 July 1990 over the exchange rate and wage bargaining, accompanied by an extremely over-optimistic assessment of the development challenge (as evidenced in the unwillingness to raise taxes before mid-1991) greatly exacerbated the adjustment problems and the ensuing financial costs. The rapidity of the economic collapse in the east, the very low productivity in all areas of economic activity, the application of wage harmonisation agreements for adjustment to western wage levels, and the extension of the western social security system have combined to produce a dependent region in the new *Länder*, whose income level has been heavily dependent on financial transfers from the west, yet whose level of production costs was unattractively high to outside investors. High levels of income transfer and of capital subsidy for new investments were therefore needed, alongside infrastructure modernisation costs and unemployment and social security expenditures. While convergence in economic performance was achieved from 1992 to 1996, from that period onwards, growth rates between east and west have paralleled each other and then widened, implying a divergence once more. It is clear then that the catch-up between east and west is not a matter of a half-decade, as government spokesmen in the early unification period implied, but one of many decades.

The fact that one-half of incomes in the east has been provided by transfers, less than one-half of transfers from the west have been invested in infrastructure and economic and social physical capital, and that only one-half of the costs of these transfers was met by taxes and charges, the remainder through debt, all imply that there would be very serious public finance consequences (Paqué, 2000). For the first years of unification there was a very rapid build-up of deficits and debt: tax increases did not take effect until mid-1991 and later, and hefty rises in social insurance charges began in 1992 and 1993. It was, however, only in 1994 that budget consolidation in the form of restraining budget deficits really began, while the build-up of debt proceeded rapidly until mid-decade. Of course, these imposts on incomes, primarily in the west, reduced disposable income, reduced consumption and burdened the cost of labour, in the form of social security charges. They therefore acted to depress the rate of growth in the economy, in spite of the positive stimulus of public borrowing and the evident modernisation of the economic base in the east. Room for budgetary policy manoeuvre became very tight, and Finance Minister Theo Waigel (CSU) struggled to contain deficits for a major part of the 1990s. The emergency budgets and the creative accounting required to ensure that Germany met the Maastricht Treaty convergence criteria in 1997 for entry to the single currency remain in the popular consciousness, long after memories of other budgetary battles have faded. Likewise, the Employment and Social Affairs minister for many years, Norbert Blüm (CDU) struggled with benefit cuts and pension reforms, in an effort to control the ballooning costs of the welfare system during the 1990s. Even for the year 2002, a federal budget deficit of 2.7 per cent is possible, perilously close to the 3 per cent limit of the eurozone's Stability and Growth Pact (*Handelsblatt*, 4 December 2001).

With hindsight, it is very easy to focus on the initial errors of diagnosis, the political unwillingness to raise taxes and the facility with which costs were transferred to the social insurance system. It is undeniable that the nature of the economic challenge was seriously underestimated in the early post-unification period and that the ensuing costs were therefore amplified. A good case can also be made that the transfer of federal German economic and social institutions, such as the collective bargaining and social welfare systems, often held to be too rigid, hampered, rather than assisted, the adjustment mechanisms in the east. However, unification was without precedent and its achievement, in spite of the social costs, the financial burden and the disappointed hopes in the east, must be underscored. The quality of physical infrastructure in the east, though variable, is now in some cases of world quality, and there are showcase manufacturing plants of the highest technological level. Of course, the manufacturing base is far too small and too little export-oriented, but there are other assets in the east, such as its much more flexible labour market than in the old *Länder* (Paqué, 2000).

This analysis of the financing of German unification sets the scene briefly by elucidating the economic consequences of unification, the creation of a dual economy and the macroeconomic effects; it then details the initial funding provisions, and the funds and welfare support put in place at the time of unification. Particular attention is paid to the Solidarity Pact I negotiations of 1993, which arranged for the incorporation of the new *Länder* into the States' Financial Equalisation System, so providing at least a modicum of financial stability for the east German *Länder* and their municipalities. The public finance costs, the rises in tax and social insurance contribution, the strains on the welfare state and the budget-driven reduction in welfare provision are highlighted, before the recent revisions to the Solidarity Pact and Equalisation System are sketched, which give a funding perspective to 2015 or 2020. This long horizon, stretching well into the future, gives a sense of the continuing financial costs, which must, even in moderate measure, restrain the growth rate in Germany. There has been considerable success over the last ten year period in constraining the burgeoning costs without any crisis. Nevertheless, public asset sales, spending restraint and welfare reform continue to frame the public agenda, while the costs of unification are slowly but progressively absorbed.

German Economic, Monetary and Social Union and Initial Financial Provisions

As a result of the seriously deteriorating economic situation in the GDR following the opening of the Wall in November 1989, a set of rapid policy decisions were taken by a small cabinet committee of the Federal government in February 1990 to extend economic, monetary and social union to the East. Events were sealed by the election in March 1990 of the first CDU-led government in the GDR under de Maizière, and serious negotiations on the State Treaty for economic unification of the two parts of Germany commenced. There was concurrently a somewhat muffled debate in the West over the terms under which economic and monetary unification should take place: there were warnings by Lutz Hoffmann, chairman of the DIW research institute (which soon came to appear prescient), a stated preference by Karl-Otto Pöhl, president of the *Bundesbank* for a less favourable rate of currency exchange, and a warning letter from the Advisory Council of the Economics Ministry over a too rapid unification of the two economies (Sinn and Sinn, 1992; Ghaussy and Schäfer, 1993; Hoffmann, 1993). Despite this, fateful decisions were taken in haste against a rapidly deteriorating background, but there remained considerable optimism in government circles over the future adjustment capacity of the East German economy. The State Treaty introduced economic, monetary and social union on 1 July 1990. This set the terms for the currency exchange, it extended the West German economic and social constitution to the GDR, established a social market economy in place of a centrally-administered, command economy and exposed East Germany overnight to West German and world market competition. Private property was established, the old monopolistic *Kombinate* (combines) were to be broken up, the Deutschmark and the western monetary and banking order were instituted, and the Federal German labour market order and welfare state arrangements thenceforth applied. Unification produced a dual economy overnight, with rapid falls in output and employment in the east and an induced boom in the west. Employment in the east shrank rapidly from 10 million to 6.6 million, while employment in industry shrank from 3.6m to 660,000. By the depth of the depression in mid-1992, industrial output collapsed to 60 per cent of its level in the first half of 1990. Meanwhile, west Germany experienced an inflationary boom, as a result of the sharp rise in demand for its capital goods and consumer products. As a large part of the extra demand was fuelled by debt-financed government spending, the western half of Germany quickly experienced excess demand and overheating of its economy, with inflation peaking at 4.5 per cent in mid-1992. This then caused the *Bundesbank* to step in, with recession-inducing high interest rates. The causes of the rapid collapse in the east lie in the at least fourfold overvaluation of the eastern exchange rate upon the currency exchange, the very rapid wage inflation as a result of the wage harmonisation agreements signed in winter 1990–91, the obsolescent and polluting nature of perhaps 30–40 per cent of east German industrial capacity, and the collapse of Comecon trading from 1 January 1991 (Siebert, 1992; Sinn and Sinn, 1992; Ghaussy and Schäfer, 1993).

Of course, with hindsight, it is easy to conclude that the Federal government had very seriously underestimated the nature of the task involved in economic unification, and that deeply-flawed policy choices had been taken during 1990. The economic and social costs of a hurried transformation have been plainly apparent over the ensuing decade and will now stretch well into future decades. In spite of a range of warning voices, both the need to act quickly and a misguided optimism led to fateful policy decisions, whose impacts soon became apparent. Government spokesmen, in particular Chancellor Kohl, whose expression of 'blühende Landschaften' (blooming landscapes) echoed down the years, and his Economics Minister of the time, Helmut Haussmann (FDP), continued to express strong confidence that East Germany would achieve an economic miracle upon the introduction of the Deutschmark with economic unification, comparable to the events of 1948–49, which themselves were held to be the starting point of West Germany's 'miracle'. No rise in taxation would be needed to pay for the task of rebuilding in the new states and this policy orientation formed an important plank in the December 1990 election programmes of the CDU/CSU-FDP coalition parties. In fact, the historical parallels were very weak indeed and were based on very faulty economics. The introduction of the DM in West Germany in 1948 and the attendant liberalisation had taken place in a world that was reopening to trade and one where the incipient Korean crisis would give a rapid boost to West German exports. Equally, in spite of the cartels, concentration and economic controls affecting West German industry under the National Socialists, a quite recognisable capitalist order was still in place in 1948. In contrast, the challenge for East Germany to transform forty-five years of a deeply-distorted centrally-planned economy, from an exaggerated level of economic concentration into the huge, monopolistic *Kombinate*, where the population had lost much sense of the profit motive and market behaviour and where exposure to the rigours and price structures of the world economy was tightly controlled, was of a wholly different nature. This was particularly so as the new states were absorbed overnight into an open world trading system and had to adapt to the highly-developed and complicated legislation of the West German economic constitution (Siebert, 1993). Perhaps in 1990, government speakers merely wanted to express their faith in the ability of the German people to build on their obvious strengths of order, industry and technical application.

The Legal Provisions and Instruments for Financial Support to the East

The State Treaty on Economic, Monetary and Social Union came into force on 1 July 1990 and immediately ushered in the unification of the two economies, in terms of their economic constitution, their monetary arrangements and their labour market and social welfare provisions. East Germany was exposed overnight to western and world competition. From a financial viewpoint, article 26, paragraph 2 of the treaty applied the western budget structures to the east, including a federal budget and tax structure, the creation of a free-standing social insurance system, the separate status of publicly-owned enterprises, and the application of clear subsidy rules. Of course, in key aspects, territorial authorities in the east had to be created from scratch, since the existing institutions had largely been a shell under the highly-centralised GDR constitution. Article 27 of the State Treaty imposed borrowing limits on territorial authorities and on the *Treuhandanstalt* (which had been created in March 1990 to restructure and in part privatise the vast GDR state assets in industry, commerce, services, land and buildings). Critical in the present discussion is article 28, which specified transfers from West Germany to support the state budget of the GDR and to pump-prime the full range of social insurance schemes. Thus, for the first half of 1990, DM 22 bn was allocated, rising to DM 35 bn for the whole of 1991, with a supplementary DM 750 million to support the pension insurance system which was introduced in 1990 and DM 2 bn for this purpose in 1991, as well as DM 3 bn for unemployment insurance. The Treaty also provided in article 26, paragraph 4 that all income deriving from privatisation should be allocated for the purposes of structural economic adjustment and for budget support in the GDR (Bach and Vesper, 2000: 195). As will be seen, these allocations soon proved to be wholly insufficient for transformation and for income support in a situation of mass unemployment.

Alongside these direct allocations from the federal and *Treuhand* budgets, a number of key parallel, 'shadow' funds were created or drawn upon to support the transformation in the east. Principal among these was the German Unity Fund, which was seen as the main instrument for funding adjustment in the east, donated with bond-financing of DM 115 bn at the outset. Its expenditure was planned to fall rapidly over time. The Unity Fund was, in particular, intended to fund infrastructural development and to pump-prime the social insurance funds, so putting a social safety net in place. Since the east German *Länder* were not to form part of the States' Financial Equalisation System (*Länderfinanzausgleich*)[1] until the beginning of 1995, the Unity Fund would operate as a partial substitute until the end of 1994. Other funds, in addition to the *Treuhandanstalt*'s own allocation and revenues, were as follows:

-the *Kreditabwicklungsfonds*, which assumed the inherited GDR state debt and State bank balance sheet losses due to the terms of the currency conversion;
-the *Erblastentilgungsfonds*, which assumed the inherited public housing sector debt of the GDR, and which came to assume the *Kreditabwicklungsfonds* and *Treuhand* debt on 1 January 1995;
-the existing budget of the Federal Labour Office became responsible for unemployment benefit, short-time working, early retirement and retraining costs;
-the European Recovery Programme (ERP) Special Funds bore much of the cost of aid for the establishment of small- and medium-sized enterprises, R&D assistance and regional investment aid[2];
-the Joint Task (*Gemeinschaftsaufgabe*) 'Improvement of regional economic structure', funded by federal and land governments, provided standard regional development assistance;
-the Federal Railways and the German Bundespost (to be split later into primarily *Deutsche Telekom* and the *Deutsche Post*) had infrastructure renewal budgets of at least DM 100 bn each for east Germany over the 1990s.

Finally, the east German *Länder* and municipalities also had prime responsibilities for infrastructure renewal, industrial promotion, housing renewal and social assistance, even as they struggled to establish themselves in the west German mould, with only a weak pre-existing basis in the form of inherited GDR structures. To this catalogue of treaty provisions, one should add some key innovations of the Unification Treaty, which came into force with political union on 3 October 1990. These provided much greater detail about the implementation of the west German pension and health insurance systems in the east, they spelled out the objectives of the *Treuhandanstalt*, (so strengthening the priority given to privatisation of State productive assets) and specified that confiscated property be returned (*Restitution*) to previous owners where possible in place of monetary compensation. This latter significantly delayed economic restructuring in the east and has also had financial consequences in that many aspects concerning the return of property remained unresolved.

Clearly, the financial policy orientation underlying this approach assumed that the economic costs of unification could be contained and would fall over time. The decision not to raise taxes, but to rely on debt-financing and eastern asset sales as the prime sources of revenue reflects the excessive optimism over the scale and speed of transformation and the rate of economic catch-up with the west: it also reflected a proper assessment that a proportion of the costs of the extraordinary historic opportunity of unification should be spread over generations by a rise in public debt. The emphasis on capital subsidies as a major development instrument is also clear from these provisions: direct wage subsidies to sustain employment were never seriously considered, since they were feared to have wage inflationary effects and substitution effects between those on subsidised and those on regular work contracts (Flockton and Esser, 1992).

The first recognition of the depth of the transformation crisis and of the scale of its costs occurred in the early months of 1991. The Eastern Recovery (*Gemeinschaftswerk 'Aufschwung Ost'*) emergency programme was announced shortly after there had been street demonstrations in east Berlin against the closures of renowned east German names, such as the *Interflug* airline and the *Wartburg* car works. A particular urgency was injected into the situation with the assassination over Easter 1991 of the president of the *Treuhandanstalt*, Detlev Rohwedder, by Red Army Fraction terrorists. The German Unity Fund was topped up twice (rather than the declining support planned), and the DM 21 bn Eastern Recovery programme was introduced to fund renovation and modernisation projects, and also job creation schemes by the eastern *Länder* and municipalities. This implicitly recognised that the economic collapse had dealt a devastating blow to the budgets of territorial authorities there and, concurrently, the eastern *Länder* were absorbed fully into the value-added tax revenue structure of the *Länder* (Bach and Vesper, 2000: 195). The Federal government also decided to raise the levels of aid for business investment in the east, thus more than reversing the planned reductions. The 12 per cent general investment grant applicable throughout the new *Länder* (20 per cent for small firms) was extended to last to the end of 1998, though falling in stages, to 8 per cent and then 5 per cent, but in addition a 50 per cent special tax allowance on investment expenditures was instituted, applicable from June 1991 and running to 1997/1999 (according to the type of development). Finally, the Joint Task's regional aid, in the form of discretionary investment grants, also applied to a maximum of 23 per cent of the investment value. Cumulated, the grants covered one-third of the investment cost, and including the tax relief, up to one-half of a project cost could be covered (Deutsche Bundesbank, 1998b). Subsidies to the east then rose very strongly as a result, rising from DM 19 bn in 1991 to DM 34 bn in 1996, only to fall gradually to DM 29 bn in 1999, as a result of the phasing-out of the very favourable tax allowances on investments there (Deutsche Bundesbank, 2000: 22; Bundesministerium für Finanzen, 2001).

Over the first half of 1991, the question was increasingly posed as to how long Germany could avoid tax increases. The deficits were rising rapidly and public debt was accumulating at an alarming rate. In June 1991, tax decisions were taken and there were, concurrently, hefty rises in social insurance contributions, to meet eastern social welfare expenditures. The Solidarity Surcharge ('Soli') was instituted in mid-1991 at first for one year, at a rate of 7.5 per cent on all income tax, investment income and corporation taxes due. It was accompanied by a two stage increase in mineral oil tax, a rise in VAT and a rise in insurance tax. In 1993, a 30 per cent withholding tax on all interest incomes was instituted, although the tax-free allowance on savings income was raised. Later, in 1995, the 'Soli' was reintroduced at a rate of 7.5 per cent, falling to 5.5 per cent in 1998, although the tax revenue shortfall arising from this was made up partly by a rise in VAT by 1 per cent point to 16 per cent (OECD, 1998, 2001). Alongside these direct and indirect tax increases, however, there were sharp rises in social insurance contributions, as will be elucidated below.

Economic Collapse, Renewal and the *Treuhand* Privatisations

As has been seen, the first two years following economic union saw the creation of a dual economy, with a 'straw fire', evanescent boom created in the west and deep depression in the east. The Bundesbank's action in raising interest rates so steeply cut the overheating, engineered a recession and heavily influenced the re-orientation of budgetary policy towards deficit containment. The high German interest rates of 1992/93 also helped plunge the EU's Exchange Rate Mechanism into crisis, forcing out weaker currencies from the system. A recovery in the east can be dated from 1993, when regional GDP growth rates of 8 per cent to 9 per cent can be seen, and growth rates in productive industry reached 12 per cent to 15 per cent annually. Only in 1997, with the slowing of the western economy and, in particular, as a result of a construction industry crisis in the east following the ending of the special tax reliefs on investment from 1997, did the growth rate in the east fall to that of the west and then sink below it. In the years since 1997, there has therefore only been a sluggish aggregate performance in the east, and a divergence rather than convergence in growth can be observed. The variable successes in the manufacturing sector there have not been able to offset the deep recession in construction. In the present discussion, this points to continuing very heavy income transfers and 'second' labour market support funding. Effective (open and disguised) unemployment in the east has rarely fallen below 30 per cent, with registered unemployment generally staying at 17 per cent or more, with the remainder made up by special labour market measures. In the first eighteen months after unification, for example, up to 2 million benefited from the short-time working provisions, even when there was zero work to be done. A significant part of the older workforce were then moved to forms of early retirement (discussed in more detail below) and others were placed in retraining or job creation schemes (Flockton and Esser, 1992; Deutsche Bundesbank, 1998a). As will be seen, the support costs for the insurance funds, the Federal Labour Office and the federal subsidy to the Office all represented large income transfers to the east. The privatisation policy of the *Treuhand* has been the subject of bitter debate (Nick, 1995; Arbeitsgruppe, 1992; Lange and Shackleton, 1998), but in the present context, one has to stress the build-up of losses by the privatisation and restructuring agency. Instead of asset sales forming a major source of revenue to cover the transformation costs in the east, the financial balance sheet was wholly negative. Under the reform communist government of Hans Modrow in early March 1990 in the GDR, the state assets to be allocated to the *Treuhand* were estimated to be of DM 1000 bn in value. *Treuhand* President Rohwedder downgraded this estimate to approximately DM 600 bn in December 1990. However, when the *Treuhand* closed its doors at the end of 1994, the final debts were estimated at DM 275 bn. Sales revenues totalled only DM 74 bn. Meanwhile, during the first five years of the decade, federal subsidies to the *Treuhand* were running at DM 30 bn annually (Deutsche Bundesbank, 2000: 21). It is apparent that rather than being a source of revenue, the *Treuhand* itself incorporated all the very transformation difficulties of the east German economy.

The 1993 Solidarity Pact, the Federal Consolidation Programme and the States' Financial Equalisation System

By the Spring of 1993, it was transparently clear that a longer term re-ordering of the financial dispositions among the Federal government and states would be needed, not least to incorporate the new *Länder* into the States' Financial Equalisation System in a way which would secure their future financial soundness. At the same time, a re-orientation of the national budgetary stance was imperative, so as to rein back the ballooning deficits and debt. It had been commonly thought that the western *Länder* had escaped easily from the main burdens of funding unification (which had fallen primarily to the German Unity Fund, the federal budget and to the social security funds), but the expiry of the Unity Fund at the end of 1994 posed the difficult question of how the new *Länder* could be absorbed into the States' Financial Equalisation System from January 1995. The Federal government therefore sought by triangulation of these conflicting interests, in the form of a 'Solidarity Pact', to reach a re-ordering of financial arrangements within the federal system, while at the same time reining in its own deficits.

The Federal Consolidation Programme of Spring 1993 provided for the full integration of the east German *Länder* into the States' Financial Equalisation System from 1995 and so offered a secure, longer-term funding basis for the *Länder* and municipalities there. This was decisive for the funding of adjustment and transformation, whether of infrastructural and housing modernisation, economic promotion and technology transfer or job creation schemes and the funding of social assistance. The Consolidation Programme had two main constituent elements, a re-ordering of the Equalisation System and, secondly, the extension of the *Erblastentilgungsfonds* (Inherited Burdens Amortisation Fund). The latter would take over the *Kreditabwicklungsfonds*, a part of the debt of the east German housing system, and the debt of the *Treuhandanstalt*, which was closing its doors at the end of 1994. The *Deutsche Einheitsfonds*, though to be closed at the end of 1994, would continue to have its own amortisation arrangements. Here the debt service burden, previously borne 50:50 by the Federal government and the western states, would in future be borne more by the latter. (Bach and Vesper, 2000: 196)

The Solidarity Pact negotiations can be interpreted in terms of the vertical allocations between the Federal government and the *Länder*, the horizontal equalisation among the states, and the provision of large-scale supplementary transfers by the Federal government. (Bösinger, 1999) The negotiations agreed firstly on a transfer of DM 57 bn for the year 1995 from the federation to the states, to be followed by an equalisation between the old and the new *Länder*. This would ensure that the new *Länder* and their municipalities would receive payments per inhabitant of 105 per cent of the west German level, so as to meet their rebuilding and modernisation objectives. The re-ordering involved changes to both the vertical and horizontal transfers. Firstly, the *Länder* share of the VAT revenues was raised from 37 per cent to 44 per cent: this had the consequential impact not only that the new *Länder* could be incorporated in the system, but also that the 'horizontal' financial disparity between the states was reduced. Concurrently, the rate of equalisation among *Länder* was lowered, which permitted the net contributing states to retain a higher marginal rate of their extra tax revenue earned.

The significant expansion in the supplementary transfers made by the Federal government reflected, however, the key responsibility of the national government to ensure that all-German disparities are reduced. On the one hand, the Federal government agreed to expand its investment aid for economic modernisation and social facilities support (under article 104a, clause 4 of the Constitution) from DM 6.6 bn in 1995 to DM 10.4 bn in 1999. Secondly, it expanded its three forms of special supplementary transfer (*Bundesergänzungszuweisung*), which are designed to enable the horizontal equalisation among the States, and therefore of transfers to the east, to reach appropriate levels. The Special Needs (*Sonderbedarf*) supplement was by far the largest, in recognition of the particular financial needs of the eastern *Länder* to fulfil their duties, and here the transfer rose from DM 14 bn annually in 1995 to DM 22 bn in 1999. The shortfall (*Fehlbedarf*) transfer was also important in covering any final gap, and to ensure that 90 per cent of such a gap was closed: here the provision was for a rise from DM 3.5 bn in 1995 to DM 3.8 bn in 1999. As Bach and Vesper (2000: 197) show, the final outcome was one where the western *Länder* had to raise their contribution level to the equalisation system. Within a larger envelope of funding, including VAT rises and the 'Soli' revenues, the *Bund* made savings of DM 5.8 bn in the first year of operation, the new *Länder* received an extra DM 8.5 bn annually, and the western *Länder* had to pay an extra DM 4 bn. This helped secure the funding basis of the eastern *Länder*, although their debt accumulation has continued at a strong rate over recent years and they have very large continuing physical capital investment needs, as will be elucidated below. It has to be said that these Solidarity Pact I negotiations did little to reform the underlying mechanisms of the Equalisation System and shortly after the introduction of the revised system in 1995, the main contributors among the western *Länder*, notably Bavaria and Baden-Württemberg, with partial support from Hesse and more recently Rheinland-Palatinate, opened discussions among themselves with the objective of lodging a formal complaint with the Federal Constitutional Court against the design of the system. Reform would be tied up with the renewal of the programme of transfers to the east required at the latest by 2004, and so the Solidarity Pact II negotiations of 2001 would come to take place against a background of pressures for *Finanzausgleich* reform.

Deficits, Debt and the Tax Burden

As stated previously, total public transfers to the east had reached DM 1.179 trillion (DM 888 bn net) by the end of 1997 (Deutscher Bundestag, 1997) and a further DM 1 trillion had been transferred by west German and international private investors. (Of these public transfers, the Federal Labour Office had paid DM 199 bn, the pension insurance system DM 80 bn, the western *Länder* and municipalities DM 66 bn, the German Unity Fund DM 160.7 bn and the EU DM 41 bn. Separate from this calculation, there remained the repayment costs of the DM 360 bn Inherited Debt Amortisation Fund). It has to be admitted that any assessment of the scale of net transfers raises definitional questions and would in any case pose difficulties of calculation. The federal finance ministry and the *Bundesbank*, for example, assessed public transfers at DM 140 bn annually over the 1990s or 4.5 per cent of west German GDP, while others such as Bach and Vesper (2000) estimated more conservatively at DM 110 bn. Any estimate should be net of tax revenues raised in the east and interest paid in the east to western lenders, but it is also clear that west German producers have benefited significantly from eastern demand, and so there has been a significant multiplier effect on western activity. The taxes raised on this heightened western activity should be credited to the east, as should the tax allowances granted largely to western investors who availed themselves of the special tax depreciation measures granted on investment in the east. Finally, one should include only federal expenditures which exceed 'normal' spending, although some federal programmes previously justified by the division of Germany now represent a saving. For example, the cuts in promotional aid to the eastern edge of the old Federal Republic (*Zonenrandgebiet*) and to west Berlin, including the VAT reduction in west Berlin, helped reduce subsidies paid to west Germany from DM 59 bn in 1991 to DM 48 bn in 1995 (Deutsche Bundesbank, 2000; 22). It will be apparent that any assessment is heavily dependent on the assumptions adopted. Notwithstanding these qualifications, the successive years of high budget deficits led to a rapid accumulation of debt. Prior to unification, in 1989, West German debt amounted to less than DM 1,000 bn or 41.3 per cent of GDP. Rapid debt accumulation in the first half of the 1990s led to a debt level of over DM 2,000 bn by 1996 and threatened the fulfilment of the Maastricht convergence criteria for membership of the EU single currency. It rose to DM 2,346 bn by the end of 1999, or 60.6 per cent of GDP. (In this latter year, however, there had been a rise in commitments, as the federal budget assumed full responsibility of the debt occasioned by the railway reform and of the Inherited Debt Amortisation Fund). Broadly, one-half of this increase in state debt can be associated with unification costs narrowly defined and it was the federal budget itself which had assumed the prime responsibility for the debt and interest servicing. Interest payments had, therefore, risen from 12 per cent of federal revenues in 1989 to 19 per cent ten years later.

As noted above, the turnaround in policy on taxation occurred in mid-1991, with the institution of the Solidarity Surcharge, the withholding tax and successive increases in indirect taxes, such as mineral oil tax and VAT. Later, towards the second half of the 1990s, the pendulum swung towards tax reform and the abolition of certain taxes. Thus, for instance, the property tax and the local trade capital tax (*Gewerbekapitalsteuer*) were never introduced in the east and were abolished in the west in 1997 and 1998, respectively. There were also attempts at tax simplification by the simultaneous eradication of the thicket of tax allowances and the lowering of tax rates. This was the case for the 1996 Annual Tax Law (*Jahressteuergesetz*), the 1997/98 major tax reform (*Grosse Steuerreform*) under Finance Minister Waigel and, finally, the 1999–2002 Tax Reduction Law of the Red-Green coalition. Also worth mentioning is the 1994 *Standortsicherungsgesetz* (Law to Secure Production Location), which cut top corporation tax rates and top income tax rates on commercial incomes (OECD, 1998: 69; OECD 2001: 52). To a varying extent, these successive tax reforms under both CDU-CSU/FDP and under Red-Green governments sought to reduce the effective marginal taxation rates on corporations and incomes from commercial activity. There has therefore been a notable shift within a broadly constant tax revenue share of GDP, which has burdened indirect taxation and wages tax, while relieving company taxation (Bach and Vesper, 2000: 215).

An Over-burdened Welfare State?

The rise in social insurance contribution rates deserves particular attention. Partly to fund the higher costs in the east of unemployment benefits, the special labour market measures, the widespread use of early retirement, the favourable pension arrangements and the securing of the health system there, social security contributions rose rapidly in the first half of the 1990s. Many of these functions can be considered 'versicherungsfremd' (outside the direct responsibility of the insurance system) and should have been supported by the tax system. In the face of reluctance to take responsibility for a rise in direct and indirect taxation, the CDU-CSU/FDP governments of Chancellor Kohl permitted rises in social insurance contribution rates. Thus, unemployment insurance rates rose from 4.3 per cent of gross earnings in April 1991 to 6.5 per cent at the beginning of 1993 and pension contribution rates rose from 18.7 per cent in 1991 to 20.3 per cent in 1997. It was only by the subsequent raising of VAT and the introduction of the ecology tax in 2000 that further rises in pension contribution rates have been avoided (OECD, 2001). Of course, there are serious long-term structural problems affecting the welfare system in Germany, as in other European countries, and successive governments from the mid-1980s have grappled with the mounting pension costs (for a discussion of reforms such as those of 1997 and 2000, see Toft, 1996, and Konrad and Wagner, 2000) and have sought in several attempts to rein in health expenditure (Seehofer, 1996; OECD, 2001). In the face of slowing productivity growth, high unemployment, an ageing population and escalating health supply costs, the German welfare system, as elsewhere, faces fundamental structural difficulties (Flockton, 1998). However, it is incontrovertible that German unification has put the system under very serious medium-term strain, partly because of a reluctance to make the tax system bear its full share of the unification costs. This has raised labour costs (since social insurance payments are largely borne by the employer and employee alike) and has led to popular fears that funding of the welfare system may be unsustainable.

The 1997 study by the German Institute for Economics Research (DIW) makes clear that in the three main areas of the welfare system, surpluses earned in west Germany (in spite of rising unemployment there) were exceeded by ballooning costs in the east (DIW, 1997). The pension insurance system in the west, for example, recorded surpluses of DM 71.1 bn in the period 1991–97, while there was a DM 75 bn shortfall in the east. The early retirement provisions in the new *Länder* had been exceptionally generous, in the form of early retirement benefit (*Vorruhestandsgeld*) and benefit to bridge the gap between employment and the onset of retirement (*Altersübergangsgeld*), as a way of ameliorating mass unemployment by pensioning off workers early, encouraging part-time work by the older workers and removing the older, long-term unemployed from the unemployment register (*Arbeitslosenstatistik*). By the end of 1995, for example, 750,000 ex-employees in the east had taken early retirement. The revised Employment Promotion Law of 1 January 1995 also put pressure on the pension system, as it eased the path of the older unemployed worker to take early retirement and so shifted the cost from the Federal Labour Office to the pension insurance funds. The Labour Office also faced losses of DM 70 bn in the first half of the 1990s, however, in spite of unemployment insurance fund surpluses of DM 116 bn accumulated in west Germany. The deficits had to be met by a rundown of the Office's reserves and by large subsidies from the federal budget (Deutsche Bundesbank, 1998a). Finally, in the health sector, there were not solely the costs of pump-priming the health funds, but specific regulations in the east also burdened their budgets. The revised Employment Promotion Law of 1995 in article 157, paragraph 3, for example, allowed a 20 per cent reduction in health insurance contributions paid in respect of the unemployed to be met by the funds themselves. The strain this caused has been a contributory factor in forcing an amalgamation of the eastern and western fund systems.

A detailed catalogue of the cuts in eligibility and the value of welfare benefits would scarcely be useful in this context, but it has to be said that there have been numerous changes over the years, so as to restrain the expenditure dynamic of the social welfare system in periods of slow growth and high unemployment. Reductions in unemployment benefit, in unemployment assistance for those without accrued entitlement (*originäre Hilfe*), a slower uprating of social assistance, a reduction in income support for ex-students and ex-army conscripts (*Unterhaltsgeld*), and the restriction of child-rearing benefit to those on lower incomes, have been put in place in order to restrict the financial imbalances (Otremba, 1999: 23). In other areas, where costs were borne largely by employers, the Kohl governments also sought to make savings in the period 1996–98, for example by cutting bad weather payments for construction workers and sick pay provisions

Overall, therefore, as a result of the tax changes and the rise in social insurance costs, net incomes in west Germany over the 1990s have been rising slowly and have only just exceeded inflation. In real terms, western take-home wages and salaries have risen slowly, except for the early boom period and short bursts of wage inflation in 1996, for example. To an extent, these low net wage increases reflect labour market weakness as well as high levels of compulsory deductions: they have, however, restrained consumption and therefore the growth rate of the economy itself.

The 2001 Solidarity Pact II Negotiations and the Reform of the States' Financial Equalisation System

As noted above, the states principally contributing to the Financial Equalisation System lodged a formal complaint with the Constitutional Court three years after the 1995 incorporation of the new *Länder* into the system. The complaint held that the system was discriminatory, in that after reallocation it significantly changed the relative ranking of states according to their financial strength per head. Particular mechanisms in the system favoured the city states, for example, while the incorporation of the financially weak eastern states had left those revenue-strong western states in a much weaker relative position after transfers. The complainants claimed that states should have a higher marginal rate of retention of extra tax revenue earned, as an incentive for effective tax gathering and as a reward for sound financial management: the present system left them with only 10 pfennigs for every extra mark raised. They focussed their criticisms on the heavy per capita weighting of 1.35 for city states, the so-called harbour 'burden' and on the very high rate of the equalisation to be achieved (namely, no state should receive a revenue per inhabitant less than 95 per cent of that of the other states) (OECD, 1998). One might add, however, that one aspect of the mechanism favours the richer large states, namely, the fact that only one-half of the tax revenue strength of the municipalities is taken into account: were this to be fully taken into account then the transfer to the east would be approximately DM 5 bn larger (Vesper, 1998). The Federal Constitutional Court decided in November 1999 that a reform of the system was to be agreed in two stages. Firstly, by the end of 2002, the Bundestag should vote on a law which would enunciate the underlying principles of the equalisation system and, secondly, further legislation should spell out in detail the revised system which would come into force from the beginning of 2005. Among the principles to be revised were the division of VAT between the federal and *Land* governments and in parallel the system of supplementary transfers (*Ergänzungszuweisungen*), the city state weighting and the municipal tax revenue weighting. Overall, no *Land* should have a net financial strength less than 95 per cent of the average. While a fundamental reform could potentially threaten the financial base of the eastern *Länder*, nevertheless, the Court was clear in insisting that the system should fully sustain all *Länder*, enabling them to fulfil all their functions (*Handelsblatt*, May–June 2001, various).

The reform of the Equalisation System has been closely tied to the negotiation of the Solidarity Pact II, which will continue federal financial assistance to the east after the expiry of the present scheme in 2004. The special federal investment assistance and the scale of east Germany's continuing investment and operational needs are intrinsically linked to the federal supplementary transfers and to the horizontal transfers in the Equalisation System. During 2000 and 2001, there was considerable sabre-rattling and tactical manoeuvring by the state prime ministers in the east, so as to gain a continuation of the level of transfers at broadly present volumes until 2015 or 2020. Concurrently, the richer opposition-ruled western states publicly questioned the interstate financial transfer arrangements in other areas, such as hospital investment spending within the health system and the federal labour office budget. However, in part this reflected political posturing ahead of federal elections in September 2002 (OECD, 2001; *Handelsblatt*, 2001, various). The pressure was on the Federal government to settle the Solidarity Pact II issue well in advance of the election period in order to shore up its electoral base in the east. Various studies have sought to assess the future capital needs of the eastern *Länder* by estimating the shortfall in provision compared with the average for the west. Such studies must make assumptions about the inherited capital stock of the ex-GDR, its age, value, and rates of depreciation and decommissioning. Clearly, in some areas of provision, facilities in the east are more favourable than in the old *Länder*, but primarily in economic overhead infrastructure there still remain large deficits, in spite of the exceptional levels of investment of the 1990s. The DIW (2001) estimates an eastern gap in infrastructure and other public capital provision of DM 200 bn (at 1991 prices), while other studies, based on much narrower assumptions, estimate a shortfall of approximately DM 100 bn. Over a ten to fifteen year time-scale, this would require funding commitments of at least the levels of the last decade.

It will be of no surprise that in mid-2001 the Federal government agreed to continue the flows of transfers to the east at approximately current levels (*Handelsblatt*, 26 June 2001). Against the background of such independent studies of investment needs, and importantly, given the political imperative to retain voters' allegiance in the east against the predations of the Party of Democratic Socialism (PDS), a continuation of current policies would be the expected outcome. After much posturing, the richer western *Länder* also appear to have abandoned their aggressive rhetoric over a reform of the Equalisation System: rather, a compromise reform in small steps, which raises the proportion of tax revenue retained, after equalisation, is now to be expected, without a fundamental restructuring of the system. The June 2001 compromise appears to have done little to clarify the system whereby there are overlapping responsibilities between the Federal government and the *Länder* (as in the 'Joint Task') and mixed financing between the levels of government. However, it has at least enabled agreement to be reached on the level of funding for the east to 2015 under the Solidarity Pact II. A total of approximately DM 56.8 bn annually will be transferred to the east, of which DM 21 bn will take the form of federal supplementary transfers and the remainder will comprise VAT revenues and direct transfers in the horizontal equalisation between the *Länder* (*Handelsblatt*, 26 June 2001).

Constrained Growth and Future Financial Commitments

During the later years of the 1990s, there was an open debate in Germany over whether the budgetary, tax and social insurance contribution burden was constraining economic growth and, therefore, exacerbating the high unemployment of the period. It was as if the Federal Republic was in a position of constrained growth, as the continuing high unemployment further depressed demand and exaggerated the financial pressures on the welfare state. Of course, the diagnosis differed according to the economic and political orientation of the analyst. Neo-keynesians such as the DIW research institute or certain spokesmen of the SPD (as highlighted by Oskar Lafontaine in his first decisions as Finance Minister in autumn 1998) claimed that excessive budgetary restriction and consolidation of deficits was depressing demand (Lafontaine, 2000). Market liberals on the other hand, such as the majority of the Council of Economic Advisors, demanded more consolidation of deficits, so as to regain investor confidence and to permit a lowering of tax and social insurance rates, which were held to burden the cost of employment and harm incentives (SBGE, 1998). To recap, after the initial, major policy errors of the first two years, budgetary policy became more restrictive from 1993 and supported the tight monetary policy then pursued by the *Bundesbank,* permitting a budgetary easing from 1994. The net budgetary stance, whether stimulative or restrictive of demand, depends on the balance between the influence of cyclical forces of the tax revenues and social benefits paid, against discretionary expenditure increases or cuts. The resulting German budgetary policy was mildly expansionary in 1995 and 1996 but became restrictive from 1997 onwards, particularly as 1997 was the test year for the Maastricht Treaty convergence criteria, which set upper budgetary limits for entry to the single currency. In the later years, the budgetary stance was more restrictive, as shown by the consistent reduction in the so-called 'structural deficit', leading to its elimination in 1998 (SBGE, 1998: Table D2).

As Otremba makes clear, German economic performance over the ten years of 1989–1998 was at least as good as that of the EU average and could bear comparison with the federal German performance over the 1970s and 1980s, albeit that this was often sluggish (Otremba, 1999: 22). Measures such as the state share of national expenditure, the tax and social insurance contribution share of national income and the state deficit as a percentage of GDP, all compared as favourably in 1998 as in 1989. (In years such as 1993 and 1994, the performance of these measures was poorer, but these excesses were later clawed back). Overall, in Otremba's view, there have not therefore been excessive deficits and the build-up of debt over the ten year period reflected the historic challenge and opportunity of unification. The deficit measures, calculated on a national accounts basis, are not distorted by the large-scale privatisations and asset sales in west Germany (not to mention the *Treuhand*) pursued partly to restrain state deficits. However, in the case of the state debt statistics, one should bear in mind the run-down of state assets which was pursued alongside the mounting indebtedness.

There can be little doubt that the tax and social insurance burdens and the interest charges on state debt have exerted some depressive effect on employment, consumption and investment, and therefore on GDP growth. They create a sense of insecurity among households and investors and, in particular, have damaged faith in the long-term stability of the pensions and health systems, so leading to greater saving and reduced consumption. However, the impact has not been decisive for the fluctuating but disappointing economic performance over the period – in budgetary terms, the structural deficits were cut, but the cyclical 'automatic stabilisers' were allowed to operate. The causes of unemployment in west Germany are primarily structural, but they include external influences on export demand, such as the emerging markets crisis, the Russian default and the US recession. Of course, looking purely on the expenditure side, one must recall the cuts in social benefits and in subsidies in west Germany, which had the effect that one-half of the transfers to the east were covered by such expenditure cuts (Otremba, 1999: 22; Deutsche Bundesbank, 2000: 20).

These financial burdens of unification have restrained growth somewhat in recent years and have, as we have seen, sharpened the challenges faced by the German welfare state. However, other factors have played a greater role in the rather disappointing growth and employment performance nationally. The continuation of the transfers to the east at broadly current levels until at least 2015, as demonstrated by the June 2001 compromises on the Solidarity Pact II and the recasting of the States' Financial Equalisation System, shows that these budgetary costs will stretch well into future decades. However, in so far as they reflect infrastructural and productive capacity investments, the modernising effect in the east is for all to see, while other commitments sustain skill retraining or incomes and so lay the bases for growth and underpin solidarity between the two parts of Germany.

Notes

1 The States' Financial Equalisation System seeks to ensure that there is a fair distribution of tax revenues among all levels of the federation and geographically, as an expression of cooperative federalism. As a result, revenues among the Federal government, *Länder*, and local authorities are subject to a complicated system of redistribution, which meets the constitutional imperative of the promotion of uniform living conditions throughout the territory. Vertical redistribution among the Federal government, the *Länder* and the local authorities covers the allocation of the joint taxes, which are income and corporation tax and VAT. All levels of government also have their own taxes to which they have exclusive access. Income tax is also subject to a vertical redistribution between a *Land* and its local authorities, which recognises unequal tax-raising power at the local level. Horizontal equalisation occurs among the *Länder*, so as to assure equality of living conditions, which is defined by number of inhabitants, weighted for special characteristics, such as the city state weighting. Equalisation horizontally is conducted in two stages, of which the second stage brings the tax revenue per inhabitant in financially weak *Länder* up to at least 95 per cent of the average. Finally, the grants-in-aid made by the Federal government are supplementary transfers which ensure the reduction of disparities and top-up the previous allocations to ensure the desired outcome. A detailed discussion of the system can be found in Owen Smith, Eric (1994), *The German Economy*. (London: Routledge), pp 68–75.
2 See Chapter Five in this volume on small and medium-sized business in eastern Germany.

Bibliography

Arbeitsgruppe Alternative Wirtschaftspolitik (1992) *Memorandum '92. Gegen den ökonomischen Niedergang: Industriepolitik in Ostdeutschland.* (Cologne: Papyrossa)

Bach, Stefan and Vesper, Dieter (2000) 'Finanzpolitik und Wiedervereinigung- Bilanz nach 10 Jahren', DIW *Vierteljahresheft zur Wirtschaftsforschung*, no. 2, pp. 194–224

Bösinger, Rolf (1999) 'Die Neuordnung des bundesstaatlichen Finanzausgleichs 1995', *Finanzwissenschaftliche Schriften*, vol. 93, (Frankfurt/Main: Peter Lang Verlag)

Bundesministerium für Finanzen (2001) 'Subventionsbericht 2001', *Handelsblatt*, 30 July

DIW (1997) 'Vereinigungskosten belasten Sozialversicherung', *Wochenbericht*, Deutsches Institut für Wirtschaftsforschung (ed.), no. 40, pp. 725–729

DIW (2001) 'Zum infrastrukturellen Nachholbedarf in Ostdeutschland', *Wochenbericht*, Deutsches Institut für Wirtschaftsforschung (ed.), no. 20, pp. 293–298

Deutsche Bundesbank (1998a) *Monatsbericht*, January, statistical tables

Deutsche Bundesbank (1998b) 'Zur Wirtschaftslage in Ostdeutschland', *Monatsbericht*, April, pp. 41–53

Deutsche Bundesbank (2000) 'Subsidy trends in Germany since the start of the nineties', *Monthly Report*, December, pp. 15–30

Deutscher Bundestag (1997) 'Jahresbericht zum Stande der deutschen Einheit', *BT-Drucksache*, no. 13/8450

Flockton, Christopher and Esser, Josef (1992) 'Labour market problems and labour market policy' in Smith, Gordon *et al.* (eds.), *Developments in German Politics.* (London: Macmillan), pp. 281–302

Flockton, Christopher (1998) 'Germany's long-running fiscal strains: unification costs or unsustainability of welfare state arrangements?', *Debatte*, vol. 6, no. 1, pp. 79–93

Ghaussy, A. Ghanie and Schäfer, Wolf (1993) (eds.), *The Economics of German Unification.* (London: Routledge)

Handelsblatt (2001) regular reports during May and June

Hoffmann, Lutz (1993) *Warten auf den Aufschwung.* (Regensburg: Transfer Verlag)

Konrad, Kai and Wagner, Gert (2000) 'Reform of the public pension system in Germany' in *DIW* (Deutsches Institut für Wirtschaftsforschung) *Discussion Paper*, no. 200

Lafontaine, Oskar (2000) *The Heart beats on the Left.* (Cambridge: Polity Press)

Lange, Thomas and Shackleton, J. R (1998) *The Political Economy of German Unification.* (Oxford and New York: Berghahn)

Nick, Harry (1995) 'An unparalleled destruction and squandering of economic assets', in Behrend, Hildegard (ed.), *German unification: the destruction of an economy.* (London: Pluto), pp. 80–118

OECD (1998) *Economic Survey of Germany.* (London: OECD)

OECD (2001) *Economic Survey of Germany.* (London: OECD)

Otremba, Walter (1999) 'Finanzpolitik 1989 bis 1998 – die Dämme haben gehalten', *Wirtschaftsdienst*, no. 1, pp. 18–25

Paqué, Karl-Heinz (2000) 'Die ostdeutsche Wirtschaft nach zehn Jahren deutscher Einheit: Bilanz und Perspektiven', *Wirtschaftsdienst*, no. 7, pp. 398–401

SBGE (1998) 'Vor weitreichenden Entscheidungen'. *Jahresgutachten 1999 des Sachverständigenrates zur Begutachtung der gesamtwirtschaftlichen Entwicklung*, 18 November, table D2

Seehofer, Horst (1996) 'Die dritte Stufe der Gesundheitsreform', *Wirtschaftsdienst*, no. 2, pp. 59–62

Siebert, Horst (1992) *Das Wagnis der Einheit.* (Stuttgart: DVA)

Sinn, Gerlinde and Sinn, Hans-Werner (1992) *Jumpstart. The Economic Unification of Germany.* (Cambridge, Massachusetts, and London: MIT Press)

Toft, Christian (1996) 'The German pensions debate: historical context and current debate', *Debatte*, vol. 4, no. 2, pp. 95–115

Vesper, Dieter (1998) 'Länderfinanzausgleich: neuer Verteilungsstreit zwischen West und Ost', DIW *Wochenbericht*, no. 7, pp. 133–141

Chapter Three

The Party of Democratic Socialism as Political Voice of East Germany

Peter Barker

The beginning of the second decade after unification is a suitable time to be summing up the development of the Party of Democratic Socialism (PDS) in Germany, especially after the election of 2002. Since the decision was taken not to dissolve the Socialist Unity Party (SED) at the Special Party Congress in December 1989, but to hastily re-label it as the SED-PDS, the party has emerged as a significant political player at *Land* level in eastern Germany. It was involved in an unofficial coalition with the Social Democratic Party (SPD) from 1994 to 2002 – and with the Greens from 1994 to 1998 – in Saxony-Anhalt, and has been part of official coalitions with the SPD in Mecklenburg-Western Pomerania since November 1998 and, most important of all, in Berlin since January 2002. Although the PDS has been represented in the *Bundestag* since the first all-German federal election after unification in 1990, achieving *Fraktion* status with a national vote of 5.1 per cent in September 1998, its presence there has only symbolic value.[1] However, the loss of *Fraktion* status in September 2002 and the reduction of its representation in the *Bundestag* to two direct seats represents a severe blow to its ability to project itself nationally.

It is at *Land* and local government level that the PDS has made its political mark. The political successes in the east, even taking the setbacks of 2002 into account, underline the primary function of the PDS as a representative of eastern German interests. It is now commonplace in discussions of the PDS that it is still a regional, 'milieu', party whose prime influence has rested (over the period since unification) on its ability to articulate eastern German interests in a way that the other political parties with their western roots and structures, have been incapable of doing. Numerous commentators, whether from an extremely hostile position (Moreau, 1992 and 1998; Moreau and Lang, 1994 and 1996), or from more sympathetic or objective viewpoints (Neugebauer and Stöss, 1996; Patton, 1998; Yoder, 1999; Probst, 2000; Sturm, 2000 and Hough, 2002) have come to the conclusion that the PDS has increasingly played this role over the 1990s and will continue to play this role in the short to medium-term future. Where they tend to differ is in their prognoses about the possible shelf life of the PDS given the rapid changes in eastern German society. Some, such as Moreau, predict or hope for a relatively short period of PDS influence, certainly at national level, pointing to the rapid 'westernisation' of the eastern *Länder*, the decline in the eastern population as a result of continuing westwards migration, and the repeated failure of the PDS to increase its vote in the west much above 1 per cent, or to establish credible membership organisations in the west. This view has gained strength with the loss of their most effective leaders, Lothar Bisky and Gregor Gysi, in 2000, and their election losses in the national election and state elections in Saxony-Anhalt and Mecklenburg-Western Pomerania in 2002. Some are even prepared to repeat the rather rash predictions of 1991 and 1992 of an imminent demise of the PDS. Others see a longer-term future for PDS influence in German politics, especially at *Land* and local level in the east and mostly regard this influence as positive, since it helps, in their view, to bind certain sections of the east German population, which are sceptical of western institutions, into an engagement with Germany as a whole, while at the same time not depriving them of their GDR biographies and identity. This view, that the PDS has a longer-term future was strengthened by the Berlin result in October 2001, which saw the PDS increase its vote in east Berlin from 39.5 per cent in 1999 to 47.6 per cent and in west Berlin from 4.2 to 6.9 per cent. It is possible that the setbacks of 2002 represent a significant turning-point in this respect.

Despite the first significant evidence of PDS support increasing amongst the electorate in west Berlin – it achieved 16.9 per cent of the vote in the western district of Kreuzberg in 2001, and a PDS politician, the former head of the *Bundestag* parliamentary group Gregor Gysi, becoming deputy mayor of Berlin in January 2002, it is still the case that the PDS is a predominantly eastern party, with its only significant electoral representation in the east. A number of theories have been advanced to explain why this should be so. These theories have recently been summarised by Meredith Heiser-Durón (Heiser-Durón, 2001) who based her categories on those laid out by David Patton (Patton, 1998).

The 'Milieu' Theory

The 'milieu' theory, namely the view that the PDS appeals primarily to those voters who have a positive attitude to certain features of life in the GDR, such as full employment and female economic emancipation, is one which is mentioned by most commentators. It is certainly true that the PDS arose from a particular milieu (SED party members) and that the membership of the party is still overwhelmingly dominated by former SED members – still around 90 per cent. The evidence from elections, however, especially those in the latter part of the 1990s, has shown that the backgrounds of PDS voters are far more diverse. In the 1998 federal election, 44 per cent of the youngest age groups (18–24 and 25–34) voted for the PDS (Infratest Dimap, 1998), and none of these voters would have been old enough to have become SED members before

1989. The ability of the PDS to attract voters in the youngest category became even clearer in the 2001 Berlin election; here over 30 per cent of voters under twenty-four voted for the PDS, the largest per centage achieved by any party (*Frankfurter Rundschau* 2001a). These voters can have only dim memories of the GDR and were more likely to be attracted to the PDS by other factors such as its opposition to German involvement in the American-led, anti-terrorism coalition in Afghanistan. Unfortunately for the PDS, Chancellor Schröder took a large number of these votes due to his clear statement before the election in 2002 of his opposition to a possible war against Iraq. The 'milieu' theory is therefore one which has lost validity as the sole explanation for the PDS's rise in popularity until 2002, although there is undoubtedly still a significant group, especially amongst the membership, to which this category still applies.

The 'Loser' Theory

The second theory, that the PDS attracts the 'losers' of unification, is one which has been repeatedly put forward to explain the continued popularity of the PDS amongst certain voters. There is no doubt that the continued high level of unemployment, still roughly twice as high as in the western part of Germany, is a significant factor. The economic 'losers' of unification are still very much in evidence and have an influence beyond the individuals involved. They symbolise the disappointments of unification, despite arguments that the structural difficulties of the east German economy have made the workforce in the east more flexible than its western counterpart (McFalls, 2001). The term 'loser' is, of course, a difficult one. Analyses of PDS voters have shown that the party attracts a disproportionate number of the educational elite: in the 2001 Berlin election, the PDS had the highest percentage of voters (29 per cent) with the *Abitur* (school-leaving qualification at eighteen or nineteen) (*Frankfurter Rundschau*, 2001a). Some of these are undoubtedly representatives of the old GDR bureaucratic and academic intelligentsia, which lost status and influence after unification, but some are from a much younger age group, which in earlier times would have been more likely to have voted for the Greens (Golz, 2001: 924).

Nevertheless, the disappointments of unification still play a role in the attraction of the PDS as a protest party, and it will be interesting to see whether its greater involvement in government will affect its popularity in this respect. There is already evidence from the 1999 local elections in Mecklenburg-Western Pomerania that the PDS's involvement in power there, and the failure of the state government to stimulate economic growth, adversely affected its vote, which fell by 2.5 per cent (Heiser-Durón 2001: 257). This trend became very clear in 2002, when the PDS lost heavily in Mecklenburg-Western Pomerania (minus 8 per cent) in the state election and in Berlin, where in September 2001 it had achieved its highest vote of 22.6 per cent in the election to the Berlin parliament. In the national election in 2002, its vote was halved to 11.3 per cent in Berlin, however, compared to the national election in 1998, it was only down by 2 per cent.

The Representation Gap

Further theories put forward by Patton relate to the failure of the western parties to produce consistent electoral performances in the eastern states, thereby producing a representational gap. Although the SPD and CDU have consistently polled higher votes than the PDS, electoral support has been volatile. In recent state elections in Saxony (1998), Thuringia (1999) and Saxony-Anhalt (2002), the SPD has fallen into third place behind the PDS, only just achieving double figures (10.7 per cent) in Saxony, while the CDU lost over seventeen per cent of its vote in the 2001 Berlin election, and with 23.7 per cent of the vote only just managed to finish ahead of the PDS (22.6 per cent). The drop in the CDU vote in the eastern *Länder* was widely credited as one of the main factors in the CDU loss of power in 1998. In the 2002 election, however, both the SPD and the CDU increased their vote, mostly at the expense of the PDS.

The position of the small western parties (FDP and Alliance 90/Greens) in the east has been particularly precarious. Although both parties emerged from the 1990 *Land* elections with representation in the state parliaments, and in some cases, such as Brandenburg, Saxony-Anhalt and Thuringia, as members of coalition governments, its representation was only of short duration. By 1994, the FDP had disappeared from all eastern states. However, they managed to come back into the state parliament in Saxony-Anhalt in 2002, and because of the poor showing of the SPD (20 per cent), became the junior partner in a coalition with the CDU. Alliance 90/Greens were represented in the Saxony-Anhalt parliament from 1990 to 1998, but in 1998 they even lost this toe-hold in the east, so that the 'Magdeburg Model', in which the PDS 'tolerated' a Red-Green government, became a minority SPD government tolerated by the PDS. Despite improvements in 2002, the FDP still suffers from the lack in the east of their only core voters, the independent middle class, and the perception that it only represented the more well-off voters; this perception was initiated by the FDP's role in a number of decisions taken during the unification process such as that on the restitution of property. The large membership that it had acquired from the former Block party in the GDR, the LDPD, soon melted away, leaving it with an organisation dominated by western imports. Alliance 90/Greens quickly reverted to being a western-dominated, post-materialist party, after its difficult merger with the remnants of the citizens' groups from the GDR in 1993. The eastern, former citizen movement representatives, were, with only a few exceptions such as Gerd Poppe, quickly side-lined, and it is only in a few pockets in the east, such as Berlin Mitte, that the Greens have an active membership with viable organisational structures. The winning of the

Greens first directly elected seat in a national election, in the east-west constituency of Kreuzberg-Friedrichshain in Berlin, may, however, herald an
upturn in their fortunes in the east.

According to the theory of the 'representation gap', the PDS has been able to
exploit its position as the only home-grown political party, which, despite its
dubious history, is able to attract voters who are suspicious of western-dominated structures and organisations. The two *Volksparteien* (people's parties)
have increased the advantage that the PDS has in this respect by tending to
depend on western imports who, in some cases, such as Werner Münch (CDU)
in Saxony-Anhalt, became mired in scandal, or on eastern leaders, such as
Gerd Gies in the same *Land*, who turned out to have had Stasi connections. On
the other hand, Kurt Biedenkopf, CDU premier of Saxony since 1990, came
from the west, although he was very clearly not a creature of the CDU party
machine in Bonn. Only very few SPD figures from the east – exceptions are the
current president of the *Bundestag*, Wolfgang Thierse, and Manfred Stolpe,
premier of Brandenburg until 2002, and after September 2002 Schröder's
new commissioner for the east – have been able to improve their profile within
the SPD.

The Vacuum Theory

This thesis has gained momentum since the advent of a Red-Green federal government in 1998 and the attempt by the Chancellor, Gerhard Schröder, to
move the SPD ideologically into the political centre. With the adoption of economic and social policies, which have lost many of their socialist attributes, the
PDS has been able to occupy a position on the left of the political spectrum,
which has been vacated by other parties. In many cases, it has stolen elements
from earlier Green and SPD political programmes.

The most obvious example is the question of German involvement in NATO
military operations outside Europe. The first major test came with the Kosovo
crisis and the bombing campaign in Serbia. The PDS was the only party in Germany to unequivocally oppose German involvement in this operation,
although large sections of Alliance 90/Greens also expressed their opposition.
The ability of the PDS to represent pacifist viewpoints, and in some instances
anti-American sentiment, became clearer with the Afghanistan crisis. Alliance
90/Greens was now part of a governing coalition with the SPD and was forced
by Schröder to sanction Germany's involvement in the anti-terrorism coalition.
A small group of Green MPs did vote against the bill sanctioning the deployment of German forces in November 2001, but enough Green MPs, under pressure from the party leadership, in particular the Green Foreign Minister Joshka
Fischer, voted in favour, which enabled the government to achieve a slender
majority in the *Bundestag*. The PDS meanwhile, despite some slightly ambiguous statements by Gysi during the 2001 Berlin election campaign, was the only

party to oppose this bill *en bloc* and as a result undoubtedly picked up votes in this election from disaffected Green and SPD voters. The SPD's adoption, however, of an unequivocal anti-war stance in relation to Iraq before the 2002 national election certainly undermined the PDS's claim to be the only anti-war party of the left. The PDS therefore has more work to do to re-establish its claim to be the only credible party of the left, especially in western Germany.

Two Germanys or One?

Some of the reasons for the continued electoral success of the PDS until 2002 can therefore be attributed to the failure of western political parties to successfully occupy the political vacuum left by the collapse of the political system of the GDR. For a variety of different reasons, some of them mentioned above, this has meant that the PDS's success was primarily due to its ability to fill that vacuum and to represent eastern interests more effectively than the other political parties. However, a turning-point came with the floods in Saxony in the summer of 2002. Prompt action by the Federal government and financial support for the victims of the floods meant that Chancellor Schröder and the SPD were perceived as the political forces that had the power and the will to change circumstances in the east. The crucial question then is whether 2002 represented a turning-point or whether easterners will harbour significantly different interests from those of western Germans for the foreseeable future: if the former, then are we talking about a relatively short period of time, while the latter implies a semi-permanent state of affairs in which the eastern part of Germany will function differently from the rest of Germany. As yet, nobody is able to answer these questions effectively. It is questionable whether social scientists are in a position to establish the extent of eastern adaptation to western structures and mindsets, or how far eastern structures are in the process of adapting the western imposed structures to local conditions. Some trends are already visible, such as the ability of some groups in the labour market to adapt quickly to flexible work patterns and attitudes in the modern economy (McFalls, 2001). All commentators agree, however, that the continued presence of the PDS in all the eastern parliaments has meant that the post-unification political landscape, which has developed in the east, is different from that in the west. Three parties dominate the eastern political landscape: the SPD, CDU and the PDS, with the last party only marginally behind the other two up to 2002. Whereas governing coalitions in the western *Länder* are mostly formed by an alliance between a large and a small party (CDU or SPD with Alliance 90/Greens or FDP), thus providing a variety of possibilities, in the east the only possible variations after 1998 were a single party with an absolute majority as in Saxony, a grand coalition between the CDU and the SPD as in Brandenburg, or an SPD/PDS coalition. It was only in 2002 that a reversion to a western-style (CDU/FDP) coalition in Saxony-Anhalt appeared. The political landscape in the east is therefore still decidedly different from that in the west, with the PDS having a role in the government of two of the six eastern states (including Berlin).

Regional or National Party?

The PDS could therefore rest on its achievements in the east and remain as a regional party aiming primarily to represent eastern interests. There is, however, clear evidence that the leadership of the party was not content with this strategy before 2002. The PDS loudly proclaimed its aim, from 1993, of becoming a modern, all-German socialist party, even though its strategy in the west has been almost universally seen, even by itself, as a disaster. (Sturm, 2000: 229–32). The notion of establishing itself as an all-German party still underlined the general thrust of the recent draft programme and the 'Leitantrag' (Main motion) for the party congress in Dresden in October 2001: 'This country needs a strong democratic-socialist party'. (Leitantrag, 2001: 1) Yet, behind the all-German rhetoric, it was significant that in the 'Leitantrag', a substantial section was still assigned to the specific position of eastern Germany: the section is entitled, 'From the periphery of Germany to the middle of Europe: The East as a factor for the future – maintain solidarity and strengthen self-determination'. (Leitantrag, 2001: 4–5) Also the greater prominence given to extra-parliamentary activities in this paper could reflect the party's desire to provide a channel for frustration amongst easterners with western-dominated representative democracy: We therefore want more than ever before to become the partner of extra-parliamentary, social and political movements'. (Leitantrag, 2001: 2) In the draft programme, however, references to specific east German interests were not as prominent, but lurked behind the thrust of the document, which is critical of capitalism, and the general attacks on government policy (Programm, 2001). In its rather torturous efforts to update the 1993 programme – an attempt to draft a completely new programme failed as a result of opposition from more traditional groups in the party to jettisoning the 1993 programme – the same configurations that shaped the development of the PDS over the 1990s, with the possible exception of the very early period, again became clear: programmatic statements directed to the whole of Germany and linked to a political agenda to the left of the SPD, but combined with political action reflecting the specific circumstances of eastern Germany. The shock of defeat in September 2002 has, however, caused the party to re-emphasise its position as a party of opposition with its centre of gravity in the east. This became clear at the party conference in Gera in October 2002. The reformist leadership, which until 2002 had dominated programmatic discussions despite the election of a more traditionally minded leader, Gabi Zimmer, in 2000, was ousted entirely from leading positions in the party at Gera. Calls to revert to the position of a regional party representing eastern interests were loudly articulated. Also, opposition to involvement in state governments was strongly expressed.

This is in stark contrast to the mood in the party after the 2001 Berlin election. The success of the PDS in Berlin, and the fact that it has a significant role in the government of a western political territory, cannot be taken as a sign that the PDS has broken out of its limited role as the political representative of east German interests because of the substantial part that the eastern electorate plays in a united Berlin. Nevertheless, the main proponent within the PDS for concentrating on becoming an all-German socialist party, and Gysi's campaign manager, André Brie, emphasised at the beginning of the campaign its potential for representing an historic breakthrough for the PDS in its struggle to gain acceptance with western voters: 'This election can deliver a breakthrough for us in the West. The election campaign has a great symbolic importance. It concerns the capital which was divided and which is still culturally and socially divided'. (*Neues Deutschland*, 2001). The significance of the Berlin vote was recognised by the other parties, and the fear of a Gysi win, and a possible formal coalition between the SPD and the PDS, was reflected in the decision of the CDU to recruit Günter Schabowski, a member of the Politbüro in the GDR whose press statement on 9 November 1989 brought about the premature opening of the Wall, to head their own forum 'Innere Einheit' (Inner Unity) for the campaign and afterwards. The FDP recruited Bärbel Bohley, a prominent citizen movement activist from 1989/90 and Gysi opponent, to their campaign. It is likely, however, that Berlin will remain an exception in the Berlin Republic by allowing the PDS to gain an electoral toehold in the west. Although Gysi became deputy mayor of Berlin in January 2002, his resignation after an expenses scandal in August 2002 has had a profound effect on the party's standing. The reduction of PDS representation to two members of the *Bundestag* also means that it has little opportunity to appeal to western voters at a national level.

Despite these setbacks, it remains the case that the PDS's strength lies in the perception of around a fifth of the east's voters, with tacit support from a further section of the electorate, maybe as high as twenty per cent, who do not vote for it, and that their own interests are best served by maintaining the strong presence of the only homegrown political party, however contentious its history, at *Land* and local level. Over the 1990s, the PDS strengthened its position in the towns halls with exactly 200 mayors by the end of 2001 (including district mayors in Berlin), some in important towns such as Hoyerswerda and Merseburg. It won an important *Landrat* (Head of an administrative district) election on the island of Rügen in September 2001, bringing its total to three, and regained the mayorship of the town of Sassnitz. The 1998/9 Landtag elections confirmed its growing political status in the east, replacing the SPD as the second force in Saxony and Thuringia. The formal coalition in Mecklenburg-Western Pomerania in 1998 and its continuation in 2002, which, despite a few hiccups, such as the decision by the SPD premier, Harald Ringstorff, to vote for the pension reform bill in the *Bundesrat* in 2001, rather than abstaining, as had been agreed with his PDS partner, has been remarkably stable. Ringstorff has frequently restated his view that a coalition with the PDS provides for more stable government than grand coalitions with the CDU (*Frankfurter Rundschau*, 2001b). However, the death of the 'Magdeburg Model' in Saxony-Anhalt in 2002 and the strong drop in its eastern vote in the national election in 2002 may mean that the PDS reached the highest point of its influence in the political system in 2001.

At local level, the PDS does still, however, exploit its strength in a whole range of bodies which represent specific interests, such as tenants groups. Two recent campaigns have served to underline the readiness of the PDS to get involved in local issues, thus strengthening its image as the party that engages with social issues at grassroots level. The first, in Brandenburg in 2001, concerned the *Land* government's decision to make their promise to guarantee all children a kindergarten place, dependent on budgetary considerations. The campaign against this decision, which was run by the kindergarten organisation, Kitas, was strongly supported by the Brandenburg PDS. Some have even suggested that the closeness of Kitas to the PDS was a key factor in the ruling by the Land Constitutional court in September 2001 that the government's decision was not unconstitutional. The second example concerns the decision by the Saxon government in August 2001 to close one of the Sorbian mother-tongue schools in Upper Lusatia. Again the PDS played the leading political role in opposing this decision, although the SPD subsequently joined the campaign. This support is perhaps more surprising than the involvement in the Brandenburg campaign, since the Sorbian families affected by this decision are highly conservative Catholics, natural supporters of the CDU. The campaign against the decision by the Saxon government ultimately failed, but this episode provided a prime example of the ability of the PDS to ally itself, in local campaigns, with groups whose political sympathies lie elsewhere.

It is at the local level that the membership strength of the PDS is most apparent, despite the constant drop since 1990; in the year 2000 it was down to 84,000 (69,000 excluding Berlin), roughly half the size compared with 1991. This membership strength, which is still stronger than the other major parties in the east – CDU 57,630, SPD 27,742 (excluding Berlin) – is, however, under threat from the fact that 80 per cent of the membership are over sixty, and only 2 per cent are younger than 30 (Staud, 2001: 8). Even though it was able to attract younger voters in elections until 2002, it is not able to persuade them to become members – it has to be said however that its position in this respect is no different from that of other parties. The likelihood is therefore that the membership will shrink considerably over the next ten years and the party will miss, in particular, the organisational contributions of the so-called 'Turbo-Rentner', the pensioners, very often people who were forced into early retirement, who are the core of PDS activities at local level. The ability of the PDS, therefore, to continue to play the role of active support for local groups is likely to diminish over the next few years. It will, rather, have to depend more on its presence in the media and on regaining electoral success in order to maintain its position. Also, it is clear that the process of adaptation to west German structures will continue, as well as continuing emigration westwards, which will diminish further the need for a specific representative of east German interests. Although the unemployment rate in the east has stubbornly refused to come down significantly, and is still roughly twice as high as that in the west, there are some hopeful signs with the decisions by several car manufacturers, such as BMW, to site new plants in the east. The need for the PDS to break out of its mould and develop into an all-German party is therefore as great as ever, although there are still significant obstacles to this, which were particularly apparent in 2001 with the fortieth anniversary of the building of the Berlin Wall and the fifty-fifth anniversary of the creation of the SED.

The PDS and the History of the GDR

The PDS's attitude towards the history of the GDR, and in particular the role of the SED in that history has been crucial in a number of respects. It determined its semi-pariah status within the political institutions and its relations with other political parties, in particular the SPD. Its recent statements on the 'forced' merger of the KPD and the SPD in April 1946, and its tentative comments about the Berlin Wall, which fell short of straight apologies, may have been enough to assuage the strong doubts within the SPD leadership about entering into power at Land level with the PDS, even in such a sensitive political arena as Berlin, but it is clear that the PDS leadership has had to tread very carefully with its own membership in the way it handles these sensitive historical issues. In neither case has the leadership been able to present unequivocal apologies, despite condemning both the instrumentalisation of the SPD by the KPD and the inhumane consequences of the Wall; in both cases this condemnation has been relativised, with the KPD-SPD merger being described in a statement by the party's executive as 'der ernst gemeinte Versuch vieler überzeugter Sozialdemokraten und Kommunisten, durch diese Vereinigung die Ursachen der Niederlagen von 1914, 1918 und 1933 zu überwinden' (a serious attempt by many convinced social democrats and communists to overcome by means of this merger the reasons for the defeats of 1914, 1918 and 1933), (PDS, 2001) and the building of the Berlin Wall being called a form of 'Selbstschutz' (self-defence) by the party's chairwoman, Gabi Zimmer, to prevent the GDR from bleeding dry. (*Frankfurter Rundschau*, 2001c) The tentative nature of both statements reflects the need of the leadership to retain the support of the traditional wing of the party, which was estimated in the mid-1990s as being between a third (Bisky) and a half (Modrow). (Sturm, 2000: 156) It could however be that the leadership is overestimating the strength of traditional feeling in the party: an internal poll conducted amongst its members in May 2001 indicated that sixty-nine per cent of the membership felt that there was 'zu viel DDR-Geist' (too much of a GDR feeling) in the party (Staud, 2001: 8). In this context, it is significant that the preamble to the coalition agreement between the SPD and the PDS in Berlin contains specific statements on the forced merger of the KPD and the SPD, the suppression of the 1953 uprising and the building of the Berlin Wall in 1961. The sensitivities surrounding the history of the Cold War in Berlin are still very much alive and were reflected in the fact that no opinion poll in west Berlin before the election produced a majority in favour of PDS involvement in the government of Berlin.

Part of the PDS's role, amongst other things, is to provide representation for the forty-year history of the GDR and the experiences of its population within this history. A poll conducted in 1997 revealed that a sample of 1,500 east Germans put positive aspects of life in the GDR, such as full employment (89 per cent), social security (85 per cent), employment of women (84 per cent), far ahead of the negative aspects, such as SED dictatorship (38 per cent), restrictions on travel (62 per cent) and spying on colleagues (5 per cent) (Winkler, 1997: 49). It therefore cannot afford to be seen as totally accepting the western line on such sensitive issues as the Wall or support for military action by NATO in the Balkans or against terrorism without running the risk of alienating substantial parts of both its membership and voters, despite the fact that numerous polls show that only a very small minority hanker after a return of the GDR. Its failure to appear as anything other than a representative of eastern interests, however, has the knock-on effect of preventing substantial parts of the west German electorate from seeing it as anything other than a party incapable of representing western interests, thereby restricting its support in the west to fringe groups on the left. A failure to have made concessions on its attitude towards significant events in the history of the GDR would have made a coalition with the SPD in Berlin impossible and prevented the PDS from making any progress in western Germany.

As yet, the PDS has not progressed beyond its original function of acting as a conduit for eastern aspirations and frustrations. The fact that the PDS assumed a formal role in the government of Berlin, only twelve years after the collapse of its predecessor, has in fact had the opposite effect, by alienating significant proportions of both the west and east electorate and forcing the PDS back into a defensive position. Signs of a violent reaction to possible PDS involvement in government in Berlin were already apparent in the ceremonies to mark the fortieth anniversary of the building of the Wall in August 2001. The PDS, as in previous years, took part in these ceremonies, but this time protestors removed the wreaths laid by the PDS. There is still a substantial proportion of the electorate in the east, a number of polls suggest that it is not the majority, as well as the majority of western voters, who strongly resist the notion of the PDS representing anything beyond what they regard as a backward-looking GDR-fixated, eastern mentality. Attempts by the PDS to break out of this mould are regarded by such groups as cynical electoral manoeuvring. As has been the case for the last thirteen years, the PDS is still in a process of transition, relatively sure of its role as a representative of eastern interests – although this confidence has been undermined by the loss of support in 2002 – but unsure of what its ultimate position in the all-German party landscape is going to be, or even if it is going to survive as a significant political player at national level at all.

Note

1 The PDS was able to obtain representation in the *Bundestag* in 1990 after the Constitutional Court ruled, on 29 September 1990, that the East and West German electoral areas should be treated separately as far as the five per cent hurdle was concerned. 1994, it achieved four direct mandates in east Berlin, which provided the other route to representation, even though its vote fell again below 5 per cent nationally.

Bibliography

Der Spiegel (2001) Interview with Ralf Christoffers, 13 August , p. 59

Frankfurter Rundschau (2001a) 'SPD und CDU werden vor allem von "kleinen Leuten" gewählt, bei den Jungen dominiert die PDS', 23 October, p. 5

Frankfurter Rundschau (2001b) 'Im Osten Deutschlands ist das keine Exotik', Interview with Harald Ringstorff, 24 December, p. 4

Frankfurter Rundschau (2001c) 'Die PDS will "die Partei der Einheit sein", 19 June, p. 4

Golz, Hans-Georg (2001) 'Machtworte' *Deutschland Archiv* vol. 1 34, no. 6, pp. 921–24

Heiser-Durón, Meredith (2001) 'PDS Success in the East German States, 1998–99: "Colorful Calling Card from the Forgotten Communist Past?"' in McFalls, Laurence and Probst, Lothar (eds), *After the GDR. New Perspectives on the Old GDR and the Young Länder*, (Amsterdam-Atlanta GA: German Monitor no. 54)

Hough, Daniel (2002) *The Fall and Rise of the PDS: 1989–2000*. (Birmingham: Birmingham University Press)

Leitantrag (2001) 'Nur Gerechtigkeit sichert Zukunft! Es geht auch anders! Strategie und Programmatik der PDS bis 2003. Leitantrag an den Dresdner Bundesparteitag der PDS', 6–7 October. (Berlin: PDS)

McFalls, Laurence (2001) 'Die kulturelle Vereinigung Deutschlands. Ostdeutsche politische und Alltagskultur vom real existierenden Sozialismus zur postmodernen kapitalistischen Konsumkultur', *Aus Politik und Zeitgeschichte*, no.11, 9 March, pp. 23–29

Moreau, Patrick (1992) *PDS: Anatomie einer postkommunistischen Partei*. (Bonn-Berlin: Bouvier)

Moreau, Patrick (1998) *Die PDS: Profil einer antidemokratischen Partei*. (Munich: Hanns Seidel Stiftung)

Moreau, Patrick. and Jürgen Lang (1994) *Was will die PDS?* (Frankfurt am Main: Ullstein)

Moreau, Patrick and Jürgen Lang (1996) *Linksextremismus. Eine unterschätzte Gefahr*. (Bonn-Berlin: Bouvier)

Neues Deutschland (2001) Interview with André Brie, 7 August

Neugebauer, Gero and Richard Stöss (1996) *Die PDS. Geschichte, Organisation, Wähler, Konkurrenten*. (Opladen: Leske + Budrich)

Patton, David (1998) 'Germany's Party of Democratic Socialism in Comparative Perspective', *East European Politics and Societies* , vol. 12, no. 3, pp. 500–526

PDS (2001) press statement, 7 May

Probst, Lothar (2000) *Die PDS – von der Staats- zur Regierungspartei. Eine Studie aus Mecklenburg-Vorpommern.* (Hamburg: Verlag Dr. Kovac)

Programm (2001) 'Programm der Partei des Demokratischen Sozialismus. Entwurf', Berlin 27. April 2001

Staud, Toralf (2001) 'Die roten Panther', *Die Zeit*, no. 25, 13 June 2001, p. 8

Sturm, Eva (2000) *'Und der Zukunft zugewandt'? Eine Untersuchung zur „Politfähigkeit" der PDS.* (Leske + Budrich: Opladen)

Winkler, Gunnar (1997) *Sozialreport 1997: Daten und Fakten zur sozialen Lage in den neuen Bundesländern.* (Berlin: Verlag am Turm)

Yoder, Jennifer (1999) *From East Germans to Germans? The New Postcommunist Elites.* (Durham and London: Duke University Press)

Chapter Four

Challenges to *Rechtsstaatlichkeit* in the Berlin Republic: The Kohl Affair and the Stasi Legacy[1]

Anthony Glees

Introduction

In the Federal Republic of Germany the principle of the *Rechtsstaat* may currently be seen to be under threat in two discrete areas – both very different from each other, but both sinister and impacting on German political culture. One has to do with the apparently endemic propensity of some German political leaders to use cash corruptly, or improperly, to realise major political ambitions and projects. The other stems from the lacklustre pursuit of former East German Communist human rights abusers by the German authorities since the 1990s (mirroring the failure by earlier federal governments to address the numerous domestic consequences of National Socialism). The use of cash for corrupt political purposes and the more dangerous failure to call human rights abusers to account are, ultimately, both attacks on German civil society and the system of justice which upholds it.

Both these matters, each of which in its own way calls Germany's commitment to lawfulness into serious question, converge – somewhat bizarrely and unexpectedly – on the so-called Stasi archives in Berlin supervised by the Federal Commissioner for them, Frau Marianne Birthler. This is because this unique set of documents (which record many of the chilling acts of the secret police and intelligence service right up to its dissolution a decade ago) contains evidence about both of them. The archive holds the records of not only the persistent persecution of political dissidents and the appalling catalogue of human rights abuses by the East German authorities from 1949 until 1989, but also of key aspects of the financial wrong-doing of several leading West German politicians. Their transgressions, where uncovered by the Stasi, were retained for future blackmailing purposes. These files include documents which may well throw significant light on the financial dealings of Helmut Kohl (and his circle). He argues that the release of this material will allow illegally obtained evidence to damage him (even if it provides relevant facts about the operation of his 'system'),and many Germans feel the German Communist past should no longer trouble them. There is pressure, therefore, on both these counts to let the past be the past. To do so, however, will do great damage to German political culture and the fundamental commitment to public lawfulness in German political life, which has sustained it since its inception in 1949 (Clemens, 2000: 25).

There is cause for concern here, but no reason to panic. As long as Germany's political class remains vigilant and retains its basic attachment to the rule of law, the failings of individual German politicians pose only a limited threat to the well-being of the Federal Republic. At the same time, even a limited threat may ultimately make the *Rechtsstaat* weaker when facing future challenges, and can only strengthen the growing trend towards public disillusionment with democratic politics, and the major established parties, which has been a feature of German political life since 1990 (Stöss, 1990: 15–24).

This latter point has been recently addressed in an important essay on the current condition of civil society in reunified Germany, written by the present Federal Chancellor, Gerhard Schröder. He has taken as his starting point a deep concern at what he sees as 'a general dissatisfaction in Germany with "politics"' (Schröder, 2000: 18–21). He argues firmly that it is to be attributed 'first and foremost' to 'dissatisfaction with specific political personnel'. He continues: 'in the present case, it can be rather precisely associated with the crisis that has befallen the Christian Democratic Union (CDU) as a result of its financial scandals and their incomplete resolution'. The Chancellor does not offer any specific remedy to the CDU or the German electorate; whilst it was plain he was referring to Helmut Kohl and other leading Christian Democrats, he does not mention them by name and he suggests that this particular issue is not merely part of a wider problem (which used to be called *Politikverdrossenheit*), but that it could be best addressed by the slightly vague nostrum of encouraging citizens 'to return to politics', thereby producing an answer to the 'major' issue of 'how to organise security and justice'. Yet, quaintly, he defines his Government's role not as a determination to apply the law firmly, or even reassert high moral values in public life, but much more hazily as 'the state steering civil society towards the structures of the modern economy' (Schröder, 2000: 21).

It seems pertinent to note that having raised the issue of financial scandals, and the need to deal with them fittingly in a legal sense (which is presumably what he meant by the phrase 'the incomplete resolution' of the matter), Schröder concedes that the fundamental problem facing German civic culture has do with 'specific political personnel' and what he styles the demands of a 'modern economy' rather than any systemic problematic. Certainly, his focus on Kohl was timely and it may indeed be the single issue which at present most taxes Germans concerned with the way in which affairs of the German state are conducted. Kohl, after all, had taken on the notion of civil society by contravening not merely the 1994 law on party funding but, far more seriously, the German Constitution. Article 21 of the Basic Law obliges parties to publicly account for the sources and use of their funds and their assets which, as we shall see, the ex-Chancellor has repeatedly refused to do for the CDU. It is hard to exaggerate this point (to which we will return).[2] Yet the Kohl affair, which may indeed, as one American scholar claims, be the 'biggest scandal in post-war German political history' is but one problem facing German political culture, and it is emphatically about more than a few aberrant individuals. It is, in short, about the absolute need for political leaders to uphold the lawfulness of German political life by insisting that the law be fully obeyed – and having the courage to demand that public wrongdoing be properly punished (Clemens, 2000: 25–50).[3]

If we accept that German political culture – *any* political culture – ought to be as healthy as is possible, and if we accept that it is more than just a 'psychological' idea 'which refers to what people think about politics...not to actual political behaviour', generating instead the basic criteria for what is acceptable in politics, then its well-being is indeed under threat if lawfulness is not maintained (Hague *et al*, 1999: 468: 135–153).[4] Lawfulness has quite rightly become a core Western political value. Even a country like the United Kingdom, which lacks a formal written constitution (its devolved governance exists simply as the outcome of an Act of Parliament and may be revoked by Parliament in Westminster at any time – as was seen during the 2000 suspension of the Northern Ireland Assembly) nevertheless strongly supports the centrality of the concept of the rule of law. The British Government, for example, introduced the European Convention on Human Rights into British law in autumn 2000, a clear signal of where it stands on the issue. Indeed, it is a consequence of this fundamental commitment to lawfulness that at the 1999 Cologne Council (at which the European Union heads of government agreed the Agenda 2000 document which, amongst other things, sought to regulate the eastern expansion of the European Union), the key importance of the rule of law – *Rechtsstaatlichkeit* – was emphasised.[5] Ever since the 1993 Copenhagen Council, the pivotal role that the liberal democracies of the EU now give to the rule of law and human rights has been underlined.[6] As the very first condition of future membership of the EU, the Commission stipulates that 'any candidate country' must demonstrate that 'it has achieved stability of [sic] institutions guaranteeing democracy, the rule of law, human rights and the respect for and protection of minorities...' Regular monitoring by the Commission of these and the other requirements was instituted – and takes place.

In recent years, all western governments have placed an ever-increasing emphasis on the rule of law, or *Rechtsstaatlichkeit*, as a required defining dynamic of modern western governance. For the political scientist (rather than the constitutional lawyer), this may be defined as governance conducted under conditions of lawfulness which guarantee the human rights of the individual citizen and oblige those with power to be accountable for what they do with it. It follows – or it is meant to follow – that those who have gained political power must accept that they must act in accordance with the rule of law in the pursuit of policy and must not abuse the rights of those subject to their power. The term 'rule of law', it should be stressed, is not a vague theoretical concept, but has been firmly and specifically defined, and formally set down, in several key conventions and charters.[7]

Corruption is, of course, illegal. Germany is not the only polity in which corruption exists. Scandals in the United States (where President Clinton issued pardons on leaving office to those with whom he was financially and personally connected) and in France (where the dealings of the late President Mitterrand and some of his close associates have recently been investigated) show that there is nothing specifically German about its current concern with the lawfulness of its political actors. In recent years, the British political system has been damaged by a series of serious financial scandals, some of which, such as the Ecclestone or Robinson affairs, have involved a barely legal convergence of party finance and Prime Ministerial roles, as well as the bribery of Members of Parliament by public companies and influential individuals. Nor is Germany the only state which sometimes fails to uphold the rule of law if to do so may cause embarrassment to present or past political leaders. Britain's own poor record in failing to bring to trial a number of individuals involved in serious human rights abuses of one form or another is a matter of record.[8] Some of those left untouched by Britain willingly performed tasks for Communist intelligence services, and thus for regimes who abused the civil rights of their own citizens, including human rights activists, who were at that time refugees in the UK from the Central and Eastern European states now applying for membership of the EU;[9] others had willingly been involved in mass murder organised by Nazi and Fascist regimes.

As far as Germany is concerned, it could be argued that not only is it not different from other Western polities in this regard, but that previous acts of corruption in German political life may have darkened the reputation of the Federal Republic without undermining its commitment to lawfulness (one might add that Kohl's own previous financial dealings underscore this point). Why, then, does it seem under increased scrutiny today? For one thing, of course, the mere fact that it has happened before makes it worse now. For another, in contemporary German political culture, Kohl has come to represent much more than just a former Chancellor. He is properly seen as a symbol of national unity, a founding father of a new and still emerging political culture, reflecting the processes of 'dual transformation' which his strategy for unity prompted (Nickel, 2000: 106–123). Unity did not merely change eastern Germany; it also changed western Germany as well. In the vast melting pot of this new political culture, Kohl's championing of unity (and European integration) forms a significant part (for which he has received and merited great honour). Unity was, however, also the assertion of the superiority of West German political culture over that of East Germany, or, put another way, the victory of a *Rechtsstaat* over an *Unrechtsstaat*. Kohl's financial unlawfulness will inevitably feed into Germany's civic culture, and citizens of the New *Bundesländer* may wonder at the strength of a political system which cannot make him account for what he has done.[10] They may be forgiven for undergoing 'dual disillusion- ment' since unification in 1990: once at the failure to deal with the crimes of the former German Democratic Republic, and then again at the corrupting behaviour of the Chancellor of unity.[11]

When we add to this an already existing and sizeable level of dissatisfaction with the west German party system in the new *Bundesländer* (not to mention the growing problem of neo-Nazi activity which is, perhaps, the most virulent expression of a dissatisfaction with the concept of the *Rechtsstaat*), it is plain that the new Germany faces difficulties which extend far beyond the behaviour of rogue 'personnel'.[12] Indeed, the *Rechtsstaat* depends on far more than simply its political leadership. Whilst it is perfectly true to say that Kohl's wrong-doing must have far less impact on the long term health of German civil society than the wrong-doing of Communism in Germany (which current research shows went far wider and far deeper than was hitherto suspected), in both cases there has been a patent failure to address it, which makes the wrong-doings worse. In both cases, the remedy may indeed be the same: to bring the wrong-doers to justice. If the *Rechtsstaat* is to regain its position as the defining dynamic of Ger- man civil society, the principle of accountability must be upheld both in the case of aberrant politicians and the wrong-doers in the GDR. A culture of polit- ical impunity, in which a blind eye could always be turned to individual and systemic political wrongdoing, would be nothing short of a disaster for Ger- many. Only one thing could conceivably be more damaging to German politi- cal culture than the passive toleration of political lawbreaking – popular support for the lawbreakers (and of this there is already some indication, both in the growing sympathy for Kohl, and the growing support for the Party of Democratic Socialism, the PDS, the successor to East German Communism, outlined below).

If the *Rechtsstaat* today faces a challenge to its credibility, then this is in part because Kohl's wrongdoing intersects with a wider crisis of lawfulness in respect of the treatment of East Germany's Stasi past. Indeed, the entry of the former East Germany into a new German Republic in 1990 (thanks in large part to Kohl himself), which also obliged Germans to confront the legacy of Communism, has hugely amplified this point. In 1990, lawfulness became a central principle for all Germans now in the new Federal Republic and one which differentiated this German state in the clearest possible way from both the Third Reich, which preceded it, and from the Communist German Democratic Republic, alongside which it was forced to live before taking it over in 1990.

This chapter argues that the lawfulness of the Federal Republic is indeed under threat even if the size of this threat should not be exaggerated and even if the fundamental stability of the Federal Republic has not been called into question. 'Berlin is not Weimar' – at any rate, not yet. But the threat now exists. In February 2000, at the height of the allegations against Helmut Kohl, *Infrat-*

est polls showed that 51 per cent of Germans were satisfied with their democracy. In September 1998, that figure had been 58 per cent. A decline of 7 per cent in Germans satisfied with their state may not be a catastrophe – but it is certainly indicative of a crisis. *Infratest* also reported that in June 2000, 70 per cent of all electors believed that Kohl should relinquish his *Bundestag* mandate (indicating widespread disapproval of his malfeasance) but by January 2001 (that is before the Cologne Court, charged with investigating Kohl, reached its verdict in February) that number had sunk to only 41 per cent. It seems reasonable to believe that many Germans ceased to care whether or not Germany's longest serving Chancellor had broken his country's laws even before finding out whether or not he had done so.

After the verdict reached on 28 February 2001, in which the Court agreed to suspend further proceedings in return for a DM 300,000 fine (implying that its preliminary investigation confirmed at least an element of wrongdoing – since otherwise no penalty would have been called for), the number wanting Kohl to step back from political life sank still further. A majority of German citizens clearly discounted the gravity of the offence and saw in it no bar to future participation in the law-making processes of the German Parliament.[13] Even without the historical precedent of the Weimar Republic, where corruption almost certainly helped to undermine the first German attempt at democracy, it is hard to see how democratic practice and civil society can flourish in the Berlin Republic if its leading citizens are able to evade accountability for their political actions in public life and if voters cease to find this worrying. In theory, few countries take lawfulness more seriously in formal terms than the Federal Republic, as the briefest examination of its constitution makes plain.[14] Yet in practice even the courts seem unwilling to press the point. The Cologne Court's verdict on Kohl explicitly cited the Chancellor's 'fifty years of *engagement* in public affairs' and 'his uncontested record of merit in creating a European zone of peace' as reasons for exercising 'lenience' in his case which indicated, perhaps only to cynics, that political success outweighed unlawful political activity. Ought any German court, *any Western* court to use political successes to mitigate cynical and sustained law-breaking? The conclusion which ordinary citizens may be inclined to draw from this is not simply that whatever is politically successful is also legally acceptable ('*Recht ist was den Politikern nutzt*'), but also that the laws themselves are actually not to be taken seriously.

At the same time, we should not ignore the fact that Kohl, despite his power and reputation, was challenged and was brought to account. This was because many ordinary members of the German political class (especially in the media but also in all parties) did take the view that the existence of CDU illegal funds should not be swept under the carpet. Even if *Rechtsstaatlichkeit* is the primary responsibility of the lawmakers, its secondary supporters in the political class are no less vital to its maintenance.

The Kohl Scandal

The case here, then, is that unless *all* political offences against *Rechtsstaatlichkeit* are seriously pursued, *Rechtsstaatlichkeit* as a political concept will itself be undermined. The Kohl scandal indicates just this (Pflüger, 2000; Leyendecker, 2000; Schäuble, 2000). There is, of course, no direct linkage between the sustained, brutal and – at times – deadly wickedness of the GDR and the illegal seediness of a corrupt *camarilla* which included, apart from Kohl and his mysterious benefactors, only a handful of middle-ranking party officials. It is not the argument here that they are anything other than two important if distinct, examples of challenges to the supremacy of the *Rechtsstaat*. Nor is it certain that the Kohl affair truly is 'the biggest scandal' in the history of the Federal Republic, an epithet which should probably be reserved for the failure to bring Nazi and Communist human rights abusers to justice. What the two issues share is that both are crass examples of a lack of political and judicial will to make individuals involved in the business of governance account for their wrong-doings. It does not follow that every political wrong-doing has the same value. What does matter is the principle of accountability.

As far as the corrupt use of party donations is concerned, it is evident not merely that at least two key laws (one in the German Constitution and a 1994 elaboration of this) were broken at the very highest levels of German government, but also that the law-breakers, of whom at least one was also a lawmaker, were convinced they would never be caught. The seriousness of this charge becomes apparent when its implication is understood: the law-breakers were plainly confident that the *Rechtsstaatlichkeit* of the Republic – its very Basic Law – could safely be circumvented, and did not therefore themselves believe much value needed to be attached to the concept. Since Kohl says the matter is now closed, its final clarification may well now depend on the Stasi's record of Kohl's activities. There is bitter irony in the fact that the unlawfulness of one German regime may illuminate the unlawfulness of another, fundamentally lawful one. It seems likely that, given the apparently deliberate destruction of Federal records in the Chancellor's Office in September 1998 (before Gerhard Schröder was elected the new Chancellor), the Stasi archive could therefore not merely yield the final truth on German Communism, but will also indicate the health of the *Rechtsstaatlichkeit* of the liberal Republic before 1998. This is, it should be emphasized, the second time that Kohl has been obliged to face charges of unlawfully using political donations as bribes for political advantage. His first brush with the law on 'black funds' had almost precipitated the premature end to his political career. As one author wrote before this current scandal broke: 'Noone could have foreseen that, without Gorbachev, Kohl's Chancellorship would chiefly have been known as the government that presided over the worst corruption that west Germany had ever experienced' (Glees, 1996: 207–213).

The Stasi's files on Kohl are likely to be substantial and comprehensive. One hundred of Kohl's phone lines in the Chancellor's Office were tapped by the Stasi as were the private lines of Frau Weber, Kohl's personal secretary, and Friedrich Bohl, the Minister in charge of his Office. They were monitored by forty-eight stations in Berlin and Czechoslovakia. In all, Peter Lux, the officer in charge, produced some 19,000 pages recording seven years of conversations from 1982 to 1989. It is on the use of these files, then, that the future reputation of Germany and her political leadership will, sooner or later, rely. It is still not clear whether they will be fully examined by lawyers and researchers, although at the time of writing, this seems increasingly unlikely. They are currently embargoed, and subject to an injunction based on Kohl's assertion that, as a victim of the Stasi, his files should not be open to public scrutiny without his permission, which he is not disposed to give (interestingly, previous legislation governing research into the Stasi files specifically exempted major historical figures from the 'victim exclusion' clause). If the files continue to be closed, it will inevitably suggest that the liberal democratic elites in Parliament (and the courts of the Federal Republic) will have chosen 'the absence of conflict' rather than the 'presence of justice' by turning a blind eye to the Stasi record (Frei, 1997; Herf, 1997). Indeed, the net effect of the Kohl affair has been that new regulations have been drawn up restricting the use of the archive.[15] There seems no doubt at all that Kohl, supported (some might believe incomprehensibly so) by the Federal Minister of the Interior, Otto Schily, is winning the fight for the integrity of his reputation.[16] In March 2001, some CDU *Bundestag* members, led by Erika Steinbach, called for him to be re-nominated for a major Party post. Only the tragic death of his wife prevented him from being called upon by his Party to play a 'massive role', as had been promised, in the Berlin elections later that year.

It is, of course, perfectly fair to point out that the facts about Kohl were illegally obtained by a secret service dedicated to the maintenance of an unlawful Communist regime, that Kohl was certainly a Stasi victim – and that two 'wrongs' do not make one 'right'. No serious analyst of German politics can believe that it would not be infinitely better for German political culture were Kohl to name his donors and give a full account of the uses to which he put his 'black' funds, obviating any need to rely on Stasi papers. His steadfast refusal to do so, however, raises the question as to the lesser of the two evils in this matter, and in this respect it is hardly possible to deny that German political culture would suffer less damage from a proper use of the archives than from a continued silence and cover-up. The Stasi files – the *only* secret service files open to the general public in their entirety and extending right up to the collapse of the GDR – are therefore a major resource for all those who believe in upholding lawfulness in general, and in discovering the truth about Kohl in particular. The necessity of upholding lawfulness only becomes fully apparent when citizens are able to gain knowledge of the true facts about policy-makers and their policies, particularly when they have used power and secrecy to avoid transparency. Political pressure seems set to move increasingly in the opposite direction, denying the citizen the opportunity of enforcing accountability on those who have acted unlawfully. Laws governing the use of the Archives, originally developed to protect the citizen from a government's abuse of its power (by making it crystal clear how police states operate), now appear capable of being used to protect an abusing government from the rights of its citizens to understand this and seek their remedy in a court of law. This, at any rate, is the view of a senior archivist in the Stasi archive.[17]

The apparent lack of interest in seeing the lawfulness of the CDU's financial dealings tested in the courts as expressed by Chancellor Schröder, described above, has plainly been picked up by the courts themselves. The February 2001 decision not to proceed further in the matter and to ask Kohl to pay a fine, of which 50 per cent was to be donated to a charity of his choice, and fifty per cent to go to the State combined with the explanation that 'the economics of trials' dictated the need for closure was hardly a happy one.[18] In effect, the court had bartered the *expense* of a trial against the provision of *justice*, seeking to dilute this truth by offering a sop to charity (itself a dubious 'sweetener' of a sort). Although it was reasonable to point out that even if Kohl had been convicted, he would have been fined rather than jailed, the decision has allowed him to claim he has been deemed 'innocent' of any wrong-doing.

Not every leading German believed that the Cologne Court's decision (which may be challenged) implied a victory for the principle of lawfulness. A prominent Social Democrat, Franz Müntefering, the Federal Minister of Transport, Construction and Housing, bitterly attacked what he claimed was improper permission for Kohl to persist in 'lawbreaking'.[19] Adding that Kohl 'remained true to his own precept that cash' – he used Kohl's own term, *Bimbes*, for this – 'could sort everything' he concluded that justice had not been done. Kohl's actions, of course, were widely criticised, even within his own party: as we shall see, Richard von Weizsäcker believed he had done great damage to justice in the Federal Republic. Thomas Kielinger, one of Germany's leading journalists, was equally scathing in his criticism of Kohl's unlawful behaviour (Kielinger, 2000, 12–13).

Even if only technically, Kohl has now been exonerated. He has been relieved of the obligation to name the donors of the money that he used for 'black' funding purposes. Yet irrespective of whether his exoneration by the courts will stand the judgement of history, a fundamental question about the current condition of German politics has been begged and must now be answered. It is whether this decision and its consequences will strengthen or weaken German civil society, whether it will sustain or undermine public confidence in politicians and politics in the very sense in which Chancellor Schröder expounds the issue. It might be argued that to permit politicians to break the law and, when found out, escape prosecution by handing over cash would, as Müntefering suggests, simply intensify popular cynicism about politicians and the political system. To demonstrate that lawfulness in German politics is not merely a question involving the CDU and Helmut Kohl, but has affected the SPD and the Greens (one of whose leaders, Joschka Fischer, was recently under scrutiny for his actions as a student radical in the 1970s and for his statements about this early in 2001) serves to confirm that the struggle to maintain the *Rechtsstaat* must indeed be a major cause in German political life today. Eastern Germans might indeed be forgiven for seeing some linkage between the half-hearted pursuit of Stasi and SED human rights abusers by two Kohl administrations and his own record of corrupt political action within the 'system' he controlled, even though there is almost certainly no connection between them. Even so, perceptions are always important in politics.

Kohl, who resigned as honorary chairman of the CDU on 19 January 2000, was also investigated by a *Bundestag* Committee of Inquiry chaired by Volker Neumann, the conclusions of which are still awaited. Kohl repeatedly told the committee that he could not remember any details concerning the affair (mirroring his earlier comment in respect of the Flick affair that he had suffered a 'blackout' when receiving cash in an unmarked envelope) (Glees, 1987 and 1989). In November 1999 the ex-Chancellor was obliged to admit having received about DM 1 million in undeclared party donations between 1993 and 1998. He had been forced to go public following a statement made on 4 November by the debonaire Walther Leisler Kiep, a former Treasurer of the CDU, who had already been convicted of illegal fundraising in 1991 (receiving a suspended sentence of eighteen months), that CDU cash had been laundered through Swiss bank account (Clemens, 2000: 37).[20] Kiep had been caught thanks to the persistence of the Augsburg public prosecutor who discovered evidence of missing millions in the tax returns of an arms dealer Karl Heinz Schreiber who resided in Canada. Schreiber's bank accounts led directly to the CDU. Yet Kohl's refusal to name the donors is in itself an offence under German party law, which requires anyone donating in excess of DM 20,000 to be publicly identified. In December 1999, the federal public prosecutor began a criminal investigation of this matter, parallel to the Neumann inquiry which concluded, in May 2000, that sufficient grounds for criminal prosecution existed which were then halted by the Cologne Court the next year.

The *Bundestag* is also looking into these and other allegations predating German unification in 1990. These include the funding of CDU campaign activities by the industrial giant Siemens 'out of gratitude for its huge profits in business with East Germany'.[21] It had already been suggested that the east German interests of Elf, the petrol company, had provided cash for Kohl, but it seemed plausible that Siemens's payments related to its actions in the 1980s, that is before the SED fell, when it illegally helped the East Germans to build computer chips, and that the donations made after 1989 were intended to keep Siemens out of the courts.[22] It was also surmised that Kohl may have benefited from SED cash which had been sent out of the GDR prior to its collapse. Some DM 430 million were allegedly transferred to Hungary from where the BND, the German secret intelligence service, passed it on, again allegedly, direct to the

CDU.[23] What compounds the seriousness of these allegations is that they indicate that within a few years of his having been given the benefit of the doubt over claims that he had acted corruptly in the 'Flick Affair', Kohl had in fact carried on regardless and re-offended almost at once (Glees, 1987; Glees, 1989).

Kohl has vehemently denied both the Elf and the Communist cash allegations (dismissing the latter, but only the latter, as 'idiotic'). Yet if this were the source of the cash, it could provide one explanation as to why Kohl has sealed his lips, along with the attempt to seal the archives. Even so, some CDU members appear to accept Kohl's own judgement that since he promised the donors their identities would be kept secret, as a 'man of honour', his 'integrity' should be respected by now ceasing to try to get him to reveal the names. Whether 'integrity' may be appropriately applied to one who has sabotaged a full investigation seems far harder for some CDU members to concede, since they fear Kohl may be seeking to cover up a more persistent track record of corruption which could continue to damage the Party. There has already been one fatality as a direct result of this funding scandal: on 20 January 2000, Wolfgang Hüllen, a senior financial officer in the CDU, committed suicide as the Neumann Committee began hearing evidence. A further theory about the origin of the cash, on the face of it hardly plausible, was that it came from the former East German Communist Party, the SED, though for what precise purpose would appear to defeat even the most fertile imagination.[24] It serves simply to illustrate that anything less than the complete truth can only further muddy the political waters. What is beyond question is that business links between the CSU, the CDU's Bavarian sister party, and East European businessmen caused cash to flow corruptly from one side of the Iron Curtain to the other prior to the fall of the Berlin Wall.

It seems true that Elf had paid large sums of money to several politicians, including Agnes Hurland-Buning of the CDU (a Kohl confidante) and Hans Friedrichs, an FDP former economics minister (who had been implicated in the Flick Affair fifteen years earlier).[25] It was also true that Elf had funded Dieter Holzer, a Saarland businessman with, it was alleged, contacts to the German secret intelligence service. Nor should it be forgotten that Wolfgang Schäuble, who resigned the leadership of the CDU in February 2000, was forced to admit that he, too, had received a donation of DM 100,000 in cash from Schreiber. Schreiber had handed money to Schäuble (which the latter had at first denied) as well as to Kiep. Manfred Kanther, the hard line ex-minister of the interior and general secretary of the Hesse Christian Democrats had, together with Prince Casimir zu Sayn-Wittgenstein played a key role in channelling the cash into the CDU's 'black account' from where Kohl could spend it as he saw fit.

On at least three occasions, the Hesse CDU was told that certain generous 'bequests' had been made. One of them, the latter explained in December 1999, had been left to the CDU in the wills of German Jewish Holocaust survivors from Switzerland (though precisely what prompted their generosity was never spelled out).[26] Kanther was very well-known as a 'law and order' hardliner, yet on 14 January 2000 he was forced to admit that these so-called 'bequests' were entirely fictional. Over a number of years, he had dishonestly taken DM 8 million, invested it illegally outside the Federal Republic and then received at least DM 14.3 million and arguably as much as DM 30 million back into the CDU treasury.[27] That the fictitious benefactors of the CDU should have been described as Jews simply beggars belief.

Kohl, it may be safely assumed, believed so strongly in his mission that he did not think he could do any wrong; he was convinced his power would protect him from discovery. Even when the truth began to seep out, he refused to accept blame, still less to apologise. On 30 November 1999, he said simply 'I regret if there was a lack of transparency or control in what I did. This was not my intention. My wish was to serve the party'.[28] According to Roger Boyes, Kohl came close to admitting that the cash was used to help the CDU win local elections by funding projects with voter appeal. He had decided these matters by himself relying on his intimate contacts with hundreds of local party politicians. For obvious reasons there are only a few numbers to put on these contacts: from 1986–87 Kohl allegedly transferred some DM 2.56 million to his regionally based colleagues; in 1996 his own Rhineland Palatinate CDU was given at least DM 370,000.[29] For the final years of his Chancellorship, Kohl did not register a single contribution made to him in person. Speaking up for him, his chosen successor Wolfgang Schäuble said there was no evidence that any government decision had been influenced by this money and no evidence that any politician had gained personal enrichment from it. He announced, however, the immediate dismissal of Horst Weyrauch, the CDU's chief accountant who was also implicated in wrong-doing, which was an admission of sorts. Schäuble was soon forced to step down.

Kohl's record, once in the public domain, was attacked by senior Christian Democrats as well as other politicians. One of the first was Heiner Geissler, until 1989 General Secretary of the CDU (whom Kohl had sacked), and another the far more weighty Richard von Weizsäcker, the former President of the Republic (von Weizsäcker, 2000) There are several reasons why von Weizsäcker's critique deserves careful study. For one thing, it emanates from a man who had held several of the highest offices in the Federal Republic and knew Kohl well (but was never part of his *camarilla*). More importantly for the purposes of this study, von Weizsäcker has, for more than ten years, been a compelling and reflective critic of German political culture, well alive to the dangers that aberrant political behaviour, if not countered, becomes structuralised. Von Weizsäcker believes that the Kohl affair is, without question, a genuine crisis of German political culture and, in a specific sense, the result of political parties gaining undeserved political predominance in German political life.

He argues that when, in 1990, following unification, a commission examined the Basic Law, the one area it failed to look at was whether the constitutional and legal provisions concerning parties had proved themselves beneficial or not. This failure was, he suggests, a major mistake, not because parties were unnecessary, but because deeper thought needed to be given to the fact that individuals gain power in German politics by achieving power within parties. This could produce a 'system', one highly prone to the abuse of power and corruption, and Kohl's system, honed over eighteen years, was ultimately able to undermine faith in the constitutionality of German political life. For all his many talents, von Weizsäcker claims, Kohl pursued a relentless drive for power, subjecting his party to a rigorous and intimidating personal rule. As the only serious rival to Kohl's power in the late 1980s, and with a considerable following in the country, von Weizsäcker was particularly at risk from him. He says that Kohl unsuccessfully sought several ways of neutralising him before – with great reluctance – agreeing to 'kick him upstairs' into the office of the Federal Presidency, from which there could be no possible return to the Chancellorship, and thus no future challenge to Kohl. Kohl, he claims, had ruthlessly used networks ('*Seilschaften*') to ring-fence his authority. It was clearly understood in the CDU that solidarity with the leadership was required at all times; to contradict Kohl was known to lead to severe 'punishments'.

Von Weizsäcker insists that Kohl's words of excuse ('my wish was to serve my party') prove that the ex-Chancellor did not merely put 'service to party' above 'service to the State', but also believed that to do so was wholly proper. This compounds the fact that for Kohl money played such a critical role in his system: all of this taken together, von Weizsäcker concludes, boils down to great future danger for Germany. The former President accepts that no-one believes Kohl profited personally from all the cash that floated around, but that cash, and Kohl's reaction to his wrongdoing, are the measure of his attitude towards the basic political values of justice and of honour. As Chancellor, he had sworn on oath to uphold the Constitution, but had nonetheless persistently taken money illegally. He had then sought to justify his refusal to name the donors by saying he had given his 'word of honour' that they would not be revealed. His definition of 'honour', von Weizsäcker insists, is in reality just 'a base refusal keep his lawful promise to the *Rechtsstaat*'.

In von Weizsäcker's view, it is this failure to understand the nature of political honour which is the most pernicious aspect of the 'System Kohl'. It represents, he argues, a low point in German political culture which must now be overcome. What could political honour mean, he asks, if the most powerful man in Germany, the father of its unity, refuses to honour the law? The former President concludes his critique – characteristically – by seeking an institutional rather than a legal remedy. In future, no person should be allowed to be Chancellor for sixteen years, and be able to so confuse his own political ambition with the well-being of the state he serves. Even so, he accepts that German political culture has to rely on values that it cannot itself create; they have to pre-exist it. Civil courage, he believes, which is part of the Christian Democratic heritage, must assert itself.

There are, however, two further points which von Weizsäcker could have made but did not. The first is that the Basic Law ascribes a central role to the political parties in the liberal democratic state order. Kohl's manipulation of his party was, therefore, a direct attempt to manipulate the Basic Law.[30] The *System Kohl* was, in effect, if not a *coup d'etat* then most certainly a *coup* against the *etat*. Secondly, however, and perhaps more fatefully, Kohl's 'system' may well seek future justification by pointing to the success of unification and asking Germans to set his 'service to his party' against rising east German prosperity, which may have been the purpose of the corrupt practices. In this way, Kohl could argue, he had always sought to do the best for the east Germans.

To do wrong to achieve a 'greater' good has been a standard excuse of politicians through the ages. It is, however, because of the purpose and essence of *Rechtsstaatlichkeit* that this argument is deemed an unacceptable one. One wrong can never make a right. Furthermore, it offends the very people it claims to assist. More than economic advance, the east Germans deserve *Rechtsstaatlichkeit*.[31] Indeed, they have earned it. For it was the demand for the *Rechtsstaat* (something East Germans did not have under Communism) which, more than any other idea, inspired the dissidents of the 1980s. Their insistence that peace meant nothing without human rights was an expression not just of their own political will but of a long German tradition of liberalism and constitutionality – one which, to its credit, survived forty years of Communism. The ordinary east Germans who recall the corruption that existed in the GDR deserve to see that a clear line can be drawn between the *Unrechtsstaat* that was the GDR and the *Rechtsstaat* that ought to be the Berlin Republic. Bärbel Bohley's important if astringent comment should not be forgotten: '*Wir wollten Gerechtigkeit; dann kam der Rechtsstaat*' ('We wanted justice and then came the rule of law') carrying with it a charge from one of the most doughty Germans of the twentieth century, that justice and the *Rechtsstaat* proved to be not one and the same. That the distinction she draws should be so readily visible today is a telling comment on the Federal Republic.

The Political Failure to Address the Stasi Legacy

If Kohl's illegal use of cash for political ends represents one real threat to the lawfulness of the Federal Republic, the failure to properly pursue those who abused the rights of their fellow Germans under German Communism is another. It is an irony that the 'Stasi archive' in Berlin, were it to be exploited fully, might provide the key to a solution of both of them. For, remarkably, the files stored here provide evidence on each of them. The death of Erich Mielke in June 2000 – at liberty, a free citizen of the new Federal Republic – drew public attention to the fact that Mielke, a dedicated and ruthless Stalinist murderer, was never put on trial for the thousands of killings, and the hundreds of thousands of human rights abuses for which he had been responsible.[32] He had been able to live out his days in a spacious flat in Hohenschönhausen (round the corner from one of his most vile jails), protected by a cohort of his former employees. He had repeatedly urged his men 'to act in the interests of Communism without regard to legal formalities or scruples' (under GDR law) and had stressed 'the need to "hack off the heads"' of those who opposed it.[33]

His personal attitude towards the rule of law was neatly stated in a tape-recorded conference on how to treat Stasi double agents who had cheated on the GDR. Mielke declared: 'We know that a wrong-doer can infiltrate our ranks. We do realise this. Were I to discover someone like this, he would not be alive tomorrow morning. I'd have a very short hearing, of course, because I'm humane. That is why I take this line. But let us be clear about why we have to be so hard. Some say "don't execute, no death sentences". All this is absurd, Comrades. They are swine. Execute them. Without laws, without legal trials and procedures and so forth'.[34] More than one hundred kilometres of the Stasi's own documents bear witness to the wickedness of his policy of deliberate and organised terror. Yet the only offence for which he was tried and convicted was a murder he had committed some sixty years earlier in the dying days of the Weimar Republic. Found guilty in October 1993 and sentenced to six years, he was released in August 1995 having served only two years – in the hospital wing of Moabit prison.

It is true that in 1991 he had also been indicted, together with Erich Honecker, of the deaths of forty-nine people seeking to flee to the West. Proceedings were postponed, however, when Honecker fled to the USSR and, on his return, were abandoned altogether, since it was said that Honecker was likely to die before a verdict could be reached. Honecker was permitted to flee to Chile in 1993 and died there, unrepentant, in 1994 (this had been the second time Honecker had escaped justice: he had been charged with corruption and treason in the post-revolutionary GDR but its subsequent collapse permitted him to avoid a trial) (McAdams, 1996). It is also true that other GDR leaders were not just indicted but forced to serve sentences (though whether they were in keeping with the offences committed may easily be questioned). Egon Krenz, on the other hand, was sentenced for six and a half years (confirmed in November 1999) for his part in the killing of would-be refugees who tried to cross the frontier with west Germany (the charge was 'incitement to murder') and his colleagues, Günter Schabowski and Günter Kleiber, had their three year sentences confirmed at the same time. It was not clear how long any of them would remain locked up. Krenz's sentence was confirmed by the European Human Rights Court in March 2001.[35] Markus Wolf, Mielke's much-feared secret intelligence supremo, despite twice being found guilty by German courts, has so far avoided jail altogether. Characteristically, Wolf condemned the Strasbourg decision on British radio as a vindication of 'retaliation rather than reconciliation', saying that those killed by East German border guards whilst seeking to flee East Germany were no different from soldiers killed 'in any war'. Most vociferous amongst those seeking to ensure that the appalling human rights record of the GDR is not forgotten, and that its perpetrators face justice, are the various victim associations and self-help groups.[36] *Help e.V.*, for example, assists some 1500 victims per year, including those taken to camps in the USSR, and political prisoners of both the Third Reich and the GDR. *Help* points out that although it deals with Germans, the extent of the terror practised on the people of Europe was enormous. In addition to the victims of Nazism, it recalls that by the time Leonid Brezhnev died, the Soviets alone had opened some 165 camps with seventeen million prisoners and ten million forced labourers (Help Report, 1999, 51). The German victims of Stalinism, it suggests, number at least a quarter of a million killed deliberately or through neglect, as well as two million victims of Red Army rape, resulting in thousands of female deaths (Help Report, 1999: 55). The Federal Ministry of the Interior estimates that from 1949 to 1989/90 some 25,000 were killed in GDR prisons, either deliberately or through neglect, 170 were executed for political crimes, some ninety-seven died at the border, 500 were forced into suicide and 127 people were killed in connection with the 1953 uprising (Help Report, 1999: 77). The respected Museum at Checkpoint Charlie, however, estimated that 943 people were killed whilst fleeing to the West, that over one million East Germans spent a period in prison for political offences and that from 1948–88 some 2,901,000 refugees fled from the GDR to the West (Help Report, 1999: 78). The Stasi were given five jails of their own in East Berlin and another seventeen throughout the GDR, along with the full complement of normal prisons available. What is more, the Stasi's crimes were by no means confined to the territory of the GDR. Serious wrong-doing took place in the Federal Republic and also in many nations throughout the world, including the United States and the United Kingdom. Whilst cynics might argue that all states, whether democratic or Communist, possess and use secret intelligence and security services, it would be quite wrong to equate them with the activities of the Communist ones. These were wholly aimed at undermining liberal democracy, and above all its supporters in East Germany. They must not be confused with those Western intelligence and security services who tried (at least partially) to prevent this and sought to sustain the East German dissidents.

The Stasi supported an extensive programme of obviously unlawful subversion against the West (Gauck, *et al.* 1991). It regarded this struggle as a war behind 'the invisible front' (Knabe, 1991: 254–9).[37] The purpose of this fight, as we shall see, was first and foremost to safeguard Communist rule in East Germany and elsewhere behind the Iron Curtain. It was a policy designed to defend the GDR, but its tactics were offensive: using the 'sword' as well as 'shield'. Even so, its aims should be not confused with military ones: the Stasi was an intelligence organisation, not a military one. The Stasi did possess a paramilitary capability, a 3,500 man commando force code-named 'S workers' under Mielke's personal command, but their remit seems to have been attacks on individuals and installations in West Germany and perhaps the training of revolutionaries, including Irish ones (Knabe, 1999: 254–9).

All the evidence we have come to possess since 1990 shows that the Stasi made a direct input into both the foreign and domestic policy of the GDR. It is important to understand, as Joachim Gauck (Frau Birthler's predecessor as Commissioner for the Stasi Archive) has made plain, that the Stasi was not 'controlled' by the political leadership but constituted its core base; in part, it was the leadership (Gauck, *e. al.* 1991: 72). As Gauck explains: 'the question of who controlled whom was never asked because the state apparatus, the party apparatus and the security apparatus had been smelted into an intimately-linked union'. It was, in addition, also a key, if not the core, part of the political executive because it was able to coerce GDR citizens into compliance with GDR law.

The arguments used to justify the failure to deal more robustly with those who perpetrated these abuses (where they still survive) are three-fold. First, that the past should be forgotten in the interests of 'social peace' and the integration of new and old *Bundesländer.* What was once an act of political unlawfulness at best and repressive brutality at worst becomes, with the passing of time, far less unacceptable. Second, that no public good would be served by lengthy investigations into crimes associated with a particular German regime which has not existed for more than ten years and, thirdly – and most importantly – that a ruling of the Federal Court (*Bundesgerichtshof*) has determined that only those offences which were an offence under prevailing *GDR* law at the time they were committed can be tried now under Federal German law. It would, the Court decided in May 1995, be unconstitutional to permit Federal German law to be used retroactively against acts committed in the jurisdiction of the GDR which were lawful at the time they were perpetrated. Prosecutions of killings by border guards have been successful, however, because the Court refined its decision in respect of these acts, where murders were committed for political reasons, and in cases where East German lawyers can be shown to have connived with the Stasi to effect prosecutions.

This is, of course, a weighty judgement of state and it would be unreasonable to dismiss it lightly or to imagine that it could be overturned as the outcome of an academic debate, even amongst constitutional lawyers, let alone one started by political scientists. Having said this, however, it must be said that even on its own terms, the judgement seems flawed. For one thing, had such a verdict been applied to Nazi crimes, many Nazi perpetrators would have evaded justice. For another, the GDR had, on its accession to the United Nations, accepted the various UN Conventions outlawing torture (for example, UN General Assembly Resolution 39/46, 10 December 1984). This means that the use of the tortures as practised at the Stasi jail at Hohenschönhausen, to name but one location where torture was regularly used until 1989, were blatant contraventions of these Conventions. The Court, however, has declared that although these Conventions were ratified by the GDR, they were never tantamount to GDR law. This seems a doubtful ruling because it seems hard to see what ratification means, if it does not mean lawful acceptance of these

Conventions. The Federal Court seems to believe that any statement of lawfulness must be viewed from the perspective of an essentially unlawful regime, rather than from the perspective of lawfully constituted western states. Additionally, it argues that it is plain from the statements of Mielke *inter alia* that his men and women were instructed (as we have seen) to behave as if there were no constitutional limits to their powers, thus the various GDR constitutions must themselves be considered not to be *Western* constitutions but *Communist* ones, implying that they had only fictional relevance and were at best a means for seeking mercy from the SED authorities, rather than any guarantee of rights.[38] Yet one cannot help suspecting that had this test been applied in respect of Nazi concentration camp guards, for example, none would ever have stood trial in West German courts (which was, of course, not the case).

Against what seems like excessive legalistic circumlocution on the part of the *Bundesgerichtshof*, there stands the reality of about a million victims (excluding the 2.9 million who felt obliged, sometimes risking their lives, to flee to the West), and the formal statements of the GDR governments which never indicated to its own citizens that the three GDR constitutions which all guaranteed a full panoply of human rights were not intended to be taken seriously as 'constitutions' in the liberal sense (Help Report, 1999; Glees, 1999). Indeed, they consistently indicated the reverse – as did the texts of the constitutions themselves. Part of the problem is, undoubtedly, a more general refusal to see the GDR as a German state in which lawfulness was arbitrarily expendable in order to suit the requirements of Communism. Even today, after all that is known about the Stasi, it is still possible for Western academics to wonder whether the GDR was, at worst, a 'sterile dictatorship' (the use of the word 'sterile' is significant, implying cleanliness and not merely lack of purpose) or at best a 'failed experiment' (Fulbrook, 2000: 89ff) (where 'experiment' has a positive connotation of a well-meaning, if doomed, enterprise).[39]

What is at stake here, as with Kohl's refusal to abide by the German constitution, is nothing less than the future health of German political culture. How can the ordinary German citizen, whether from the new *Bundesländer* or the old, have faith in the lawfulness of the Federal Republic if the Republic itself seems to ride roughshod on the idea of the *Rechtsstaat*. A culture of impunity can only signify to eastern Germans that the abuses of Communism are being forgotten for reasons of political expediency. Similarly, the process of dual transformation will encourage western Germans to believe that the story of the GDR can safely be left in the history of the GDR, that the experience of forty years of a German Communist police state has no relevance for the new and unified German state. East Germans were – and are – also Germans. The political culture of the Berlin Republic belongs to them as much as to former West Germans.

It is of course *not* the case that *nothing* has been done to uphold the principles of lawfulness in respect of Communist human rights abuses since 1990. The March 2001 European Court decision on Krenz (which upheld his conviction) is to be welcomed by all supporters of the idea of liberal democracy. In 1990, four HV A (*Hauptverwaltung Aufklärung*) agents who did western interests great damage, including Dr Gabrielle Gast, a double agent and conviction Communist who worked for the Federal secret intelligence service, were jailed for six years. The others were Hagen Blau and Klaus von Raussendorf, who both worked for the Federal Foreign Office, and Dieter Popp who worked in defence planning. All were released by August 1995.[40] Frau Gast is on record as arguing that it is indefensible that she was sent to prison whereas her commanding officer, Wolf, has remained free.[41] A very recent example worth noting is that at the end of June 2000 a former East German border guard was given a life sentence for having killed a drunken West German who had come too close to the border with the GDR.[42] Another is the investigation of school teachers in East Berlin (many of whom had Stasi links before 1990 who cannot now command, it is assumed, the confidence of their pupils). Almost twenty thousand of these have now been investigated, of whom 877 were shown to have had positive links to the Stasi. One hundred and eighty four of these were dismissed. Yet in July 2000, a Berlin Court acquitted three other former *Politbüro* members of complicity in killings along the Berlin Wall, and in March 2001 (at the same time the European Court was reaching its judgement), a Berlin Court gave a former East German People's Police officer a suspended six month jail sentence for shooting a teenager in the back. The youngster had listened to Western radio. To add an element of insult to injury, the successor to the East German Communist SED, the PDS, is a coalition partner in the government of Berlin with the SED's former enemies, the SPD. Did the Federal Republic's citizens regard East German unlawfulness as wicked only when it happened in another state?

If so, then this position is, of course, not acceptable: the wrong-doings of the East German police state, and its members, cannot be expunged simply because the GDR ceased to exist in 1990. Nazi crimes against individuals and groups continue to be regarded as crimes today, more than fifty years after the collapse of the Third Reich. The Federal German Government fully accepts this, as can be seen in the compensation package it helped establish for Nazi slave labourers that is currently awaiting distribution. The very limited attempts to impose justice on the perpetrators of unlawfulness in the GDR may demonstrate what should have been more widely done, but was not. Any state which does not take the fight for lawfulness seriously will find it hard to convince its citizens that lawfulness is a prime civic value. Furthermore, to fail to follow up lawfulness in one aspect of public affairs, say in dealing with the Stasi legacy, invites speculation on its intentions in other areas of political activity. Small wonder, perhaps, that the Chancellor of German Unity should believe the law of the land did not apply to him when he saw that the law of land did not apply where more serious transgressions had occurred. It is depressing that on 2 October 2000, the third and final extension of the GDR State criminality law (of 22 December 1997) which allowed for the prosecution of medium-ranking perpetrators came to an end and no further prosecutions for crimes including manslaughter (but excluding murder) would therefore be possible.

Christoph Schäfgen, who had a distinguished career from October 1990 until 1994, heading the GDR Government criminality department at the Berlin Court (in effect a public prosecutor), then becoming head of the central office for the historical examination of the GDR's illegal acts until its closure on 30 September 1999, accepts that the impetus for continued investigations has virtually disappeared.[43] Dr Joachim Gauck, the highly respected, former head of the Stasi archives in Berlin also holds the same view. It is a view shared by many others. Elisabeth Graul, herself a GDR political prisoner and an ex-inmate of Hohenschönhausen and Hoheneck jails, has recently pointed out that to September 1999, 22,550 cases of Communist abuses were filed, of which 21,270 were closed immediately. Prosecutions followed in 506 cases (that is in 2.2 per cent of all cases filed), 877 people were brought to court, and 221 of these were found guilty (1 per cent of the total cases).[44] It is revealing to compare these figures with those relating to the punishment of human rights abuses committed by the Nazis. From 1945–92, 103,823 files were opened, but only 6 per cent of these led to convictions. Of these, 85 per cent were found guilty of minor crimes only. Only seven people out of every thousand (0.7 per cent) were brought to justice, and only five out of every thousand (0.5 per cent of the total of the cases) were punished in any way at all. (de Mildt, 1996: 20–1; Glees, 1996: 31) If the record of the Federal Republic in respect of Communist crimes is twice as good as its record in respect of Nazi crimes, then all that is being reflected is its appalling record in both.

Conclusion

No one could seriously suggest that Kohl's unlawfulness is on a par with forty years of systematic human rights abuses under Communism. It is important to place a clear hierarchy on rights, on laws and their abuse. The more we know about the way Communist 'cadres' – German, Russian, Chinese – interrogated and investigated their own people, and felt free to rob them of their liberty and dignity without scruple, the clearer it becomes that the illegal behaviour of one politician pales into insignificance when compared with those regimes that are indelibly stamped with the mark of their abuse as their *defining* characteristic (Glees, 1999: 173; Jung Chang, 1993; Ting-xing Ye, 2000).[45] Whatever social good they may have done (providing kindergartens, jobs for life and so forth) they are also quite distinct from Western liberal states. Even the view that in a hierarchy of nasty regimes, Communist ones should always be better placed than Fascist ones, can be shown to be untenable on several grounds. If Fascist ones segregated subjects on the basis of race and credo, Communist ones segregated people on the basis of class and credo. Indeed, in Stalinist Russia and Communist China, at any rate, class was given an ethnic rather than a social value. Children of bourgeois parents were considered second rate citizens, even if they were fully fledged Communists or Red Guards. In the case of Germany's bitter political history, this should not be taken to mean that there were no distinctions between German Communism and German Nazism. It is fair to point out that there has to be a difference between the GDR and the Third Reich, since there were clear limits to the GDR's abuse of its power, and limits to its use of terror. There were some things that the Stasi would not do. Yet even these distinctions require thoughtful qualification: important similarities in style and content bind the two German dictatorships of the twentieth century. The Stalinist attitude towards the bourgeoisie and the upper class, widely held in the GDR, was actually *racial* in a genetic sense: individuals could not escape their class origins whatever their material status. In Communist China, similar views prevailed: bourgeois behaviour was seen as the product of a bourgeois *ancestry* which persisted long after the bourgeoisie as a class had been destroyed. This was the rationale that lay behind the wanton terror and destruction of the Cultural Revolution.

The failure to properly purge the crimes of the Communists in East Germany and the belief of Helmut Kohl and his circle that the Constitution of the Federal Republic and its due democratic process could be safely ignored, do not mean that the Federal Republic is not (and was not) a *Rechtsstaat*. The very fact that there is open criticism of the propensity of ordinary voters in the Federal Republic to forget unpleasant realities when casting their ballots, and that the media, lawyers, academics and tax officers are free to bring Kohl's misdeeds to the attention of citizens proves that, at its core, Germany is still a *Rechtsstaat*.[46] The current guardians of *Rechtsstaatlichkeit* are, however, these professionals, supported by honourable politicians such as von Weizsäcker, but not, alas, those who used party advantage to wound and undermine the basis on which lawfulness rests. In a political culture which shies away from adversarial conflict and strives for consensus on as many issues as possible, the insistence that unlawfulness be exposed, its perpetrators punished, and the documentary evidence of wrong-doing be exploited to the full, is the only sure means of resisting the abuse of constitutional liberties wherever and whenever they occur.

Notes

1 Thanks are due first and foremost to Frank Zwicker and Dr Rüdiger Stang of the Stasi Archive in Berlin for their invaluable help in tracing relevant papers and addressing numerous archival queries, and to former President Richard von Weizsäcker for two interviews: Berlin, 12 March 2000 and Frankfurt/Main, 11 October 2001.
2 See the updated German Constitution (Basic Law) of 16 July 1998 at www.uni-würzburg.de/law/gm00000_.html and note 37 below.
3 Clay Clemens is here not concerned with the implications of Kohl's unlawful behaviour on the *Rechtsstaat* but on the CDU and his own reputation. See too Clay Clemens and W. Pater-

son (eds.) 'The Kohl Chancellorship' *German Politics* Vol. 7 No. 1 1998. Whilst attention is drawn in this most useful text to the existence of a 'System Kohl', there is no indication here that corrupt practice lay at its heart. Although articles by Karl-Rudolf Korte (pp. 64–91) and Clemens (pp. 91–120) contain references to Kohl's 'suspicious' habits and 'rather subtle measures' in order to 'keep the machinery going', neither mention the role of money, and even the Flick Affair is ignored.

4 Hague, Harrop and Breslin argue that political culture is simply a psychological concept which 'does not refer to political behaviour – indeed behaviour may conflict with prevailing attitudes'. Whilst individuals may indeed not behave in accordance with political culture, the behaviour of *politicians* must in part define political culture and must also impact more widely on what is generally held to be acceptable political behaviour.

5 As early as 1993, accession of new states was conditional on their satisfying both economic *and* political criteria. The latter were defined as 'stability of instituitons guaranteeing democracy, the rule of law, respect for human rights and the protection of minorities'. http://europa.eu.int/comm/enlargement/intro/criteria.htm

6 http://europa.eu.int/comm/enlargement/intro/criteria.htm

7 They include: the UN Charter of June 1945, the General Declaration on Human Rights of December 1948, the international agreement on civil and political rights of December 1966, various agreements on the banning of discrimination on the grounds of race, religion, political belief and gender, as well as the various European conventions on human and basic rights including the European Convention of November 1950, the second protocol of May 1963, the fourth protocol of November 1963 and subsequent protocols, the European agreement on the prevention of torture and inhuman or degrading forms of punishment of May 1994, and further protocols arising from the agreements arising from the CSCE process. Special emphasis should be laid on the International Agreement on civil and political rights of December 1966 (which was incorporated into German law in 1973). This Agreement sets precise limits on what governments may and may not do. It is clear that human rights abuses and the corrupt use of political power are to be seen as illegal acts contrary to UN agreements and conventions. See Karl Josef Partsch (ed.), *Menschenrechte: Dokumente und Deklarationen* (Bonn, Bundeszentrale für politische Bildung: 2. aktualisierte und erweiterte Auflage: 1995) pp. 31, 32, 37, 44, 52, 107, 117, 220 ff (esp. pp. 219–282).

8 General Pinochet (gravely implicated in human rights abuses in Chile) was permitted to return home to avoid trial; Konrad Kalejs (a leading member of one Nazi *Einsatzgruppe* who committed wartime atrocities in Riga) was quite literally encouraged to leave for Australia to evade prosecution under the 1991 UK War Crimes Act (he died in November 2001); another alleged Nazi war criminal, Anton Gecas, (now also dead) was able to avoid extradition, and several uncovered agents of Communist intelligence services have been granted immunity from prosecution on a very limited knowledge of the activities of these individuals.

9 This was debated in Parliament on 21 December 1999, *Hansard* Vol. 341 No. 22 cols 182–188. Interview with Sir Stephen Lander, Director General of the Security Service, and officer concerned with Stasi, Thames House, 03 March 2000.

10 This was, for example, a point repeatedly made at a conference on these matters (*Demokratische Grundwerte*) organised by the Friedrich Ebert *Stiftung* and the *Institut francais de Dresde* in Dresden on 21 January 2000.

11 The tragic death of Frau Hannelore Kohl at the beginning of July 2001 was believed by some media commentators, without any hard evidence, to have been caused in part by her inability to cope with the evidence of aspects of her husband's political behaviour.

12 In 2000, almost 16,000 right-wing extremist attacks were registered, an increase of 58.9 per cent on the previous year. Fifty per cent of these attacks took place in the new *Bundesländer* although only 21 per cent of Germans live there. March 2001 www.tagesschau.de

13 For the verdict of 28 February 2001 see www.olg-köln.nrw.de/home/presse/urteile/lg-bonn.ht. For *Infratest* see www.infratest.de

14 An updated German Constitution may be conveniently examined at www.uni-würzburg.de/law/gm00000_.html

15 Regarding the so called 'Lex Kohl' Frau Marianne Birthler, head of the Stasi Archive, has sanctioned new regulations severely limiting access to documents concerning 'historical persons'. *Eckpunkte der Richtlinie für die Herausgabe von Stasi-Unterlagen über Personen der Zeitgeschichte sowie Funktions- und Amtsträger an Forscher und Medien* (paras. 32–34 of the Stasi Files Law), 09 March 2001. The second person to make use of these new regulations was the celebrated ice-skating star, Katarina Witt who on 28 May 2001 won an injunction preventing public scrutiny of the extent to which she profited from her close relationship with the Communist regime.

16 '*Stasi Akten Streit: Kohl klagt weiter*' in *Der Spiegel* 14 March 2001 at www.spiegel.de

17 Interview with Dr Stang, Stasi Archive, Otto Braun Strasse, Berlin 12 November 1999.

18 *Die Welt* 02 March 2001 and elsewhere.

19 Münterfering's term was 'Kohl lebt im fortgesetzten Rechtsbruch' – ('Kohl lives in a continuous state of breaking the law'). *ARD Tagesschau* 02 March 2001.

20 *The Sunday Times* 30 January 2000.

21 *The Times* 30 May 2000.

22 *The Times* 30 May 2000. Uwe Lüthje, a CDU employee, admitted having accepted large donations from Siemens in the 1980s and early 1990s amounting to almost DM one million.

23 *The Times* 30 May 2000.

24 *The Sunday Times* 07 May 2000.

25 *The Sunday Times* 09 January 2000.

26 *Die Zeit* 20 January 2000 pp. 11 ff.

27 To put these figures into some sort of perspective, it is worth noting that through totally legal means, in 1999 the CDU received DM 76.6 millions. Hans Herbert von Arnim *Die Zeit* 20 January 2000.

28 *The Times* 01 December 1999.

29 *The Times* 25 January 2000.

30 Article 21 paragraph 1 of the Basic Law states that 'the political parties participate in the forming of the political will of the people' (see updated German Constitution with 46th amendment 16 July 1998 at www.uni-würzburg.de/law/gm00000_.html). See also Gunlicks, Arthur B., 'The financing of German Political Parties' in Merkl, Peter H (ed.), *The Federal Republic at Forty* (New York: New York University Press, 1988) and Kommers, Dieter P., 'The Basic Law of the Federal Republic of Germany' ibid. The process of *Umwegfinanzierung* – evading the law – that German parties adopted during the 1970s clearly persisted in the CDU to 1998/9. Article 21 paragraph 1 adds that parties 'have to publicly account for the sources and use of their funds'. Only donations of less than DM 600 do not have to be declared (1967 Party Funding Law). Parties, however, wanted more than this, and businesses did not want to be named since tax deductions were often the only reason that donations were made. Evasion, therefore, took a number of forms: charities that benefited from tax deductions were used as a front for donations, money laundering in overseas accounts took place, adverts in party publications were sold at inflated prices. In 1977–78, 105 firms were charged with making illegal donations to the CDU and donations fell from DM 12 million in 1977 to DM 12,000 in 1978. The CDU was forced to take out a loan of DM 24 million, whilst the SPD owed its creditors DM 51 million by 1980.

31 At a seminar in Dresden on 21 January 2000, organised by the Friedrich Ebert Stiftung, at which the author was a speaker, many participants made the point that – to them – Kohl had betrayed the values of the German revolution of 1989/90 and that the corruption of the SED leadership was mirrored by his own.

32 *Der Spiegel* 26 June 2000.

33 Ibid.

34 Erich Mielke: partial transcript of tape-recorded discussion at an officers' seminar on 19 February 1982; authenticated and documented by the Stasi Archive in the Otto Braun Strasse.
35 22 March 2001.
36 Amongst the most prominent are: the *Gedenkstätte Berlin-Hohenschönhausen*, the *Gemeinschaft ehemaliger politischer Häftlinge*, the *Stiftung Haus der Geschichte, Zeitgeschichtliches Forum Leipzig*, the *Stiftung zur Aufarbeitung der SED-Diktatur*, the *Robert-Havemann-Gesellschaft*, and HELP e.V. *Hilfsorganisation für die Opfer politischer Gewalt in Europa.*
37 Knabe's is the standard descriptive work on the Stasi's organisation and history, although it has very little indeed to say about the Stasi's campaign in the UK. It is based on a meticulous study of the Stasi's own organisational analyses, and skilful cross-matching of material has produced unique data which will ensure that it remains the starting point for any research into the Stasi's activities for many years to come.
38 This is the view of Christoph Schäfgen interviewed in *Stacheldraht* Nr 9 1999 quoted in the *HELP Report.*
39 Fulbrook implies the Communist experiment was not ignoble in origin ('a state ostensibly founded on the desire to create a classless, egalitarian society in which all human beings would be emancipated from the oppressions of capitalism...instead developed into a sterile dictatorship, failing even to satisfy physical, material and environmental needs, let alone the human desire for freedom...'); she adds 'Marxism has provided a set of morally informed goals. It must be the task of the historian to analyse why certain ideals were so distorted or perverted in practice; and why, ultimately, the experiment failed'. This type of prose may seem to some observers as an attempt to divert scholarly attention away from the brutality of everyday Communism in East Germany by focusing on the alleged ideals of the regime.
40 See Roger Boyes in *The Times* 18 August 1995
41 On the *History Channel* 15 February 2001.
42 *The Times* 01 July 2000.
43 In *Der Stacheldraht* Nr 6 1999 quoted in HELP *Report.*
44 ibid.
45 For two recent accounts of human rights abuses under Chinese Communism – and the similarities and differences between Chinese and East German Communism see Chang 1993 and Ting-xing, 2000.
46 This a point forcibly made by Bernhard Schlink in *The Reader* trans. C B Janeway (London: Phoenix, 11th edn, 1999). Schlink is a lawyer and a writer. Thanks are due to Sophie Mitchell for this observation.

Bibliography

Chang, Jung (1993) *Wild Swans Three Daughters of China.* (London: Flamingo)
Clemens, Clay (2000) 'A Legacy Reassessed: Helmut Kohl and the German Finance Affair', *German Politics*, vol. 9 no. 2, pp. 25–50
de Mildt, Dick (1996) *In the name of the Volk* (The Hague: Kluwer)
Frei, Norbert (1997) *Vergangenheitspolitik, Die Anfänge der Bundesrepublik und die NS-Vergangenheit* (Munich: Beck)
Fulbrook, Mary (2000) *Interpretations of the Two Germanies 1945–1990* (London: Macmillan)
Gauck, Johannes with Knabe, Hubertus *et al.* (1991) *Die Stasi-Akten* (Hamburg: Rowohlt)
Glees, Anthony (1987) 'The Flick Affair: a Hint of Corruption in the Bonn Republic', *Corruption and Reform*, vol. 2 no. 2
Glees , Anthony (1989) 'Political Scandal in the Bonn Republic', *Corruption and Reform* , vol. 3, no. 3 (1988/9)

Glees, Anthony (1996) *Reinventing Germany: German Political Development since 1945* (Oxford and Washington DC: Berg)

Glees, Anthony (1999) 'Social Transformation Studies and Human Rights Abuses in East Germany after 1945' in Flockton, Chris and Kolinsky, Eva (eds.), *Recasting East Germany: Social Transformation after the GDR* (London: Cass), pp. 165–189

Hague, Rod, Harrop Martin and Breslin, Shaun (1999) *Comparative Government and Politics: an introduction*, 3rd edition, (London: Macmillan)

Herf, Jeffrey (1997) *Divided Memory. The Nazi Past in the Two Germanies* (Cambridge, MA and London: Harvard University Press)

Hussock, Peter Alexander (1999) (ed.), *Help Report: Selbstdarstellung, Dokumentation, Information* (Berlin: Hilfsorganisation für die Opfer politischer Gewalt in Europa – Help)

Kielinger, Thomas (2000) 'Power at any Price' *The World Today* April 2000

Knabe, Hubertus (1999) *West-Arbeit des MfS: Das Zusammenspiel von 'Aufklärung' und 'Abwehr'* (Berlin: Ch Links Verlag)

Leyendecker, Hans (2000) *Helmut Kohl, die Macht und das Geld* (Göttingen: Steidl Verlag)

McAdams, A James (1996) 'The Honecker Trial: the East German past and the German future', *The Review of Politics*, vol. 58, no. 1, pp. 53–80

Nickel, Hildegard Maria (2000) 'Employment, Gender and the Dual Transformation in Germany' in Flockton, Chris, Kolinsky, Eva and Pritchard, Rosalind (eds.), *The New Germany in the East: Policy Agendas and Social Developments since Unification* (London: Cass), pp. 106–122

Pflüger, Friedbert (2000) *Ehrenwort. Das System Kohl und der Neubeginn* (Stuttgart: DVA)

Schäuble,Wolfgang (2000) *Mitten im Leben* (Munich: Bertelsmann)

Schröder, Gerhard (2000) 'Civil Society: Redefining the Duties of State and Society' *Deutschland,* no. 5.

Stöss, Richard (1990) 'Parteikritik und Parteiverdrossenheit', *Aus Politik und Zeitgeschichte.* B 21, 18 May

Weizsäcker, Richard von (2000) 'Macht, Recht, Ehre', *Frankfurter Allgemeine Zeitung* 27 January

Ting-xing, Ye (2000) *A Leaf in the Bitter Wind* (London: Bantam Books)

Chapter Five

Economic Restructuring from Below? The Role of Small and Medium-sized Business in East Germany since 1990

Christopher Flockton

The *Mittelstand* as a Source of Dynamism in the East?

The development of a new *Mittelstand* (firms of fewer than 500 employees) in the east has been a key element of the restructuring and recovery strategy for the region. Of course, the employment potential of small- and medium-sized firms (SMEs) would offer some alleviation for the collapse in output and activity in the first years after unification. However, great hopes were placed in the notion of a new *Mittelstand* in the east, which would foster an economic restructuring from below, would be the source of new entrepreneurship in the east and would sweep away the organisational and psychological inheritance of the GDR, of monopolistic *Kombinate* (combines) and a lack of self-initiative. The west German *Mittelstand* is seen as the bedrock of German manufacturing prowess, noted for its adaptability, its flexibility in respect of changing market conditions, its innovatory ability in the design and manufacture of new products (Hunsdieck and May-Strobl, 1986; Semlinger, 1997). Equally, a mixture of medium- and large-sized firms can promote an optimum specialisation in output. Over the decades, west German firms have faced continuous open competition in a relatively bracing climate: could SMEs in east Germany, therefore, show the same adaptability (Kokatj and Richter, 1992; Belitz, 1995; Hauer, 1993)? Could they expand rapidly, producing swift product and process innovations and could they show the organisational flexibility to sweep away the collapsing inheritance from GDR times?

It has to be acknowledged at the outset that the definition of *Mittelstand* is problematic and poses difficulties for the analyst. Simply, the term is used with a variety of meanings in Germany, and the data reflect this variation. Typically, the *Mittelstand* company is seen as a medium-sized engineering enterprise with an owner-manager and an essentially narrowly-based shareholding structure, often of partnership form. The owner-manager sees himself as directly responsible for his employees and so avoids the cumbersome company forms of the GmbH (limited liability) or AG (plc), which would require split management and supervisory boards and, in the case of the AG, would incur all the costs and difficulties of disclosure associated with a stock exchange listing. In fact, the *Mittelstand* comprises firms of up to 500 employees, it includes services and the liberal professions as well as craft firms (*Handwerk*) of up to twenty employees (Nicolai, 1998). In some analyses, the self-employed and their family assistants are also included. Broad definitions risk meaninglessness, especially when, for example, firms of fewer than 500 employees cover 84 per cent of total payroll employment in the east and 76 per cent in west Germany. In respect of manufacturing alone, such a definition would cover 91 per cent of payroll employment in the new *Länder* (such has been the break-up and shrinkage of the old *Kombinate*) and would cover 90 per cent of manufacturing enterprises there. Almost all eastern enterprise could therefore be regarded as of small- and medium-scale. There are additional statistical difficulties. For example, the last full industrial census took place before unification and employment data for productive industry exclude firms of fewer than twenty employees (which are grouped as *Handwerk*).

The following analysis seeks to show a full awareness of the statistical pitfalls, it ranges over productive activity broadly defined as well as manufacturing itself, and it includes the craft firms of fewer than twenty employees. In so doing, it seeks to highlight the contribution of SMEs to the transformation of productive structures in the east, numerically in terms of numbers of enterprises and their associated employment, and it assesses in some detail the range of development assistance available for SMEs in the fields of *Mittelstand* aid, regional and R&D aid. The analysis then proceeds to assess whether the scope for flexibility of these firms has led them to gain a lead in two seemingly unrelated areas: the technology intensity and innovation level of their products and, secondly, their freedom from the relatively tight constraints of the German collective bargaining machinery. With regard to the latter, a significant proportion of eastern SMEs have been able to leave the traditional wage bargaining system introduced at unification and which imposed rapid wage catch-up with the west, as a result of wage harmonisation agreements. Given the very low productivity in the east, this produced very high unit labour costs, which alone accounted for much of the enterprise insolvency, liquidation and resultant unemployment in the first half of the 1990s. In an east German setting, the much greater wage flexibility permitted when a firm leaves, or does not join, the wage-bargaining machinery offers the opportunity of tighter cost control and of more rapid employment creation, particularly in the services area. In this sense, east German SMEs could thereby be acting as a catalyst for reform in the all-German collective bargaining system. In the second area of inquiry, the degree of innovation, new product and process development, in particular the growth of high technology firms in the new *Länder*, the east could also potentially be in the vanguard, particularly because of the high rates of new business start-ups. Has there been a marked rate of product innovation, an embracing of new technology and associated rise in value-added as means to the renewal of eastern manufacturing and business services? Finally, the chapter will conclude by pointing to potential reforms in the panoply of official assistance to SMEs, whether in the *Mittelstand*, regional and R&D aid areas, reforms which could be introduced Germany-wide as a result of experience in the east.

Evolution of SMEs in the New *Bundesländer* and their Origin

Small- and medium-sized companies had been repressed in the GDR, with small industry forced to group into publicly-owned enterprises in the last main nationalisation wave of 1972 and a form of enforced co-operation was imposed on services enterprises. During the period between the fall of the Wall and economic unification there was a loosening of controls, firstly under the reform-communist Modrow government, then by the first directly-elected government headed by Lothar de Maizière. This led to a *Gründungsboom* of new firm creation, which gathered speed in the early years following unification. This foundation boom swelled in response to both the perceived shortage areas in services and the construction boom, as well as a consequence of the break-up and privatisation policies of the *Treuhandanstalt*, responsible for the restructuring and privatisation of the productive assets of the GDR state (Nicolai, 1998; DIW, 1994). The boom in new firm creation eased after 1995, partly as a result of the saturation of initial market opportunities and partly due to the much slower growth in aggregate demand from 1996 onwards, as the economy slowed down and the building industry entered severe recession.

To convey a broad picture of the evolution, several separate sources of statistical data require reconciliation. Thus, it seems that, overall, in the period 1990 to 1998, approximately 774,000 new businesses were founded in net terms as depicted by the firm registration and de-registration statistics (*Gewerbean-/abmeldungstatistik*). The very high rate of new business start-ups in the east of 15–20 businesses per 10,000 population in the eastern *Länder*, is well over double the rate for the old *Länder* (with the exception of Bavaria which had 18/10,000). Of these new businesses, 67 per cent were in services, 8.6 per cent in manufacturing and the remainder in construction and the craft sector. The IAB institute of the Federal Labour Office records that, for the period 1990 to 1998, there were 522,000 SMEs started, with 3.2 million employees. This includes *Handwerk* firms in the east, which had grown from 83,000 firms in 1989 to 157,000 in 2000. At the end of the 1990s, 1.2 millions were employed in the *Handwerk* sector. The gap between the *Gewerbestatistik* and IAB's results is due to the growth in own trading (self-employment), with family member assistance, which appears to have risen from 200,800 at unification to 492,000 ten years later. Of course, a foundation boom is followed after a lag of several years (generally, about four years) by a wave of insolvencies, such that the net new firm creations in the late 1990s were at a level only one-tenth that of 1990 (IWH, 2001: 201, 203).

Nicolai (1998; see also Brussig, 1997) estimated that, by the end of 1994, 70 per cent of the medium-sized companies (excluding *Handwerk*) had been founded since 1990, while 10 per cent had existed in GDR days, and 20 per cent had been privatised by the *Treuhandanstalt*. Turning to the *Treuhand*'s strategy of break-up of the old monopolistic combines, of privatisation and re-privatisation (restitution to previous owners), then 25,000 smaller businesses, generally in the retail, restaurant and cinema activities), were sold quickly to east Germans, a further 15,130 had been privatised, 4,510 reprivatised and 1,200 created by MBO (management buy-out) by the end of 1998 (DIW, 1994: 322; DIW, 1999b). In particular, the *Treuhand*'s MBO policy symbolised its commitment to creating a raft of small-and medium-sized industries in the east as an entrepreneurial seed-bed for change. Of all these one-time *Treuhand* firms, 70 per cent are independently-owned, but they tend to be small and are more commonly in east German ownership.

The mode of origin of the SMEs in the east has had a significant influence on the financial constraints and strategic challenges which these firms face. In general, SMEs face a very precarious life in their early years and show high rates of company failure. Typically, the problems are initially financial (insufficient equity capital, restrictive bank credit facilities), followed by marketing and product development issues and, finally, by the organisational problems of growth. In the new *Länder*, the mode of origin of the SME appears to have influenced strongly the nature of the challenges to be faced. In the cases of privatised or re-privatised enterprises, these had to restructure fundamentally and face the falling away of domestic and CMEA markets. Such companies were also weighed down by inherited debts and unclarified property titles. Where west German or foreign owners took control, products, markets and technology were decided and there were often closures of the local R&D units. However, the enterprise benefited from a certain financial security, at least in the shorter-term. In contrast, where an east German took over such an enterprise, this presented great financial risk in addition to the uncertainty in sales and product development (Herzog, 1998; DIW, 1994: 322). In the case of MBOs and newly-established firms, these tended to be free from the burden of the past, they had greater decision-making freedom and appeared expansionist and willing to take on new staff. However, they faced great financial uncertainty and were more exposed to recession, since they did not have a base of large customer firms.

East German-owned firms in particular faced tight financial constraints in the form of equity capital shortages, exhausted credit facilities, a lack of assets against which to secure bank loans (often east Germans had taken over an operation from the *Treuhand* without assuming the associated assets), and they felt discrimination by the *Treuhand* and the banking system alike. Long payment delays could also mean bankruptcy for the smaller firm. Rental and leasing costs rose strongly and such firms faced difficulties in reaching extraregional markets (Herzog, 1998; DIW, 1994: 323). There were also a host of complaints concerning the jungle of more than 400 development assistance programmes of the EU, federal and Land governments and some firms felt that the role of the commercial banks in handling public development loans conflicted with their commercial desire to lend at full interest rates (Nicolai, 1998: 87). Overall, smaller firms serving the local and regional markets could be expected to survive better, while the larger firms dependent on extra-regional export markets had to fundamentally restructure their production processes and product range, while raising productivity and controlling soaring wage costs (Herzog, 1998; Bussig, 1997).

Development Policies for SMEs: *Mittelstand* Aid, Regional and R&D Assistance

Mittelstand aid for the establishment, expansion and modernisation of SMEs in east Germany takes the form of low interest investment loans, 'capital assistance' and working capital credits, administered by the Reconstruction Loan Corporation (*Kreditanstalt für Wiederaufbau*) and the German Equalisation Bank *(Deutsche Ausgleichsbank)*, using European Recovery Programme (ERP) funds (Kokatj and Richter, 1992). These traditional western aid programmes for *Mittelstand* firms were extended to the east at unification and, through the 1990s, 70 per cent of ERP assistance has flowed to the new *Länder*. Given that firms faced great liquidity problems, capital shortage and uncertain business prospects, the ERP loan programme made up more than 60 per cent of the entire volume of development funds flowing to the private sector in the east in the first half of the decade (Deutsche Bundesbank, 1995). These loans offer very favourable terms, since they are at low interest, have a long redemption period of fifteen to twenty years, and offer a partial release from liability (up to 40 per cent by value) for the banks handling the loan. As a second pillar to this SME aid, there is capital assistance under the so-called 'twin financing' procedure. The Reconstruction Loan Corporation assistance takes the form of participation in the firm's capital by the *Beteiligungsfonds* Ost, while the Equalisation Bank's activities expand the firm's capital base by offering unsecured, secondary lending which is similar to a firm's own capital: this strengthens the enterprise's capital base, since no collateral is required and there is no debt service in the early years (Deutsche Bundesbank, 1995: 49). In the years 1997 and 1998, DM 500 million flowed annually to eastern SMEs under this capital expansion scheme (Pressedienst, 1997). In the more recent period, the focus has moved from assisting the establishment of new firms to aiding corporate expansion. Working capital credits for SMEs are also granted from ERP funds. Also in more recent years, venture capital companies have become more active in the east and the *Länder* offer capital participation through their *mittelständische Beteiligungsgesellschaften* (joint ventures for SMEs).

Given the collapse in the industrial research institutions in the east in the early 1990s, associated with the breaking up of the old *Kombinate* and given that the shrinkage in output there was producing a firm structure of essentially *Mittelstand*-sized companies, the role of state-funded R&D policy in the first decade after unification had to address the collapse of applied industrial research and to put on a more secure footing the innovation and product development capacity of the emerging medium-sized companies. To a significant degree, public R&D policy achieved this, although there are telling criticisms to be made. At the outset, there was a strong growth in expenditure by the main sponsoring ministries, the Federal Economics Ministry and the Federal Ministry for Education and Research, such that until the end of 1995 one-third of estimated R&D expenditure in the east was funded by these federal sources, falling to one-fifth in 1997. Total R&D stayed flat, however, at DM 1 bn annually over the second half of the decade (DIW, 1999a: 220; DIW, 2001b: 538). At the same time of course, under the spending constraints imposed by unification, overall German R&D spend as a proportion of GDP fell considerably, such that small nations such as Sweden, Finland and Korea achieved proportionately more (Klodt, 1998: 142; DIW, 2000a). Key features of the German publicly-sponsored R&D effort are that a significant proportion remains devoted to the public research institutions, which work somewhat separately from industry and the universities, while specific project-funding remains predominant and so leads to a very sector-specific distribution of aid and to the concentration of funding in a relatively small number of institutions and firms (Klodt, 1998: 153). Typically, approximately 28.5 per cent of federal R&D support flows to the private sector, but such is the dominance of tied-project aid that the so-called 'indirect' aid, which is granted unconditionally and quite clearly benefits the SMEs, represents only 3.8 per cent of the federal R&D spending. The effect can be seen in east Germany, which because of its more small firm structure has only 9 per cent of total German R&D personnel and where, in the enterprise sector, more than one-half of this personnel is in firms of fewer than twenty employees.

The objectives of the two federal ministries in building up research and innovation capacity in the east are clearly to raise capital spending on research, to raise the technological level of eastern output, to secure and promote a cadre of applied industrial researchers and to foster research cooperation among the smaller firms as a means of technology transfer and of achieving economies of scale among firms of small size. There are, however, notable differences in emphasis between the two ministries, with the Education and Research Ministry pursuing more advanced project-based research, while the Economics Ministry addresses the structural questions of smaller firms such as product development and promotion, patent registration, market entry and the career development of research personnel (DIW, 1998b). Over the years 1991–97 the two ministries pursued programmes of roughly equal size, totalling DM 4.627 bn in all. The Education and Research Ministry's programmes show a marked bias towards project funding, although capital and personnel assistance was also significant. Thus, in terms of capital investment, the ministry instituted a range of Technology and New Firm Centres (TGZ) as seed-beds for new, high technology firms which would act to spread new technology and innovations through the new *Länder*. Equally, in the form of the BTU *(Beteiligung in kleine technologieorientierte Unternehmen*, i.e., participation in small technology companies) and FUTOUR *(Unterstützung für Gründung und Entwicklung von Technologieunternehmen*, i.e., support for founding and developing technology companies) programmes, the ministry made grants and took share participations in young, high technology start-up companies. Among other programmes, the ministry also provided a subsidy for R&D personnel costs equal to 40 per cent of salary costs. Start-up technology firms could also turn to the ERP loans system and to investment grants of 20–25 per cent under the regional aid provisions (DIW, 1999a).

In addition, the ministry also fostered research collaboration among small companies under its programme *Förderung der Forschungskooperation in der mittelständischen Wirtschaft* (Promotion of Research Co-operation between SMEs). Such co-operative arrangements were supervised by the AiF *(Arbeitsgemeinschaft industrieller Forschungsvereinigungen e.V,.* i.e., Working Group of Industrial Research Associations) and covered up to 4,000 small firms. It did then offer opportunities for research co-operation among small firms, together with regional research institutes, which had not previously existed and which often brought small firms into the R&D community for the first time. Finally, the Economics Ministry, for its part, supported the AiF, but also devoted large sums to research personnel development *(Personalförderung Ost)*, to the promotion of innovation (IFP) and to pre-market industrial research (MVI). Its work generally favoured product development and market penetration. Since 1999, much of the specifically east German R&D assistance has been absorbed into the all-German ProInno programme. More than two-thirds of the ProInno projects are granted to east Germany, but because of the small size of establishments there, the level of spending is low and SMEs in the east derive little benefit. This is indicated in the fact that east German business accounts for only 6 per cent of east German R&D expenditure (Belitz and Fleischer, 2000: 290).

Overall, the grants and loans had a marked incentive effect among the many SMEs, which were achieving only low profit levels and in which therefore R&D was regarded as something of a luxury in the face of financial constraints. On average, the level of state support reached 20 per cent of total company R&D expenditure, with a much higher grant towards personnel costs and lower contributions to capital costs. Not only did the programmes serve to secure the position of research personnel, but in a minority of firms they helped them to start an R&D programme where none previously existed. For smaller firms, the project aid of the Education and Research Ministry was regarded as too demanding in its conditions and was associated with too much bureaucratic outlay, while, in contrast, the untied indirect aid and co-operation assistance were important means for them to acquire new technology (DIW, 1999a: 222).

At the heart of the panoply of regional development assistance are perhaps ten of the most important programmes, which cover 60 per cent of all the aid and tax reliefs granted. In principle, these instruments had also been available in the old *Bundesländer* for many years, but it is the levels of assistance and the broad coverage of the measures which show such recognition of the transformation challenge which the east has been facing. The three key measures have been special tax reliefs for corporate investment and ERP loans at low interest (discussed above in the context of *Mittelstand* assistance), each of which accounts for perhaps one-seventh of the total assistance, and, thirdly, investment grants, which account for perhaps 7 per cent of the total value of subsidies awarded. Finally, the regional aid scheme proper accounts for 3 per cent of subsidies by value. The Development Area Law (articles 2, 3, 5, 6) until the end of 1996 granted extremely favourable tax relief for investment in the region, allowing 50 per cent of the cost to be offset against the profit stream over a five year period. The 1996 Tax Law ensured that, from 1997, these rates were reduced to 40 per cent or 25 per cent depending on the type of investment, giving greater prominence to manufacturing and craft industry investments, as well as to production-related services: this was at the expense of rental housing developments, which previously had been the main beneficiaries of this type of aid. For the period 1999–2004, a shift further away from tax reliefs is evident, with further restrictions on levels of aid and eligibility. The investment grants in the recent period have gained prominence, and become more focused with time. In the early years after unification, in recognition of a generalised locational disadvantage in the east, a blanket grant of 12 per cent of investment costs was awarded, later scaled back to 8 per cent and then 5 per cent. From 1998, the grant was drawn more tightly, in that only manufacturing and production-related services could now benefit, although firms with fewer than 250 employees benefited from an automatic grant of 20 per cent of investment costs. Aid for house building and renovation in the inner cities continued with a degressive 10 per cent grant until the end of 2001 (Ragnitz, 2000: 227). Lastly, regional aid grants and ERP low interest loans were available under the 'Common Task: Improvement of Regional Economic Structure', which favoured, in particular, the SMEs in manufacturing and production-related services, permitting levels of total assistance of more than 40 per cent of the investment cost, and 60 per cent in the case of small firms. However, the *Länder* had to participate equally with the federal government in these schemes, bearing one-half of the cost.

Overall, in the period 1990–96, out of a total DM 94 bn in assistance under these regional aid programmes, it was the special tax allowances which accounted for 43 per cent of the assistance, while interest-rate subsidies accounted for 35 per cent and the investment grants for 22 per cent (*Handels-*

blatt, 1 October 1997). During these earlier years of regional assistance to the east, the programmes were heavily criticised for their indiscriminate, watering-can approach of sprinkling the bounty around, for the poor sectoral orientation of the projects aided, and for their administrative shortcomings. Most criticised was the extent to which tax relief favoured construction activity in the east, leading to a profound misallocation and a bloated construction sector. Excessive provision of rented apartment blocks and of out-of-town shopping malls for which there was no clientele was funded at a cost to the Finance Ministry, in terms of tax revenue foregone, of DM 33 bn. Further, tax relief was of benefit to profitable companies, which were largely west German concerns with subsidiaries in the east, or property companies attracting western investors. This aid scarcely benefited the east German SMEs, since profits were poor. The shift in policy towards a tightening of the reliefs and its re-orientation towards investment grants for smaller firms in manufacturing and production-related services was therefore a belated recognition of the need to secure the industrial base in the east more directly (Ragnitz, 2000). There was also significant evidence of administrative failure. The *Bundesrechnungshof* (Federal Court of Auditors) found that for the two years 1994 and 1995, DM 600 million had been paid out without justification in the form of investment grants (equalling 10 per cent of total grant expenditure), while 79 per cent of all cases of tax relief awarded showed errors (DIW, 1997: 53).

Profitability and Labour Costs

The levels of profitability and cost structures faced by *Mittelstand* firms in the east can only be interpreted from more broad-ranging studies, since these rarely address the *Mittelstand* grouping as such. It is clear that the profitability of east German firms has in very recent years been improving satisfactorily. Studies by both the *Deutsche Bundesbank* (1999) and the DIW (1998a) have concluded that only one-third of firms in the enterprise sector is still making losses. In manufacturing itself, for the year 1997, only one-half of eastern firms achieved a surplus, while one-quarter still registered losses. Overall, the manufacturing sector incurred losses equal to 1.8 per cent of turnover, compared with a profit of 1.2 per cent of turnover in the west. It appears that smaller firms with a turnover of less than DM 5 million have been enjoying good returns, while larger firms with a turnover exceeding DM 10 million have suffered losses. In part, these differences may reflect the burden of the *Treuhand* inheritance, where the remnants of the old industrial core continues to suffer restructuring and profitability problems. Thus, in 1997, 30 per cent of ex-*Treuhand* firms continued to make losses. In the old industrial core of chemicals, shipbuilding and heavy engineering, for example, unit wage costs in 1997 were twice as high as net value added per employee (DIW, 1998a). One can make a distinction between the ex-*Treuhand* firms and the subsidiaries of large western companies, which have struggled to contain their wage costs, and the newly-created firms and smaller firms, often in east German hands. These tend to have a tighter cost control. Among firms established after 1990, only 15 per cent continued to incur losses in 1997 (DIW, 1998a).

These distinctions between larger ex-*Treuhand* companies, those in western ownership, and the smaller firms, especially those created after 1990, are pertinent in relation to the control of wage costs and therefore to profitability, for small- and medium-sized firms in the east appear to have responded to the crippling wage harmonisation agreements by essentially contracting out from the wage bargaining machinery. SMEs in the new *Länder* appear, therefore, to have much greater flexibility than the larger firms and the subsidiaries of west German concerns to have pay rates which reflect more closely the actual productivity levels in the firm and its profit position. It is very widely accepted among economists that the wage harmonisation policy, together with the rapid transfer of the west German social security system to the east, dealt a heavy blow to employment and the operation of the east German labour market (Pohl, 2000; Sinn, 2000: 10). With unit labour costs rising very rapidly in the early post-unification years, reaching levels 50 per cent higher than those in the west, then falling to 25 per cent higher in recent years (DIW, 2000b), east Germany has been a very high labour cost area. Wage harmonisation agreements passed in winter 1990/91 for branches such as engineering, printing and chemicals, foresaw a wage catch-up to western levels by 1994 (which was later delayed to 1996 following a crippling strike in 1993). Convergence in very recent years, however, has slowed to a snail's pace, in recognition of the unemployment reality (DIW, 2000b; IWH, 2001). In principle, smaller firms can escape these wage pressures by leaving their respective employers' association (or never joining it), in the phenomenon known as *Verbandsflucht*. The scale of this abandonment of the western imposed collective bargaining system has given rise to comments in the press that east Germany has become a 'collective wage rate-free zone'. One may then pose the question whether this new flexibility afforded SMEs in the east represents a Trojan Horse for collective bargaining reform as a whole in Germany (Burda, 1999:7).

While studies reach slightly different results, deriving perhaps from their sampling base, there is broad agreement that, in the new *Länder*, only 26 per cent of enterprises with between 50 per cent and 58 per cent of total dependent employment remain parties to the formal collective bargaining system. This compares with 76 per cent of enterprises and of employment in 1993 (WSI, 2000; DIW, 1999b; IAB, 1999). Larger enterprises with more than 500 employees, admittedly rather scarce in the new *Länder*, are overwhelmingly members of the formal collective bargaining system, whereas small firms with fewer than twenty employees are rarely members. Important variations arise by sector and branch, with 96 per cent of organisations in the public administration, social security and healthcare branches being bound by collective wage agreements, while in manufacturing, the level is 28 per cent (IAB, 2000).

The degree to which east Germany has become a 'collective wage-free zone' is in fact hotly disputed, with industrial relations specialists (Koch, 1995; Turner, 1997) stressing that the locus of bargaining has, under the crippling financial pressures, merely moved down to the plant level, with firm and plant agreements now being negotiated with works committee representatives. Some evidence for this can be deduced from the findings of the mid-1999 IAB questionnaire. This reported that 29 per cent of firms, though not party to branch negotiating machinery, nevertheless 'oriented' their remuneration to the respective branch collective agreement. A difficulty of interpretation arises here, in that this gives few clues as to the proportion of employees covered, the wage levels and wage structures practised.

In 1999, negotiated hourly wage rates in the east lay at 91.5 per cent of the western level, with a range spanning 70 to 100 per cent by branch. However, effective gross wages lay at 79 per cent of the western level for the regional economy as a whole and at 67 per cent in manufacturing (DIW, 2001a). This reflects the longer working week at 39.2 hours in 1999 (west: 37.5 hours), the more meagre additional benefits, as well as the rarity of pay rates above the tariff wage (which, in contrast, are enjoyed by 42 per cent of westerners). The average effective wage in manufacturing is also sharply depressed for the reason that firms which lie outside the bargaining machinery pay at rates one-third lower than the tariff wage (DIW, 1999b; *Handelsblatt*, 28 February 2000). Among the SMEs in the east, a high proportion will therefore pay at rates significantly lower than the tariff wage.

The sharpest conflicts (outside of the building sector for which an effective minimum wage was introduced by the 1996 Posted Workers Law) have occurred in the engineering sector, where the mighty *IG Metall* union has sought to impose the 100 per cent wage level reached in principle in 1996. The union faces a rapidly haemorrhaging membership, which was down by four-fifths in the period 1990–97 and of *Tarifflucht*, the refusal by medium-sized engineering companies to adhere to negotiated wage levels. The Saxony engineering employers' federation, the VDMA, went so far as to enable its member firms to leave the Federation under accelerated provisions and to negotiate with the rebel Christian Engineering Union, so escaping negotiations with *IG Metall*. The response of the latter has been to impose, where it can, house agreements or recognition agreements on firms which have left the VDMA, so forcing employers to pay the tariff wage. In particular, it has managed to impose a collective bargaining discipline on subsidiaries of western firms, notably those of Robert Bosch GmbH, as well as on companies which are suppliers to the engineering giants, such as Volkswagen (*Handelsblatt*, 28 February 2000). Overall, while the picture in the east is varied, it is clear that smaller firms and those in less unionised branches outside of engineering, particularly in private services, have escaped the constraints of the wage harmonisation agreements and pay at a wage level which reflects much more closely the financial capacity of the enterprise.

A Technological Renaissance?

Have small- and medium-sized companies in the east become the vanguard in terms of new innovation, technology transmission and the creation of new products? Are there signs of a *Modernitätsvorsprung* (a modernising advantage), whereby methods, products and modes of organisation are being transformed from below to take a lead? Technology growth centres such as in the environs of Berlin, Dresden, Leipzig, Jena and Chemnitz have experienced rapid growth: there have been 17,000 high technology start-up companies established in the east since 1990, or 17 per cent of the German total. Some high technology developments have hit the headlines, such as the spectacular growth of Lintec AG, a company developed from scratch by an east German computer enthusiast, or of PC Ware AG, both of which were floated to acclaim on the *Neuer Markt* stock exchange for growth companies. Likewise, the microelectronics branch in the Dresden area has boomed around the semi-conductor plant of Infineon (previously a Siemens subsidiary) and also of the AMD micro-devices company. In total there are 18,000 employed in the Dresden area in microelectronics and a further 10,000 new jobs are expected by 2003, partly employed in the advanced microchip project part-funded by DM 187 million from the Education and Research Ministry. Likewise in Jena, the Jenoptik AG optical systems company has seen a rapid development, but there are also many small biotechnology companies as offshoots from the university. (Bundesministerium, 1998) Overall, in the high technology branches in east Germany, 15 per cent of start-ups have been in biotechnology, 17 per cent in microelectronics and a significant proportion in IT applications.

Given the fact that a significant proportion of commercial R&D expenditure in the new *Länder* is heavily supported by public funds (Bundesministerium, 1998; IWH, 1999c), one may ask what evidence there is of significant new business start-ups in the technology intensive sectors? Overall, the new business start-ups in east Germany are proceeding at twice the rate per head of population compared with the west. In R&D intensive manufacturing branches, east Germany shows an even more significant advance. Compared with a federal average of 1.72 start-ups per 10,000 inhabitants, there are 3.41 in Thuringia, for example, and in technology intensive services, the rate of new start-ups in Saxony is double that of the federal average (Bundesministerium, 1998). There is no doubt that certain of the federal development programmes have helped create centres of innovation, even if these are sometimes small. Young, high technology firms in receipt of ERP company foundation funds show quite surprisingly strong clusters around cities such as Rostock and Chemnitz, and this is closely related to the policy of Technology and New-Firm Centres (TGZ) (IWH, 1999c). Separately, the index of highly qualified employees as a proportion of all employees shows strong clusters in the Dresden area.

However, are there signs that these clusters of technology and innovation have spread more broadly to SMEs in the region, through co-operation schemes or through dispersion mechanisms more generally? Unfortunately, there are indications that there is a far lower R&D intensity in the broad mass of east German manufacturing and production-related services. This can be detected in the lower technological content of products and in the fact that a much lower proportion of output is sold outside the region. Thus, for example, the proportion of manufactured output represented by low technology-intensive products lay at 59 per cent in 1999, compared with only 44 per cent for the old *Länder* (Belitz and Fleischer, 2000: 287; DIW, 2001b: 540). Measures of R&D spending in manufacturing in the east show rates of only one-third to two-fifths of the west German rate. Especially among the small companies of fewer than fifty employees, 42 per cent did not undertake R&D of any kind (regardless of the fact that 60 per cent of industrial companies in aggregate received public funding for innovation in the years from 1992 to 1995) (DIW, 1996: 447). Finally, patenting activity in the commercial sector in the east is 20 per cent lower per head than in the west. Only 8 per cent of German patent applications came from the east in 1999.

This limited spread of technological change and innovation in the east can doubtless be explained to a considerable extent by the pattern of structural change associated with transformation. The collapse of the highly organised R&D activities inherited from the GDR, structured around national research institutes and around the *Kombinate* (for applied industrial research), had a devastating effect through to 1993, after which the situation was stabilised by the heavy public R&D programmes. Also the very fact that the enterprises which expanded rapidly with transformation served the regional market in the construction and building materials branches, in food processing and plastics has distorted the emerging technological composition and level, since these are all essentially sectors of low technological and skill requirements. The relatively weak development of business services in the east (with the exception of architects' bureaux) also reflects the relative absence there of headquarters offices and of larger firms, which would otherwise offer a ready market for their services. The relatively small size and number of firms conducting R&D and product innovation means that they cannot form the base for widespread structural change: far more greenfield development by western firms in the east is needed (Belitz and Fleischer, 2000: 288; *Handelsblatt*, 22 March 2000).

Reforms to Development Aid Policies?

Given the plethora of programmes at EU, federal and *Land* levels, which comprise more than 400 separate schemes and up to 700 partial schemes, it is essential that this thicket of *Mittelstand*, R&D and regional aid be clarified, made more transparent and effective. In particular, overlapping responsibilities between levels of authority should be eliminated. The 'watering-can' principle of spreading aid widely in an unfocused way should be abandoned and time-limited, degressive levels of assistance (reducing with time) should be introduced to cut back the 'subsidy mentality' which has grown up, and which is present not only in the east (DIW, 1997: 62).

A fairly common criticism of the regional aid schemes has been that they have been pursued without any clear overall concept, merely transferred from the west. While, in principle, stress has been laid on capital subsidies (since east Germany cannot remain a lower wage level/higher labour intensity economy indefinitely) there have nevertheless also been wide-ranging labour subsidies, at the same time as wage harmonisation proceeds apace. It was as if government agencies subsidised labour, even as trade unions pushed up its price (DIW, 1997: 52). Regional assistance (and *Treuhandanstalt* liquidity credits) helped protect the old industries, they made no distinction between industries which supplied the extra-regional market and those which were merely local, and they led to out-size developments (including speculative construction of housing and shopping malls), since a significant share of the risk was borne by the aid scheme.

The changes to the regional aid scheme, which have focused assistance much more in the form of investment grants and directed it primarily to SMEs in manufacturing and production-related services, need to be pressed further. Regional investment aid for rental housing projects needs to be abolished, so as to intensify the focus, and the indiscriminate award of investment grants in the east should be phased out by the end of 2004, when the new 'Solidarity Pact' assistance programme for the new *Länder* commences. There can be little justification for awarding an automatic grant for investment in the east, fifteen years after unification, as if a generalised regional disadvantage still exists. Firms should now be able to operate without a generalised investment subsidy. Secondly, sub-regions within the east, such as Dresden, Leipzig and parts of Brandenburg around Berlin, have almost reached western per capita levels of output and income, and differences within the east remain greater than any generalised east-west gap (Ragnitz, 1999: 2). All Germany-wide regional aid criteria should apply from 2005 and the state should narrow its focus more upon infrastructural improvement as a complement to market processes. In the 'Solidarity Pact II' discussions for the re-casting of federal assistance to the east from 2005 onwards, DM 25 bn of discretionary western assistance programmes stand for renewal. In particular, DM 6.6 bn for specified infrastructure projects and up to DM 4 bn as development aid for firms in the east remain to be re-negotiated as part of the renewed arrangements for assistance to the new *Länder* (Pohl, 2000: 223).

The general criticisms addressed to the R&D promotion programmes echo some of those pertaining to regional aid: transparency and greater effectiveness are to be desired in addition to a thinning out of the plethora of programmes at all levels. This great variety of assistance leads to higher transactions costs for smaller firms, although variety perhaps allows the programmes to meet individual circumstances better. As has already been seen, the weight of both the funding for the national research centres and for project-tied aid, acts as an obstacle to the creation of research networks whereby technology and innovations can be transferred to the enterprise level. In particular, the proportionately minor level of funding of direct benefit to SMEs constrains the rate of innovation at this level. For some, a determined incorporation of the national research centres into regional research networks and a shift to more generalised assistance, perhaps in the form of R&D tax credits, grants for technology-intensive start-up firms and public guarantees as security for the research programmes of SMEs would all address more closely the need to foster the technological and product development levels in a broad swathe of east German enterprises (Klodt, 1998: 161). At a more detailed level, specific instruments of R&D assistance have in the past come under criticism. Thus the TGZ (Technology and New-Firm Centres) have been seen as relatively wasteful in that they are often not filled with new technology start-up firms but rather simply offer commercial space with support facilities; the personnel cost subsidies have been found to fund an excessive level of personnel, some of whom are not truly research staff. This factor seems to have justified the shift to an all-German programme from 1999 onwards (Belitz and Fleischer, 2000: 290; IWH, 1999b; IWH, 1999c). While the overall very generous levels of federal assistance for R&D in the 1990s therefore moderated the devastating cut-backs in research institutions and units in the new *Länder*, the case remains that co-ordination and efficient use of aid remain of prime concern, and that aid should be degressive over time to avoid the growth of a 'subsidy mentality'.

The evidence for the previous discussion would support the somewhat disappointing conclusion that, while there have been rapid rates of new firm creation, particularly among the more technology intensive sectors in the east, this has nevertheless been of a scale insufficient to foster an effective transformation from below. Higher technology sectors have grown rapidly in the new *Länder* with significant public financial support and clusters have arisen partly in response to R&D inducements. However, new products, new technology and innovation are disseminated more slowly around the region's SMEs, principally perhaps for the reason that regional demand remains relatively slow-growing and that demand for products and business-related services is held back through the weak presence of headquarters functions and of large companies in the region. The ability to pay wage rates at less than the tariff wage is critical to firms in difficulty and to new start-ups in the more labour-intensive service activities. It also affords very significant flexibility to the broad mass of SMEs in the region. However, it is of lesser importance in the case of higher technology firms and the more technology-intensive products. Overall, the SME structure of the productive sector in the east reflects the conditions of transformation since 1990 and mirrors the regional needs of a less-developed region in Germany. Perhaps it is unreasonable to expect it to have the capacity for a self-sustained transformation. While public policy for *Mittelstand*, R&D and regional assistance has channelled unimaginably large sums into supporting the collapsing economy in the east, has fostered SMEs and moderated the severity of the impact of transformation on research and development activity, there is plentiful evidence that these instruments now should be better co-ordinated, more targeted and more selective: east Germany in the new decade has become a case for regional support according to federal-wide criteria, rather than a special case of an economy in transformation. The experience of these development assistance programmes in the east offers plentiful evidence to guide federation-wide reforms of these development programmes.

Bibliography

Belitz, Heike *et al.* (1995) *Aufbau des Industriellen Mittelstands in den Neuen Bundesländern.* (Berlin: Duncker + Humblot)

Belitz, Heike and Fleischer, Franz (2000) 'Staatliche Förderung stützt den Neuaufbau der Industrieforschung in Ostdeutschland' in Deutsches Institut für Wirtschaftsforschung (ed.),*Vierteljahresheft zur Wirtschaftsforschung*, no. 2, pp. 272–290

Brussig, Martin *et al.* (eds.) (1997) *Kleinbetriebe in den Neuen Bundesländern.* (Opladen: Leske + Budrich)

Burda, Michael (1999) *Handelsblatt*, 1 November 1999, p. 7

Bundesministerium für Bildung, Forschung und Technologie (BMBF) (1998) 'Innovationscharta für Ostdeutschland', *Pressemeldungen*, August

Deutsche Bundesbank (1995) 'Progress in the adjustment process in east Germany and the contribution of economic promotion measures', *Monthly Report*, July, pp. 37–53

Deutsche Bundesbank (1998) 'Zur wirtschaftlichen Lage in Ostdeutschland', *Monatsbericht*, April, pp. 41–54

Deutsche Bundesbank (1999) 'Ertragslage und Finanzierungsverhältnisse ostdeutscher Unternehmen im Jahr 1997', *Monatsbericht*, July, pp. 75–89

DIW (1994) 'Aufbau des industriellen Mittelstands in den neuen Bundesländern', Deutsches Institut für Wirtschaftsforschung (ed.), *Wochenbericht*, no. 20, pp. 321–329

DIW (1996) 'Gesamtwirtschaftliche und unternehmerische Anpassungsfortschritte in Ostdeutschland. 14ter Bericht', Deutsches Institut für Wirtschaftsforschung (ed.), *Wochenbericht*, no. 27, pp. 435–460

DIW (1997) 'Gesamtwirtschaftliche und unternehmerische Anpassungsfortschritte in Ostdeutschland. 15ter Bericht', Deutsches Institut für Wirtschaftsforschung (ed.), *Wochenbericht*, no. 3, pp. 45–64

DIW (1998a) 'Gesamtwirtschaftliche und unternehmerische Anpassungsfortschritte in Ostdeutschland. 18ter Bericht', Deutsches Institut für Wirtschaftsforschung (ed.), *Wochenbericht*, no. 33, pp. 571–609

DIW (1998b) 'Forschungskooperation – ein Instrument für kleine und mittlere Unternehmen zur Erhöhung des Innovationspotentials', Deutsches Institut für Wirtschaftsforschung (ed.), *Wochenbericht*, no. 44, pp. 797–806

DIW (1999a) 'Zur Förderung der Industrieforschung im Maschinenbau Ostdeutschlands', Deutsches Institut für Wirtschaftsforschung (ed.), *Wochenbericht*, no. 11, pp. 219–225

DIW (1999b) 'Gesamtwirtschaftliche und unternehmerische Anpassungsfortschritte in Ostdeutschland. 19ter Bericht', Deutsches Institut für Wirtschaftsforschung (ed.), *Wochenbericht*, no. 23, pp. 419–445

DIW (2000a) 'Verstärkte F&E Anstrengungen in Deutschland erforderlich', Deutsches Institut für Wirtschaftsforschung (ed.), *Wochenbericht*, no. 7, pp. 1–9

DIW (2000b) 'Zehn Jahre deutscher Währungsunion', Deutsches Institut für Wirtschaftsforschung (ed.), *Vierteljahresheft zur Wirtschaftsforschung*, no. 2, pp. 4–10

DIW (2001a) 'Wages in east Germany – adjustment to the west German level still far in the future', Deutsches Institut für Wirtschaftsforschung (ed.), *Economic Bulletin*, vol. 38, no. 7, pp. 219–226

DIW (2001b) 'Staatliche Förderung von F&E in der ostdeutschen Wirtschaft – eine Bilanz', Deutsches Insitut für Wirtschaftsforschung (ed.), *Wochenbericht*, no. 35, pp. 537–544

Hauer, Annegret *et al.* (1993) *Der Mittelstand im Transformationsprozess Ostdeutschlands und Osteuropas*. (Heidelberg: Physica-Verlag, Beiträge zur Mittelstandsforschung 1)

Herzog, Marc (1998) 'Determinants of entrepreneurial success in east Germany' in Hölscher, Jens and Hochberg, Anja (eds.), *East Germany's Economic Development since Unification: Domestic and Global Aspects*. (London: Macmillan), pp. 79–91

Hunsdieck, Dieter and May-Strobl, Eva (1986) 'Entwicklungslinien und Entwicklungsrisiken neugegründeter Unternehmen', Institut für Mittelstandsforschung (ed.), *Schriften zur Mittelstandsforschung*, no. 9, Neue Folge, Stuttgart

IAB (Institut für Arbeitsmarkt- und Beschäftigungsforschung) (1999) 'Betriebspanel', DIW (ed.), *Wochenbericht*, no. 23, p. 438

IAB (Institut für Arbeitsmarkt- und Beschäftigungsforschung) (2000) 'Betriebspanel', *Handelsblatt*, 27 June 2000

IWH (1999a) 'Grenzen der F&E Förderpolitik', Institut für Wirtschaftsforschung Halle (ed.), *Wirtschaft im Wandel*, no. 11, p. 3–4

IWH (1999b) 'Innovationspotentiale ostdeutscher Ballungsräume im Vergleich', Institut für Wirtschaftsforschung Halle (ed.), *Wirtschaft im Wandel*, no. 11, pp. 5–11

IWH (1999c) 'Grenzen der F&E Förderpolitik: was leistet sie in den neuen Bundesländern?', Institut für Wirtschaftsforschung Halle (ed.), *Wirtschaft im Wandel*, no. 13, pp. 12–19

IWH (2001) 'Die Unternehmenslücke zwischen Ost- und Westdeutschland – ein zentrales Problem der ostdeutschen Wirtschaft?', Institut für Wirtschaftsforschung Halle (ed.), *Wirtschaft im Wandel*, no. 9, pp. 199–205

Klodt, Henning (1998) 'German Technology Policy: Institutions, Objectives and Economic Efficiency', *Zeitschrift für Wirtschaftspolitik*, vol. 47, no. 2, pp. 142–163

Koch, Karl: (1995) 'The impact of German unification on the German industrial relations system', *German Politics*, vol. 4, no. 3, pp. 145–155

Kokatj, Ljuba and Richter, Wolf (1992) *Mittelstand und Mittelstandspolitik in den Neuen Bundesländern*. (Stuttgart: Schäffer Poeschel)

Nicolai, Wolfgang (1998) 'The role of small- and medium-sized enterprises in the new federal states' in Lange, Thomas and Shackleton, J.R (eds.), *The Political Economy of German Unification*. (Oxford: Berghahn), pp. 72–88

Pohl, Rüdiger (2000) 'Die unvollendete Transformation – Ostdeutschlands Wirtschaft zehn Jahre nach Einführung der DM', Institut für Wirtschaftsforschung Halle (ed.), *Wirtschaft im Wandel*, no. 8, pp. 223–238

Pressedienst (1997) 'Gemeinsame Initiative für mehr Arbeitsplätze in Ostdeutschland', *Pressedienst der Bundesregierung*, 12 March

Ragnitz, Joachim (1999) 'Sonderförderung Ost: ein Auslaufmodell', Institut für Wirtschaftsforschung Halle (ed.), *Wirtschaft im Wandel*, no. 7, p. 2

Ragnitz, Joachim (2000) 'Die Zukunft der Ostförderung', *Wirtschaftsdienst*, no. 4, pp. 225–229

Semlinger, Klaus (1997) 'Kleinbetriebe als Hoffnungsträger oder Lückenbüsser?', *Aus Politik und Zeitgeschichte*, no. 51, 12 December, pp. 30–38

Sinn, Hans-Werner (2000) *Handelsblatt*, 30 June 2000, p. 10

Statistisches Bundesamt (1999) *German Brief*, 28 May 1999 and 26 November 1999

Störmann, Walter and Ziegler, Albrecht (1997) 'Die wirtschaftliche Förderung in den neuen Bundesländern nach 1998', *Wirtschaftsdienst*, no. 9, pp. 513–519

Turner, Lowell (1997) *Negotiating the New Germany*. (Ithaca: IRL)

WSI (Wirtschafts- und Soziologisches Institut) (2000) *Handelsblatt*, 7 January 2000 and 3 February 2000

Chapter Six

Challenges of Participation in German Higher Education – an East-West Comparison

Rosalind M.O. Pritchard

Higher Education, Humboldt and the Soviet Model

The German concept of higher education is usually attributed to Wilhelm von Humboldt whose statue, along with that of his brother, Alexander, is displayed in front of the Humboldt University in east Berlin (see Anrich, 1956; also Schelsky, 1963). His ideal of university education has become a seminal model for institutions of advanced study in many countries of Europe and in the United States (Simpson, 1983; MPI, 1979). It originated in Berlin where an attempt was made to implement it in the now eponymous university in the eastern sector of the city. The word 'attempt' is used advisedly because as a model, Humboldt's idea of a university was never completely realised, and was often more honoured in the breach than the observance. However, like an essentialist philosophy or a religion, it appeals to an innate sense of idealism, and may embody some permanent truths bearing upon scholarship, the academic community and the life of the mind. Nevertheless, it must not be forgotten that such ideals arise from a particular set of social and political circumstances which may not be valid for all time (Ringer, 1969).

After the Second World War, and the partition of Germany, Humboldt's model of higher education was superseded but not entirely replaced in the Eastern Bloc by the Soviet model. Its founder's creed of individualism and the solitary, disinterested pursuit of knowledge was subordinated to the interests of society, particularly those of the working class under socialism. The traditional rejection of *Brotstudium* (education as a means of earning money) gave way to a strong link between education and the planned economy. The unity of research and teaching was not abandoned, but by the end of the 1980s, there were twice as many people doing research outside the universities (for example in the Academy of Science) as inside them (Last and Schäfer, 1997: 517). The need to be economically useful had begun to erode basic research, equipment was ageing, buildings were poorly maintained, and the physical conditions for research had deteriorated considerably. The unity of teachers and learners – a democratic concept in which both were seekers after knowledge rather than custodians of it – was by no means abandoned under the Soviet model. Indeed by the end of the 1980s, about 7,000 undergraduate and postgraduate students were involved in 'research' at various different levels, varying from laboratory or library work to more independent operations. This represented some 40 per cent of university R&D (ibid.: 562). However, students were managed in tightly-led groups and instructed almost as if in school *(Verschulung)*. Basic research was supposed to relate to the needs of the economy, and even the students were expected to contribute as far as possible to 'production'. Ideally, the strategy was to co-ordinate research with the *Kombinate* (large monopolistic state enterprises or combines), and the whole research process was regarded as subordinate to collective, societal interests.

The Humboldtian concept of the unity of knowledge would have required broadly-based faculties covering a whole spectrum of subjects. These existed in some GDR universities, but only a few such as Berlin, Leipzig and Dresden. In addition, however, there was a plethora of narrowly-based institutions, each with its own subject discipline and the task of delivering specific training and education which fitted into the state Plan. These were intended to aid the development of each particular geographical region, but the north-south balance was badly skewed, and the four biggest areas with 36 per cent of the population had 70 per cent of the students and 61 per cent of the higher education institutions (Buck-Bechler et al., 1997a: 60). In the present paper, we shall examine the issues of staffing, access, student life and academic structures with a view to studying and evaluating the changes which were made after the fall of the Wall.

Staff Dismissals in East German Universities After Unification

GDR university courses were permeated by Marxism-Leninism. From 1951 onwards, as a result of the Second Reform of Higher Education, all students had been required to study Marxism-Leninism at college or university – typically for about 20 per cent of their course – and to pass the examinations in this subject if they were to obtain their degree qualification. The universities were penetrated by the Secret Police who sometimes listened to lectures in order to assess whether or not they were true to the Party line, and whether they were inculcating the SED spirit sufficiently strongly. It was not enough merely to teach objectively – the teaching was supposed to propound Marxism-Leninism, and an active loyalty to the socialist state. Of course, Humanities and Social Sciences subjects lent themselves to the propagation of ideology much more easily than Mathematics or Physics, but all were expected to help build socialism. People who strayed from the approved political and intellectual paradigms were victimised (Straube, 1996: 78).

Such political control of thought and of education was a negation of academic freedom, and was contrary to the spirit of the traditional German university. After unification, the western reformers set out to develop democracy and liberal values, on the basis of the Constitution and the Unity Treaty. They could not do this in partnership with staff who were committed to quite different values, and this clash of ideology constituted one reason for inevitable staff redundancies. This 'cleansing' of the East German universities was one of the most painful and controversial aspects of the post-unification reforms. The dismissal of staff and the winding up *(Abwicklung)* of institutions was partially driven by the need to bring about academic freedom, but it was also necessary in order to make universities more cost-effective. The GDR higher education staff-student ratio was about 1:5 in the late 1980s – a level of generosity which was economically unsustainable. Moreover, the Third Reform of Higher Education in 1968 had given most university teachers the right to full-time, tenured posts, which meant that staffing within the system was relatively inflexible and immobile. Also, it led to a certain narrowness of personal horizons arising from the large percentage of academics who had spent their entire professional lives in one institution. At the end of the 1970s, 40 per cent were in this category (Burkhardt and Scherer, 1997: 289).

After the Second World War, the East Germans had been subject to an anti-fascist cull in which the percentages of higher education teachers dismissed varied from 85 per cent at the University of Berlin to 46 per cent at the University of Jena (Burkhardt and Scherer, 1997: 299). After the fall of the Wall, they became subject to a new cull in which their personal, political and academic competence were investigated. First of all, decisions had to be made about which *institutions* were to be wound up, then decisions were to be made about *individuals.*; the evaluations upon which they were based had to be completed by 1993. According to the Unity Treaty, there were three possible bases for normal termination of an individual's employment:

1. The individual's subject or personal competence were inadequate.
2. There was no further need of the individual's services.
3. The post had been dissolved as a result of change in the employment circumstances.

The Unity Treaty also contained provisions for special termination of employment which could bear on politics, but mere membership of the Socialist Unity Party was not enough to bring about dismissal: it was necessary to prove that the employee had worked for the Secret Police or the Office for National Security; or that s/he had violated principles contained in the General Declaration of Human Rights of 10 December 1948 or the International Pact of Civil and Political Rights of 19 December 1966. So much then, for the framework within which the dismissals took place.

As the statistical bases before and after the *Wende* are not comparable, no-one knows the exact proportion of people who were dismissed from service in higher education. In the whole re-structuring process, however, including academic and non-academic posts, about one third of posts were lost (Burkhardt and Scherer, 1997: 323). Between 1989 and 1994, the number of academic posts decreased from 24,500 to 13,300. Most of these were in universities, but the increase of 3,300 new posts in *Fachhochschulen*[1] has to be set against this reduction. Only abut 0.6 per cent of people had to leave their jobs because they were judged incompetent in their subjects. Only about 2,200 had to leave because they were found politically unacceptable (this represents a proportion of 2–3 per cent.), and some did not wait for the authorities to dismiss them – they left of their own accord. In the nature of things, Humanities and Social Sciences disciplines were more likely to be carriers of ideology, so the cleansing process was particularly harsh in those areas. Such subjects were staffed by females to a much greater extent than the hard sciences, and women were disproportionately affected by the cleansing. Women were thus especially hard hit by redundancies, and about 31 per cent of them were dismissed (ibid.: 333). The ratio of fixed-contract to permanent posts had been high in the German Democratic Republic (20: 80), but after unification, this changed so as to allow fewer permanent posts and more short-term contracts.[2] The role of the *Mittelbau* (academic staff of intermediate rank) which had been well-established in the GDR became much more precarious, as in West Germany. In the GDR, the majority had had permanent contracts and had been responsible for core teaching, but after the *Wende*, tenured *Mittelbau* were reduced from about 75 per cent to about 20 per cent, and their responsibilities were narrowed down. Some professors who were lucky enough to retain their posts were not assimilated into the new legal structures but had to continue as professors under the 'Old Law' – with concomitant disadvantages. Many Schools of Education came to be staffed almost entirely by westerners and the whole syndrome of the western professor coming east gave rise to general resentment. The suspicion was voiced that many of these professors, some of whom were taking up their first chairs, had not been successful in gaining promotion in the west, and had come east to better themselves at the cost of the easterners. The resentment was intensified when such professors refused to live near their place of work in east Germany, but merely travelled there on Tuesday, Wednesday and Thursday before undertaking the long journey home to family and friends. Cognitively, it was understood that such professors had husbands or wives who were unable or unwilling to give up their jobs, and children who should not be uprooted from school, but emotionally the impression remained of incomplete commitment. It should be said, however, that some of the western professors who went east did so with a sense of service and with the hope that they would be able to bring about reform. Their experience in the west had been of a scenario in which the structures were rigid and not very amenable to reform.

Change was perceived from within the former German Democratic Republic system as largely exogenous and, particularly as regards the dismissal of staff from their posts, was often experienced as discriminatory – rightly or wrongly. The number dismissed on political grounds was actually a small proportion of the whole, but the fact that a 'cleansing' did take place caused widespread insecurity and feelings of injustice. Many people asked why west German academics were not being evaluated in the same way as east Germans. The Bonn Constitution guaranteed the freedom of teaching and learning, and it became an objective of the West German reformers to introduce greater freedom into the higher education system. Under socialism, it had been necessary for a subordinate to ask the permission of a superordinate before publishing. Lecturers had been spied upon in class to determine whether they were true to the Party line, and a climate of fear often prevailed. It was, of course, very difficult to obtain permission to travel, and this affected staff from within disciplines such as modern languages. During the evaluation process after unification, insufficient account was sometimes taken of the limitations on travel, and staff were judged according to the same criteria as in the west: whether they had given papers at the most prestigious conferences, for example. They had very little exposure to western literature, and this had to be made good after 1990. Despite honest and earnest attempts to understand and take account of their isolation, they tended to be judged by the 'same' criteria as scholars in the west. Their circumstances, however, were very different, and they could not compete on equal terms.

Student Access to Higher Education

At the time of unification, the age participation rate for GDR higher education had been 12–13 per cent, in contrast with about 23 per cent in the Federal Republic (WR, 1990: 13). The demand exceeded the supply, and the close control of access to higher education was justified by officialdom on the grounds that there had to be a connection between economic planning and admission, so that the constitutionally-guaranteed right to work could be upheld. The students were supported through grants, and this was also used as an argument for the predominance of state interests over those of the individual. In socialist times, access to higher education had been an ideological issue. Workers' and Peasants' Faculties had been founded in 1946 with the aim of promoting these social groups into higher education and keeping out the middle classes which were regarded as exploitative; the avowed aim was to break their 'educational privilege', but positive discrimination in favour of the working class went along with an attempt to produce ideological conformity on their part. The children of clergymen were objects of negative discrimination because religion was regarded as a hostile ideology, and they found it especially difficult to gain a university education. The state had various stratagems for 'massaging' the official statistics in relation to the social class background of university entrants. If one parent came from a more working class background than the other, the lower designation was given, and eventually, the social origin was given according to the students' own job or qualifications. Since many of them had done apprenticeships, it was possible to make them look working class, even if their parents were doctors or academics (ibid.: 195). Despite such tricks, the policy of positive discrimination in favour of Workers and Peasants was not very successful. In 1955, the percentage of students from such families was about 55 per cent, but by the 1970s and 1980s, this had sunk to 28 per cent. It seemed that the Intelligentsia had a considerable capacity to reproduce itself – to the chagrin of the Party. This was all the more remarkable because the educated professions were paid less than skilled workers, though the use of honorific titles compensated to some small extent for what they lacked in decent remuneration.

The real point of selection was in fact not when students left school, but much earlier, when they were selected within high school for entry to the *Erweiterte Oberschule* (EOS). *De facto*, there was a four-year period of preparation for *Abitur*, though officially it should have been two (the two-year period only became a reality from 1984). There were various ways of getting round the problem of failure to gain entry to a university-preparatory track at school such as doing an apprenticeship with *Abitur*, or an *Abitur* at an evening class or by distance study. In the 1980s, about 60 per cent of those qualified to enter university had done *Abitur* at the EOS, and 30 per cent had followed the vocational route (Lischka, 1997: 165). The authorities would have liked to make the latter percentage larger than the former, but never managed it. School-produced *Abitur*-holders were under a certain socio-political pressure to accept the offer of a place in higher education, because they were part of the state Plan for the production of skilled workers; if they did not wish to enter higher education, life was made difficult for them by not allowing them viable alternatives such as completing normal apprenticeships. About 80–84 per cent of those qualified to enter higher education actually did so, thus about 15 per cent did not take up the places allocated to them. Only about 64 per cent of young people got the choice of subject they wanted, and women found it even harder than men to obtain their first choice of course (Lischka, 1997: 194, 218).

After unification, the government of the Federal Republic set out to remove the element of political manipulation from access to higher education; it also sought to increase the number of people qualified to enter universities or other third level institutions, and to expand the volume of the student body. Between 1990 and 1995, the number of people qualified to study almost doubled, increasing from 33,000 to 65,000 and representing about 35 per cent of the age cohort in comparison with about 16 per cent in GDR times (Lischka, 1997: 231). This reflected an enormous increase in the capacity of the upper secondary school, and as such must be counted an achievement. In a very short period, the new *Bundesländer* had not just reached but had overtaken the old *Bundesländer* in the proportion of people with matriculation qualifications. However, a commensurate increase in actual recruitment failed to take place. As their school careers continued, pupils seemed to be *less* rather than more willing to take up places in higher education: a survey showed that in 1995, 69 per cent of ninth grade pupils intended to do so, whereas by the eleventh grade this percentage had fallen to 60 per cent (ibid.:234). In the same year, the old *Bundesländer* had 27 per cent of the age cohort beginning higher education courses, whereas in the new *Bundesländer*, the corresponding percentage was only 19.1 per cent (though the percentage of those *qualified* to do so was 35.3 per cent) (Lischka, 1997: 239). This rather disappointing take-up rate is probably due to insecurity. The citizens of the GDR were strongly permeated by a vocational ethos: more so, certainly, than their counterparts in West Germany. An apprenticeship seems to offer a chance of a job in an insecure world where there is much unemployment, whereas higher education requires deferred gratification and the reward for many years of study is uncertain. *Fachhochschulen*, newly-founded after the *Wende*, are especially popular in the new *Bundesländer*, because they offer applied studies and seem to have contact with the world of work in a way that former GDR citizens can understand and accept.

Under the post-unification dispensation, subject choices changed somewhat, with Engineering losing in popularity, and Economics gaining in popularity. A large percentage of students (87 per cent) now state that they have been able to enrol on the course of their first choice, though not everybody is in the institution of choice (Lischka, 1997: 244). Whereas at the end of the 1980s, only 50 per cent of students attended their local higher education institution, the figure is now 64 per cent; this rise can be accounted for by the difficulty and expense of finding a place to live, so it appears that financial constraints are now emerging to replace the old political constraints. In terms of social class, the percentage of freshers from the educated classes is falling somewhat, but in 1994/95 it was still much higher in the new than in the old *Bundesländer* (58 per cent compared with 41 per cent) (Lischka, 1997: 255–6). Predictably, it is the children of manual workers who decide not to take up their places in third level education; it is those of the middle classes who are profiting from the opening up of the sector and are making use of the student loan system in order to do so. Access for women has increased: almost 60 per cent of pupils in grammar schools are girls, and more girls than boys are doing *Abitur*; the trend, which looks set to continue, is that more females than males are taking up their places in higher education, and constitute about 55 per cent of the student population. Law and Economics are particularly popular with them. Small numbers of students from the old *Bundesländer* go east to study, and this is about balanced by the numbers of easterners going west.

It is interesting to compare some of these trends with other east central European countries. Fogel and Mauch (1995) discuss the restructuring of the Czech and Slovak Republics which experienced the same politically-biased access policies as the German Democratic Republic. In 1989, the percentage of students as a percentage of the population was 10.9 per cent; now about 16 per cent of 20–24 year olds are enrolled in higher education. Almost half the graduates of academic and technical secondary schools in the Czech Republic move on to college or university, whereas the corresponding figure in Slovakia is 35 per cent (ibid.: 219). Student access there is still low compared to that in other European countries, and is 'uncertain, ... given the overcrowded conditions in existing institutions, and the attempts to increase admissions standards' (ibid.: 218). Moreover, there is still very little economic payoff for higher-level qualifications, and salaries are uncompetitive. Fogel and Mauch (ibid.: 220) point out that because, in communist times, ideological criteria applied to admissions, there are now very unified standards, and this may militate against disadvantaged groups who need special criteria.

Student Life After the *Wende*

In GDR times, the students had been formed into seminar groups which lasted for the duration of their course, and had conscious political objectives. The social relationships of the students were organised, most of them lived in hostels (often in dormitories), and had group advisers to help them with everyday problems. Each seminar group had a secretary who controlled student discipline, and ensured that tasks were fulfilled. This regimented life guaranteed security, and a rapid progress through one's course, but of course the students had little real independence, either social or intellectual. Such circumstances did little to promote critical thinking, and even though the students were materially secure, a majority were dissatisfied with their accommodation, and their student budgets.

After unification, the authorities set out to de-politicise higher education, to remove ideological pressure from students, and to promote the free development of their personalities. There was much more choice of course options, but less guidance about what ones to take; moreover, there were timetable clashes, and inter-disciplinary subjects were poorly co-ordinated, leading to a prolongation of the study period. With the dispersion of students throughout a plethora of units of study, the cosy, coherent class group broke up and with it a potent source of emotional support. Most students preferred private accommodation, but this was not immediately available, nor was it always affordable. Some 20 per cent of students lived with their parents, and although over half of them would have liked their own flats, this was possible for only about 35 per cent of them, compared to 60 per cent in west Germany (Buck-Bechler *et al.* 1997b: 519).

The burden of financing study was largely transferred from the state to the individual who became more reliant on his or her parents than previously. The German student loan system, *BAföG*, became available, and many students 'jobbed' in order to help pay for their personal maintenance. Since BaföG is means tested, the take-up rate for BAföG was significantly higher in east than in west Germany at 58 per cent as opposed to 30 per cent (Buck-Bechler, *et.al.* 1997b: 521) and the average east German student had a lower monthly income than his/her western equivalents. Naturally, having to work for a living tended to prolong the duration of study period.

In the GDR, there had been a generous state support for married students with young families. Under a pro-natalist policy, marriage was actively encouraged, and an interest-free marriage credit of 7,000 *Ostmarks* was provided if one of the partners was not yet thirty years of age. By the time they reached the end of their courses, about half of the students were married, and 40 per cent had children (Buck-Bechler *et al.* 1997b: 461) It was no disaster to have a baby before graduating. After unification, the changed financial structures quickly altered the reproductive patterns of young people, and by 1994, only 8 per cent of students were married, and only 7 per cent had children (Schnitzer, 1995).

The GDR system had some strong points. For example, the students were accustomed to progressing rapidly through their courses, in comparison with their West German counterparts. They took only four or five years to obtain a degree, in contrast with about seven years for westerners. After 1990, east Germans maintained this advantage, and continued to progress through their courses more rapidly than west Germans. There has, however, been an increase in the average age of students in the new *Bundesländer* from 22.5 years in 1991 to 23.4 years in 1994 (Schnitzer, 1995). This may be a first indication that the 'rot' of excessively long study periods is beginning to set in. It is vital for the easterners to continue to progress rapidly through their courses, because they badly need to maintain whatever advantages they can achieve in a competitive world.

Despite the climate of increased uncertainty, young people reacted buoyantly, and valued the increased freedom which unification brought about. When surveyed as to whether they regretted the old order and were critical of the new, most of them claimed that the increased climate of freedom and the extension of possibilities open to them more than compensated for the increased financial hardship and economic self-reliance. They disliked depending on their parents, but they felt well able to manage the post-unification changes (Aulerich and Stein, 1997). The majority of them feel that they are offered good study conditions, and a free choice of subject discipline. Their *Abitur* (A-level) scores are on average better than those in the west, they are usually highly motivated, and want to progress through their studies rapidly. They regard the increased personal and family contribution to their maintenance a small sacrifice for the advantages which have been attained (Buck-Bechler *et al.*, 1995).

Academic Structures and Functions

Academic structures under the post-unification regime were changed towards the pattern prevailing in the west, although this has been the subject of serious criticism by the *Wissenschaftsrat* (Council for the Humanities and Sciences). In a hard-hitting document entitled *Ten Theses*, the *Wissenschaftsrat* asserted that a fundamental reform of higher education was necessary all over Germany (WR, 1993). It pointed out the weaknesses of the system in the Federal Republic, for example over-crowding, under-financing, out-dated management structures, lack of systematic evaluation of staff, and excessively long study duration on the part of students. The *Fachhochschulen* were under-valued in comparison with the universities, teaching suffered from low prestige and loose organisation, and it was an anachronism (deriving no doubt from the Humboldtian model) that all students should be introduced to research. An education system meant to serve 5 per cent of the age cohort could not serve 30 per cent of the cohort without qualitative and substantive change. However, the *Wissenschaftsrat*, prestigious and august though it was (and is), was only an advisory and not a decision-making body. In the rush to ensure a viable system and continuity of education for the students within that system, there was no time or political will for a radical recasting of higher education on a whole-country basis. West German structures were therefore transferred to the east – flaws and all. The *Wissenschaftsrat* was charged with the important task of assessing some east German institutions, and recommending whether or not they should continue to exist or be wound up *(Abwicklung)*. The legal basis for their transformation and evaluation was provided by Articles 13 and 38 of the Unity Treaty.

Most of the important research was carried out not in the universities but in the Academies. The Academy of Sciences had sixty institutes, well over 23,000 staff and a budget of 1.4 billion *Ostmarks*. There were also Academies of Agricultural and of Building Sciences, and between them they employed about 94 per cent of R&D staff in the state sector. They were strongly oriented towards the productive sector, especially the state *Kombinate*. The *Wissenschaftsrat* evaluated the Academy of Sciences and recommended its dissolution: between June 1990 and November 1991, staffing was reduced from 24,249 to 15,836. The Academy of Educational Sciences was part of the Academy of Sciences, and it was informed in autumn of 1990 that no evaluation would be carried out on it, which in practice meant that it had no chance of survival. It would only have been possible to preserve the Academies under a federal or confederate structure which would have sanctioned different structures in east and west, but when it was decided that the unification process was to take place under Article 23 of the Basic Law, it was clear that the East would 'accede' to the West, and by implication that the structures in east and west would be expected to match. There was no way in which east Germany could preserve deviant structures, and remain apart from the west. It was also, in the western view, essential that research should be re-integrated into the universities, and if the Academy of Sciences had continued to exist, research and teaching would still have remained relatively separate. It is true that feelings of injustice existed among staff, and of course the dissolution of the Academy resulted in an erosion of the research basis of East German higher education: Mayntz (1994) estimated that in 1992, research and development were only 20 per cent of what they had been in 1989. GDR research institutions did produce work of merit, and no less a body than the *Wissenschaftsrat* drew attention to its high quality, particularly in the hard sciences which of course were less permeated by 'ideology'.

The rest of the higher education system was completely re-structured. Many of its institutions included sub-degree work, were geared to particular jobs, and had fewer than one thousand students. Only the Universities at Berlin and Leipzig, and the *Technische Hochschule* at Dresden had more than 10,000 students (Buck-Bechler *et al.*, 1997c). A large number of specialist colleges were closed because they were sub-degree institutions, and in a flexible, capitalist economy which prepared its graduates for change and adaptation, there was no place for *ad hoc* institutions that were intended to contribute to the planned economy of a socialist society. The institutions of higher education at Dresden, Rostock, Greifswald and Jena were developed into 'full-universities' with a much wider subject range than previously. Twenty one *Fachhochschulen* were introduced, and were very successful because they offered relevant, compact courses and chimed with the vocational ethos to which east Germans were accustomed; they also improved the educational network in the regions, and in this respect contributed to social justice. The Colleges of Education were mostly integrated into universities, except for that in Erfurt which served as the nucleus of a University intended to be a 'reform' institution with a structure of Bachelor's and Master's degrees instead of the long-drawn out *Diplom*. In general, it was found that it was easier to achieve innovation in new than in old foundations (Buck-Bechler *et al.*, 1997a: 112).

West Germany injected enormous quantities of money into the east German higher education system. The Higher Education Special Programmes (HSP I, II & III) extended from the stage of unification until the year 2000, and put many millions of deutschmarks into the restructuring process (Pritchard, 1999: 164–5). The money was used to help implement the recommendations of the *Wissenschaftsrat*, to open up access to students, to help female academics (in the Renewal Programme [HEP]), to help absorb some staff from the dissolved Academies of Science and of Educational Sciences, to reform existing institutions and to found new ones. All this represented a huge investment and commitment.

Conclusion

Despite its financial generosity, western Germany did not really have a grand design for the reform of higher education in the east. It transformed it so as to be consonant with its own system. The *Wissenschaftsrat*, once it had carried out its system evaluation, resumed its role of advisory body. West Germany transferred structures and strategies to the east which had patently not worked in the west itself. The Federal Republic was plagued with long study times, and there was great dissatisfaction, for example, with the first – university-based – phase of teacher training. Yet, west Germany transferred this structure to the east, despite the widespread criticisms of it.

The most distinctive features of GDR higher education had been its vocational orientation, the pastoral care of the students, the work in seminar groups, the tight structuring of the courses, and the efficient throughput of students. The vocational ethos still endures and is reflected in parents' and pupils' respect for apprenticeships which are often preferred to higher education courses. Sympathy for vocational orientation appears in the predominantly positive attitudes towards the *Fachhochschulen*. However, higher education has been un-coupled from the economy, and students are no longer expected to function as cogs in the great machinery of the socialist state. This means more freedom for them, but also more risk and more insecurity. As discussed earlier, seminar groups were experienced by some GDR students as supportive and by some as claustrophobic. They no longer exist in the same form, but the indications from surveys are that the increase in access for students, the increased freedom of speech and thought, and the greater subject choice are all adequate compensations for the loss of intimacy. Moreover, east German universities are on average much smaller than those in west Germany, and less prone to de-personalisation. East German students typically take their studies seriously, and get through their courses rapidly. This feature from GDR days still characterises them and works to their advantage. Predictably, young people have proved to be more resilient and adaptable to change than their elders. Some academics who have lost their positions were politically corrupt, but this was proven in only a small minority of cases. A great many were simply unfortunate to be teaching certain subjects in certain institutions at a certain period in history which overthrew forever the world they knew and the assumptions by which they had lived. For this, perhaps, they deserve pity rather than blame or contempt.

Notes

1 'Fachhochschulen' are institutions of higher education with structured and often vocationally focused courses that students normally complete within four years.
2 See chapter seven in this volume for a detailed analysis of staff changes and employment restructuring in east German universities after unification.

Bibliography

Anrich, Ernst (ed.) (1956) *Die Idee der deutschen Universität.* (Darmstadt: Hermann Gentner)
Aulerich, Gudrun and Stein, Ruth Heidi (1997) 'Wende gut, alles gut? Oder: Sage mir woher Du kommst? Studierende in Dresden und Dortmund sechs Jahre nach der Wende', *hochschule ost*, vol. 6, no. 1, pp. 124–144

Buck-Bechler, Gertraude, Jahn, Heidrun and Lewin, Dirk (1997a) in association with Adler, Henri and Lischka, Irene, 'Strukturen der Hochschullandschaft' in Buck-Bechler, Gertraude, Schaefer, Hans-Dieter and Wagemann, Carl-Heinz (eds.), *Hochschulen in den neuen Ländern der Bundesrepublik.* (Weinheim: Deutscher Studien Verlag), pp. 47–158

Buck-Bechler, Gertraude, Jahn, Heidrun and Lewin, Dirk (1997b) in association with Adler, Henri, Aulerich, Gudrun. and Stein, Ruth Heidi, 'Lehre und Studium' in Buck-Bechler, Gertraude, Schaefer, Hans-Dieter and Wagemann, Carl-Heinz (eds.), *Hochschulen in den neuen Ländern der Bundesrepublik* .(Weinheim: Deutscher Studien Verlag), pp. 421–536

Buck-Bechler, Gertraude, Jahn, Heidrun and Lewin, Dirk (1995) *Studienentscheidung und Studienengagement in ausgewählten neuen Bundesländern.* (Berlin-Karlshorst: Projektgruppe Hochschulforschung) February

Buck-Bechler, Gertraude, Schaefer, Hans-Dieter and Wagemann, Carl-Heinz (eds.) (1997) *Hochschulen in den neuen Ländern der Bundesrepublik.* (Weinheim: Deutscher Studien Verlag)

Burkhardt, Anke and Scherer, Doris (1997) 'Wissenschaftliches Personal', in Buck-Bechler, Gertraude., Schaefer, Hans-Dieter and Wagemann, Carl-Heinz (eds.), *Hochschulen in den neuen Ländern der Bundesrepublik.* (Weinheim: Deutscher Studien Verlag), pp. 283–356

Fogel, Daniel S. and Mauch, James E. (1995) 'Restructuring Higher Education in the Czech and Slovak Republics: An Institutional Perspective', in Mauch, James E. and Sabloff, Paula W. (eds.), *Reform and Change in Higher Education: International Perspectives.* (New York and London: Garland) pp. 209–243

Last, Bärbel and Schaefer, Hans-Dieter (1997) 'Forschung an Hochschulen' in Buck-Bechler, Gertraude, Schaefer, Hans-Dieter and Wagemann, Carl-Heinz (eds.), *Hochschulen in den neuen Ländern der Bundesrepublik.* (Weinheim: Deutscher Studien Verlag) pp. 537–602

Lischka, Irene (1997) in association with Henri Adler, 'Hochschulzugang und Bildungsbeteiligung' in Buck-Bechler, Gertraude, Schaefer, Hans-Dieter and Wagemann, Carl-Heinz (eds.), *Hochschulen in den neuen Ländern der Bundesrepublik.* (Weinheim: Deutscher Studien Verlag), pp. 159–282

Mayntz, Renate (1994) *Deutsche Forschung im Einigungsprozeß: Die Transformation der Akademie der Wissenschaften der DDR 1989 bis 1992.* (Frankfurt am Main: Campus)

MPI – Max Planck Institute for Human Development and Education. (1979) 'Between Elite and Mass Education. Transatlantic Influences: History of Mutual Interactions Between American and German Education' in: *Education in the Federal Republic of Germany.* (Albany: State University of New York Press) pp. 1–65

Pritchard, Rosalind M.O. (1999), *Reconstructing Education: East German Schools and Universities After Unification.* (Oxford and New York: Berghahn)

Ringer, Fritz (1969), *The Decline of the German Mandarins.* (Cambridge, Mass.: Harvard University Press)

Schelsky, Helmut (1963) *Einsamkeit und Freiheit: Die Idee der deutschen Universität und ihrer Reform.* (Reinbek: Rowohlt)

Schnitzer, Klaus (1995) *Das soziale Bild der Studentenschaft in der Bundesrepublik Deutschland: 14. Erhebung des Deutschen Studentenwerks.* (Bonn: Der Bundesminister für Bildung, Wissenschaft, Forschung und Technologie)

Simpson, Renate (1983) *How the PhD Came to Britain.* (Guildford: Society for Research into Higher Education)

Straube, Peter-Paul (1996) 'The Influence of the State Security Agency of the GDR on Higher Education', *European Education: A Journal of Translations*, Spring, pp. 72–83

WR (1990) *Perspektiven für Wissenschaft und Forschung auf dem Weg zur deutschen Einheit: 12 Empfehlungen.* (Cologne: Wissenschaftsrat, 6. July)

WR (1993) *10 Thesen zur Hochschulpolitik.* (Cologne: Wissenschaftsrat, 22 January)

Chapter Seven

Transformation and Injustice: Women in East German Universities

Marianne Kriszio

The transformation of the political and social system of east Germany in the wake of unification also changed the position and prospects of female academic staff in institutions of higher education. With special reference to employment conditions and personnel structure, this chapter examines how women were represented at different levels in west and east German universities before and after 1990. It evaluates in particular how the two distinct systems facilitated or obstructed women's chances of building an academic career, and how unification impacted on the employment opportunities of female academic staff in eastern Germany. Taking seniority of status and security of tenure as key indicators, the chapter shows that adopting the West German model initiated some positive developments and new opportunities in the east. However, reductions of middle-level tenured posts hit women particularly hard, since they had been well represented in this type of academic employment in the GDR and few comparable opportunities presented themselves after its demise. Taking stock of these developments more than ten years after unification, this chapter demonstrates that numerically, women remain better represented among academic staff in east German higher education than in the west. Overall, however, the West German model with its limited range of tenure-track positions, its prolonged uncertainty of establishing an academic career, its dependency of junior on senior academics, and its strong emphasis on research alongside teaching have made it more difficult for women to succeed. In the GDR, teaching and research had essentially been separate tracks. After 1990, they became two linked dimensions of an academic career. Moreover, in the GDR, female students and academics were usually also mothers and as such were entitled to special support and work-load concessions. After 1990, such concessions became a thing of the past and women could no longer combine motherhood and an academic career as easily as before. While some east/west differences remain visible, convergence constitutes the dominant trend.

Personnel Structures of East and
West German Universities before 1990

Before unification, the personnel structure in east and west German universities and other institutions of higher education were distinctly different from one another. In West Germany, reforms of university employment in the 1970s had attempted to broaden access to senior tenured positions by creating new professorial ranks. Traditionally, the title of 'professor' had been restricted to a full professor; now the additional tiers of 'associate' and 'assistant professor' were introduced. While each appointee held tenure and was entitled to define his or her own area of research and teaching independently, differentiation remained with regard to salary. Thus, C4 professors received the highest professorial salary, C2 professors the lowest (Table 7.1). For all types of professors, the traditional requirement remained in place of a completed second piece of original research in addition to a completed doctorate in their subject area. Known as a *Habilitation*, this is regarded as the formal entry point to a professorial career track, although a 2001 amendment to the relevant university legislation stipulated that from 2002 onwards, new professorial appointees no longer need to hold a second doctorate.[1]

In the GDR, the employment structure was less complex. The highest staff category was known as University Teachers (see Table 7.1) and consisted of full professors and a lower category called *Dozent*, which included ranks such as associate and assistant professor or their English equivalents of reader and senior lecturer. Both positions were tenured and, significantly, both required from its holder a completed 'Promotion B', a second doctorate equivalent to the *Habilitation*. With regard to their status and function, the east German 'university teacher' and the west German professor (from C4 to C2) represented the most senior tier in their respective academic employment context.

In 1990, about 25 per cent of academic members of staff in west German universities and 20 per cent in the east held positions within the top tier (Grund-und Strukturdaten, 1992/3: 250; Burkhardt, 1997a: 10). In both Germanies, the majority of academic staff were employed at lower levels of the personnel structure (see Table 7.1). Here, the differences between east and west were significant. In the GDR, some 83 per cent of middle rank positions were permanent posts, regardless of job title or salary group (ibid.: 11). Thus, individuals employed as senior assistants or assistants were normally employed full-time, and with tenure. In many cases, assistants were young scholars working on their first or second doctorate who could progress to more senior levels of academic employment in the same institution when they had attained the relevant qualifications. Middle rank positions, therefore, could be transitional stages in a professorial career, or could constitute a permanent academic career in itself. In the GDR, promotion could lead from *Assistent* to *Dozent* and finally to *Professor*, all of them held at the same university without risk of tenure uncertainties or relocation.

Table 7.1 Personnel Structure in German Universities

Federal Republic, 1990	*German Democratic Republic, 1989*
Professors	**University Teachers**
1) C 4 = Chair Holder and Full Professor	1) Professor (Full)
2) C 3 = Full Professor	2) Senior Lecturer/Lecturer
3) C 2 = Assistant Professor	(Dozent)
Middle rank positions (all tenured)	**Middle rank positions (all tenured)**
1) C 2 = Senior Lecturer (Dozent)	1) Senior Assistant
2) A 13–16 = Lecturer (Akademischer Rat)	(Oberassistent)
3) BAT IIa, Ib, Ia = Research Assistant	2) Assistant (Assistent)
(wissenschaftlicher Angestellter)	3) School Teacher employed in
	higher education
Middle rank positions (non-tenured)	**Middle rank positions (non-tenured)**
1) C 2 = Senior Lecturer (Dozent)	
2) C 2 = Senior Assistant (Oberassistent)	
3) C 1 = Academic Assistant	1) Academic Assistant (Assistent)
4) BAT IIa = Research Assistant	
5) Instructor for specific tasks	
(may be paid according to different	
salary groups)	

Sources: Own compilation, based on Grund-und Strukturdaten, 1992/93: 250–1; Hildebrandt, 1990: 9 and Hildebrandt, 1992: 218

In West Germany, the conditions of middle ranking academic employment in universities were vastly different. The University Framework Legislation of 1976 (*Hochschulrahmengesetz*) stipulated an expansion of tenured professorial posts and prescribed that normally, the academic middle rank (*Mittelbau*) should not be tenured. Employment at this level should be limited to a maximum of five or six years without a chance of extension, while promotion from the middle rank to a senior, professorial, position in the same university was forbidden. Thus, young academics were compelled to relinquish their places to the next generation after a certain time and, hopefully, after completing their *Habilitation*.

In the West German model, therefore, academics at the beginning of their career are forced to be mobile in order to advance. Only at the lowest level of academic employment may candidates remain within an institution and seek advancement. A research assistant, a young scholar working on a doctorate, may hold a salaried position (BATIIa) for up to six years, a limit recently extended from five, and support the teaching and research programme of a professor who acts as supervising senior academic. After completing a doctorate, a young researcher may be appointed within the same institution and even by the same professor as academic assistant. This position is known as a C1 post according to the salary level and is limited to three years, renewable for a further three years. During this period of time, an academic assistant has to complete a post-doctoral research project as stipulated by the supervising professor, or a *Habilitation*, the required qualification for professorial posts. While an academic in the GDR who had completed a Promotion B could have sought promotion to university teacher in the same institution, the West German model enforces, as mentioned above, mobility to another institution of higher education.

Moreover, the Western higher education system does not permit advancement from research assistant to academic assistant. Both positions are governed by separate contracts, have to be advertised publicly and must be open to competition. There is no linear career track from the bottom up. A research assistant who is interested in an academic career has to find a new job at the end of his or her contract. As the number of positions as academic assistant to a professor is limited, research assistants frequently seek (temporary) employment as a researcher in a funded project in order to remain in higher education. In most cases, however, contracts in research projects are limited to a maximum of three years and do not generate employment security. University legislation also does not permit individuals to hold temporary contracts for longer than five years in total within the same institution.

Employment uncertainty and enforced employment change are defining components of the West German model. Below the level of professor, there are few tenured positions, notably in subjects, such as languages, the arts or sports, that rely on instructors to deliver teaching. Overall, only a handful of tenured non-professorial positions are available. Between institutions and regions, job titles are confusing (see Table 7.1), although salary groups clearly define boundaries and difference. Thus, appointees to salary groups A13–16 may be called *Akademischer Rat, Akademischer Oberrat* or Academic Director and even, confusingly, Academic Employee. In 1990, about one third of all university positions in Western Germany were middle rank positions, and of these, less than one third were tenured. Since then, the proportion of tenured posts has dropped even lower (Kriszio, 1996a: 59f).

The Situation of Women in German Universities before 1990

At the time of unification, women occupied about 18 per cent of academic posts in west German universities (Table 7.2). Among professors, 5.5 per cent were women and just 2.6 per cent among the highest paid full (C4) professors (Grund- und Strukturdaten 1992/93: 250–61). In the GDR, women also were poorly represented at the top level of 'university teachers' but nearly twice as strongly than in the West.[2] In 1989, 9 per cent of East German university teachers were female, as women held 4.9 per cent of full professorships and 12 per cent of posts as 'Dozent'. (Hildebrandt, 1990: 9)

One set of reasons for the lower representation of women in the West German university system in 1990 relates to the structural problems of academic employment outlined above. These include prolonged insecurity, compulsory mobility between institutions and localities and the unclear career paths from research assistant or academic assistant to higher appointments. In addition, West German society made it very difficult for women to combine motherhood with an academic career. Full-time childcare for infants under the age of three is hardly on offer and not readily accepted as beneficial to children. In addition, kindergarten and school normally end at midday, forcing women to make additional arrangements for their children on a regular basis. The combined effect of these pressures has been that few female academics in west Germany have children. Although data on higher education do not include information on parental status, a study conducted in 1989 found that 60 per cent of West German female professors did not have children of their own (Onnen-Isemann and Oswald, 1991: 83). Despite these obstacles, interest among women in university careers of teaching and research has been rising. Moreover, equal opportunities policies that commenced in the 1980s appear to have produced results ten years on, albeit at the lower levels of academic employment. In 1990, 25 per cent of academic posts at the lowest salary level (BATIIa), and 22 per cent of posts at the middle level of pay in West German universities were held by women.

Table 7.2 Female Academic Staff in Higher Education in East and West Germany before Unification

Federal Republic of Germany , 1990		*German Democratic Republic, 1989*	
Professors **(as % of academic staff)**	5.5	**University teachers** **(as % of academic staff)**	9.0
C 4 Professor	2.6	Professor	4.9
C 3 Professor	6.1	Senior Lecturer/Lecturer	12.0
C 2 Professor	8.0		
Middle rank positions **in total (%)**	22.3	**Middle rank positions** **in total (%)**	35.0
C 2 Senior Assistant	10.0	Senior Assistant	17.3
C 1 Academic Assistant	16.7	Academic Assistant, tenured	40.0
BAT IIa Research Assistant	25.2	Academic Assistant,	37.8
Instructor for Specific Tasks	26.0	non-tenured	
Faculty (Academic) **Positions among total** **university posts (%)**	17.7	**Faculty (Academic)** **Positions among total** **university posts**	35.3

Sources: as for Table 7.1

In the GDR, about one in three (35 per cent) academic members of staff in 1989 were women (see Table 7.2). Similarly, one third (36 per cent) of doctorates were completed by women (Hildebrandt 1992: 220) as were 25 per cent of the second doctorate ('Promotion B') required for advancement to 'university teacher'. (ibid.) In West Germany, 28 per cent of doctorates and 10 per cent of second doctorates ('*Habilitation*') were awarded to women (Grund- und Strukturdaten, 1992/93: 232–3;259).

The different personnel structures also impacted on the position of women in the two university systems. In west Germany, professors dominate within the university hierarchy not only because their remuneration is higher but also because their rank is tenured while most other ranks are not. In the former GDR, this discrepancy hardly existed since the majority of posts were tenured (Burkhardt and Scherer, 1995). While relations between a professor and an assistant, for instance, may have been hierarchical in many aspects, the assistant enjoyed relative independence because of tenure and did not have to fear future unemployment. In fact, female academic assistants in the GDR had more job security than their male colleagues since they were better represented among tenured than among untenured post holders (see Table 7.2). This unusual fact may be due to the distribution of tenured and untenured positions in different disciplines. In the humanities, where women's employment was comparatively high, more academic staff held tenure than in sciences and engineering. Overall, the poor representation of women at the rank of professor is more important in a system where only professors hold tenure than in a system where most academic posts from the highest to the lowest level are tenured positions.

For female academics in the GDR, as for women generally, it was the norm to combine employment with having children, and working mothers could draw support from an extensive system of publicly funded childcare and a variety of special concessions (Frauenreport 1990: 138). In higher education this meant, for example, that senior staff were required to make allowances for the fact that a female assistant had to care for her children when distributing duties in teaching and research. Mothers were entitled to a reduction in their teaching load to assist them in completing their first or second doctorate thus furthering their academic career. Not surprisingly, 75 per cent of female academics in the GDR had at least one child, professors and assistants alike (Stein, 1993: 201).

Adjusting East German Academic Staffing to the West German Model

By western German standards, the number of academic posts in eastern Germany was too high. Staff reductions, therefore, were deemed inevitable, quite apart from the more complex issue that some academics had propagated GDR state ideology in their teaching while the quality and objectivity of their research did not always stand up to the criteria applied in the west German academic community (see also Chapter 6). The process of restructuring academic employment in east Germany after 1990 was informed by four key objectives:

1. To achieve a considerable reduction in the overall number of academic posts.
2. To introduce the west German system of academic employment with few tenured positions and a proliferation of non-tenured lower and middle-ranking posts.
3. To evaluate the research performance of individual scholars in east Germany in accordance with established west German standards.
4. To dismiss individual scholars whose previous performance did not match the new criteria.

Between the collapse of the GDR and the mid-1990s, the number of academic staff in east Germany declined by 25 per cent on average (Burkhardt, 1995; Buck-Bechler *et al.*, 1997). Among university teachers of professorial rank, the decline amounted to 17 per cent and to 27 per cent among the (tenured) middle ranking academic staff that had been the backbone of higher education in the GDR (Mayntz, 1994a; Petrushka, 1993). Drastic staff reductions cut across all new *Bundesländer* including east Berlin (see Table 7.3) although the *Land* Brandenburg where higher education had been underdeveloped because of its proximity to Berlin enjoyed new developments and increased opportunities (Raiser, 1998). In 1989, East German higher education had employed 37,765 academic staff; by 1995, that number had dropped to 25,929 (Burkhardt, 1997a: 22). The hardest cuts affected the *Land* of Saxony where several specialist GDR academies, such as the flagship Academy of Sports Sciences had been located and where reductions totalled 46.4 per cent (ibid.; Pasternack, 1999). In east Berlin, the number of university teachers from the GDR era was reduced by 32.4 per cent from 1,378 to 932 (Burkhardt, 1997b). Dieter Zimmer claimed that in east Berlin, cuts of assistantships and other lower level positions amounted to 68 per cent (Zimmer 1994). Official data, however, that include all academic institutions and disciplines suggest a less dramatic reduction (see Table 7.3), since cuts remained below 20 per cent in the sciences and in medicine (Burkhardt, 1997a: 15).

After 1990, the careers of academic staff in east Germany depended not merely on assumptions about suitable staffing levels, but more specifically on an evaluation of their political conduct and their official functions in the GDR. All academic staff who did not leave voluntarily because they knew that they would not pass a political evaluation (Mayntz, 1994b: 298) were submitted to scrutiny, regardless of seniority or subject. The actual procedures varied between the *Länder*, and also according to rank between professors and assistants. After unification, east German public opinion assumed that all people who had held high-ranking positions in the socialist system ought to be demoted or dismissed. In some cases, demotion did not result in job loss, but consisted of the downgrading of a person who could continue to work, albeit in a lower level position. Yet east German professors who had been SED activists not only lost their positions as head of an institute or faculty, they were also barred from holding office in public administration and so lost their jobs. The political rationale for this strict treatment lies in the system of tenure in West German higher education, where the employment status of professors is that of civil servants (Übernahmegesetz, 1992). As such, they are required to show special loyalty to the *Land* in whose service they stand and with whom the ultimate powers of appointment or rejection lie.

Table 7.3 Reduction of Academic Staff in Higher Education in East Germany, 1989–1995

Staffing Position	1989	1995	Change (%)
University Teacher	7,515	6,245	– 16.9
Middle ranks	31,393	23,037	– 26.6
Total	*38,909*	*29,282*	*– 24.7*

Source: Burkhardt, 1997a: 11; 15

Of course, a process of cleansing always also throws up injustices. In some cases, academic staff were fired because someone remembered that they had been responsible for unpopular measures against students or colleagues in the past. More significant was the disclosure that some academic members of staff had worked as agents or informers for the Ministry of State Security (Stasi) of the GDR. In other cases, however, the procedure was more formal. The new administration established guidelines, where it was stated which GDR positions could be considered 'acceptable' and which precluded any future employment as a civil servant. There was no investigation into how an individual had conducted himself; the position, not the conduct, appeared to be decisive. The political term used to characterise this formalistic approach was *Systemnähe*, proximity to the (old) political system. Overall, far more men than women lost their jobs on the grounds of *Systemnähe*. Some women, however, were affected by this rule since they had held positions as party secretary at their place of work, or had been a member of an SED committee and were thus considered tarnished by their political biography.

The main process of employment restructuring consisted of an evaluation of the quality of the academic work performed in the GDR. According to the (west) German tradition, 'quality' means quality of research and is measured by publications, while teaching hardly matters. These criteria were distinctly different from those that had been valid in GDR times where researchers had not been free to disregard state ideology and where research was not an integral part of university teaching. The evaluation of research quality was more complicated for former professors and less elaborate for former assistants, but it affected everybody. In east Berlin, for example, professors had to reapply for their own position and compete with outsiders, most of them applicants from western Germany. Special committees for restructuring and new appointments, the so-called *Struktur- und Berufungskommissionen* were responsible for the staffing, renewal of academic programs and the evaluation of former academics (Raiser, 1998: 70ff). They included members from both western and eastern Germany although their chairpersons – also known as foundation deans or *Gründungsdekane* – tended to be professors from the west. The first full professors to be appointed under this system were referred to as *Eckprofessoren*, cornerstone professors. Most, again, were west Germans. On the whole, former GDR professors believed themselves to be treated fairly. The evaluating committees also took into account that east Germans did not have the same access to important international periodicals and other research information as their western peers. In certain cases, however, west German professors took advantage of their new powers and promoted their own former assistants to professorships. Very occasionally, a young east German was chosen to replace an older east German professor.

The treatment of GDR professors who were not re-hired differed between the new *Länder*. In east Berlin, some were offered a temporary contract of up to five years. During this time, they retained their professorial title, although they lost functional rights within their institution, such as membership of committees and examination boards. In other new *Länder,* such as Saxony-Anhalt and Mecklenburg-Vorpommern former full professors were stripped of their title and downgraded to assistant. In Saxony, they were given contracts as assistant professors but kept their title. Some, however, were dismissed outright. The most frequent course of action consisted of early retirement (Mayntz, 1994b: 304).

For middle rank academic staff, the most important change was the replacement of the tenured positions by the west German system. Even those who retained their employment normally lost their tenure. Under normal conditions, changes in the personnel structure in higher education in Germany do not affect existing contracts but apply only to new appointments. Yet, east German contracts were treated differently because of the special conditions of system transformation. In this process of personnel transfer, academic staff aged between forty or fifty who had passed their evaluation and could continue in employment were compelled to accept contracts that were limited to five or six years and could not be extended.

In each institution, decisions about the evaluation of quality and personnel transfer rested with a committee. It decided who could stay in his or her position, who would be re-hired or demoted to a lower rank, whose contract would become temporary, who would be dismissed directly, and who might stay in post for a number of years, although by west German standards all positions had been filled. East German universities operated a so-called *Überhang*, an over-run of staffing targets in order to reduce redundancies and protect individuals who had passed the new quality tests from the hardship of unemployment. These staffing concessions were scheduled to end in 1996.

In the GDR, most women had been concentrated in middle ranking positions, the very tier that became exposed to the loss of tenure after unification. Many west German academics did not understand why east German women academics were so upset about the changes that took place, because they regarded it as normal that academic assistants regardless of gender held only temporary contracts. East Germans knew no such normality. They may not have become a professor under the GDR system, but they could work in a university setting and enjoy tenured positions. After 1990, they were confronted with different conditions of academic life. Regardless of gender, many older east German academics experienced the loss of their former tenured position in the wake of unification as a personal catastrophe. Their sense of dread was fuelled by fears of unemployment and also by the fear that they would be displaced by younger scholars from the west. To be demoted to a temporary contract amounted for many to a personal humiliation. Moreover, East Germans had taken employment and social security for granted and expected additional gains from the onset of freedom and democracy. When the process of system transfer failed to yield such gains, the new decisions caused upset and were held to be unfair, as east Germans felt themselves to be subordinated to unwarranted western domination.

Although the democratic movements of the GDR had called for a structural renewal of higher education before unification came into effect, none of its ideas inspired the actual system transfer that took place. The adaptation to west German structures and the work of the committees with west German experts commenced in 1991 and was largely concluded in 1993. By 1994, just 2,500 of the GDR's 7,500 university teachers who had been in post before 1989 had been re-hired as professors. In 1994, 33 per cent of the newly appointed professors came from western Germany with the remaining 67 per cent from the east. (Zimmer, 1994) One year later, the proportion of east German professors had fallen to 55 per cent, although it was higher in technical universities and specialist academies for arts and music, reaching between 58 and 71 per cent (Burkhardt, 1997a: 27).

In addition, there were clear differences between regions. In Saxony, for instance, with its concentration of technical institutions of higher education, about three in four professors in 1994 were east Germans, while in east Berlin about half of the newly appointed professors came from west Germany. The more prestigious the institution and the higher the rank, the greater the percentage of westerners, and the east/west gap has increased. In May 1994, more than half (54 per cent) of all professors and two thirds (63 per cent) of full professors at the Humboldt University in Berlin came from western Germany

(Kriszio, 1995d). Two years later, the proportion of west Germans had increased to 61 per cent for associate and assistant professors and to 70 per cent for full professors. While statistics no longer record the inner-German origins of new appointees, the practice of new professors to recruit younger staff as academic assistants or specialist researchers with whom they have worked before, tends to offer more employment chances to west Germans.

Women in Higher Education in East German Universities after Unification

The changes to employment conditions have, as outlined above, reduced the opportunities of women to build their career in academic life and introduced multiple uncertainties that did not exist in the GDR (Kriszio, 1995b; 1995c). Yet, some of the changes to the university system can be seen as gains rather than losses. Thus, under the new system, east German universities were free to establish chairs for Women's Studies. The Humboldt University in Berlin and the universities of Potsdam and Greifswald developed full-scale research centres, and in 1997, the former became the first German university to offer Women's Studies as a single honours degree programme.[3]

Table 7.4 Female Academic Staff in Higher Education in East Germany, 1996

Staffing Position	*Share (%)*
Professors overall	11.3
of these	
C 4 Professors	6.6
C 3 Professors	12.0
C 2 Professors	19.6
Middle rank positions overall	32.6
of these	
C 2 Senior Assistents	21.7
C 1 Academic Assistents	29.1
BAT IIa Research Assistents	33.2
Female Academic Staff overall (%)	27.2

Source: Adler, 1998, Appendix: 4

These developments tend to be overshadowed by the impact of system transfer on academic employment practices, because the share of female staff in east German universities declined somewhat, although not as much as had initially been feared. In 1996, 27.2 per cent of east German academics in higher education were female (see Table 7.4). Two years later, women held nearly 30 per cent of all posts in east Germany. This was more than the 24 per cent pertaining to western Germany (Grund- und Strukturdaten, 1999/2000: 224) but lower than the 35 per cent recorded for the end of the GDR (see Table 7.2). Staff losses occurred above all in the middle rank positions, where women had been strongly represented in the east. Among the highest employment tier of professor, women were able not merely to maintain, but in fact to increase their share of posts in eastern Germany compared to the GDR era. Unification unleashed fears than women would be excluded from the recast universities. These fears proved, however, to be without substance. Women were not excluded from the new professoriate although very few secured appointments to foundation chairs in the early 1990s. At the Humboldt University, 126 male and just 12 female professors had been appointed by August 1992 (Petruschka, 1993: 216). Elsewhere, similar gender imbalances prevailed. In the longer term, however, the gender gap has contracted. Yet, in transforming east German universities and hiring new professors or confirming established staff in post, members of the relevant committees did nothing to promote or retain women and may even – unintentionally perhaps – have been guilty of gender discrimination. A survey of thirty-five academics who served on such decision-making committees found that deliberations were influenced by the priorities of west German associations and academic disciplines whose criteria were applied to determine the quality of research and the suitability of applicants for appointment (Zimmermann, 2000). Since women have been poorly represented in these professional bodies, they were also poorly represented on the committees charged with recasting the east German higher education system. The few women who served on a committee were often there as representatives of academic assistants and lacked power because of their lower rank, or they served as equal opportunities officers and enjoyed only limited voting rights. Committee members from both west and east Germany were mostly male, and strongly resisted appeals to heed gender equality which they discarded as interference with the academic ethos of their respective discipline and their understanding of quality and standards. The few female professors on the various committees could plead that women should be treated fairly, but did not force the issue, since a strong commitment to gender equality might reduce the esteem in which they were held, and wanted to be held, by their male peers (ibid., 2000: 130f).

Not before the mid-1990s was affirmative action adopted for appointments to academic posts in eastern Germany, and an Equal Opportunities Office established in eastern institutions. These measures, as shall be shown below, resulted in the appointment of more women to professorial posts in east German universities than in the west. Indeed, ten years after unification, women were better represented at professorial level than they had been in the GDR (see Table 7.5; also Table 7.2). Throughout the 1990s, the number of female professors has been increasing steadily in the new and old *Bundesländer,* but remains slightly higher in the east than in the west.

Table 7.5 Female Professors in Germany in the 1990s (all types)

Year	West Germany*		East Germany	
	Absolute	%	Absolute	%
1992	1,929	6.2	317	8.3
1993	2,037	6.5	483	9.8
1994	2,172	7.0	606	10.5
1995	2,376	7.6	697	11.1
1996	2,462	7.9	723	11.3
1997	2,615	8.4	777	11.8
1998	2,773	9.0	819	12.1
1999	2,876	9.2	864	12.6

* Including institutions of higher education in east and west Berlin
Source: BLK (Bund-Länder-Kommission), 2001: 38

In the all-important middle rank of academic employment, women had occupied 35 per cent of posts in 1989 (see Table 7.2); after slight initial falls (Table 7.4) female academic employment at middle rank in eastern Germany stabilised at 33 per cent, and increased in western Germany to 27 per cent (BLK, 2000: 2–3). While east German women remain better represented at the middle level of academic employment, the gap to the west has narrowed in the decade since unification (Enders, 1996). This trend towards an east/west convergence of women's academic employment has two distinct causes. The first cause relates to the transformed conditions and employment prospects in the east which made it more difficult for young female researchers to enter an academic career. The second cause relates to expanding opportunities for women to obtain academic qualifications and secure academic appointments. Let us first examine the special conditions impacting on women's chances of employment in east German universities, and then turn to the aims and impact of equal opportunities policies in higher education generally.

East German Conditions and Obstacles to Women's Academic Employment

When the first wave of new appointments after system transformation took effect in the early 1990s, women were less well placed than men to obtain positions. Just over 20 per cent of academic assistants (C1, see Table 7.1) hired between 1991 and August 1994 were female. In medicine, women fared even worse. In 1994, one out of thirteen newly appointed assistants were women; one year later, just two out of 33.[4] From the mid-1990s onwards, however, women's employment chances have improved at the all-important entry positions of academic assistant and researcher in both eastern and western Germany.

As mentioned earlier, professors appointed to east German universities tended to appoint junior staff whom they knew and with whom they had worked before. This practice made it virtually impossible for east Germans to find employment in a department or research unit run by a professor from the west. There were other obstacles, however, obstructing east Germans' access to academic careers. While the advent of academic freedom removed the ideological shackles placed on research by the GDR regime, it also invalidated some of the research output, in particular outside the sciences and related disciplines. Thus, young east Germans who had begun work on their first or second doctorate in social science subjects or the humanities, had to rethink their work to meet the new quality criteria, or start from scratch with a new project. In many cases, supervisors had been demoted and research environments reinvented. As a result, young east Germans of both genders who had aspired to enter an academic career, hesitated to do so given the uncertain conditions confronting them, and turned to other professional fields.

The reluctance to aim for an academic career also manifested itself in a sharp fall in the number of east Germans completing doctorates at universities in the region. In 1990, 3,878 individuals had done so; in 1993, that number had dropped to 664 (BLK, 2001: 28). At the low-point, the women's share of successful doctoral candidates increased, although their overall number was just 260 (Table 7.6). Since then, numbers have increased again, and the women's share among successful candidates has crept up towards forty per cent in eastern Germany, while western Germany saw a steadier increase, albeit to a somewhat lower level.

Table 7.6 Female PhDs and *Habilitationen** in Germany, 1990–1999

Year	PhDs				Habilitationen			
	West Germany**		East Germany		West Germany		East Germany	
	Absolute	%	Absolute	%	Absolute	%	Absolute	%
1990	5,137	27.8	1,230	31.7	110	10.0	105	18.9
1991	5,373	28.2	1,272	37.0	115	9.8	58	17.6
1992	5,754	28.7	432	30.9	148	12.8	21	13.7
1993	6,178	30.3	260	39.2	156	11.8	16	16.0
1994	6,483	30.9	506	36.4	186	13.4	14	15.2
1995	6,622	31.2	427	37.8	195	13.8	16	13.0
1996	6,581	30.7	523	37.1	188	12.6	20	17.4
1997	7,004	31.7	766	36.3	258	16.0	15	12.1
1998	7,411	32.5	817	39.7	266	15.4	27	14.1
1999	7,196	33.0	990	36.1	305	18.1	35	14.6

*) 'Habilitation' is a second book-length piece of original research, which was, until January 2002, required before a candidate could apply for a chair or hold any type of professorial post
**) Including institutions of higher education in west and east Berlin
Source: BLK , 2001: 28; 32

At the level of second doctorate or *Habilitation*, women's participation in these in east Germany collapsed as far as absolute numbers are concerned from 105 in 1989 to a low point of fourteen in 1994 and thirty-five in 1999. In terms of percentage, the changes have been less dramatic, declining from 18.9 per cent in 1989 to 14.6 per cent in 1999, since higher numbers progressed to the second doctorate in the GDR in line with higher staffing levels in the university system at the time. Since one of the after-effects of unification had been to deter young east Germans from attempting a doctorate, the potential pool for completing a second doctorate also contracted (Burkhardt and Scherer, 1993). Since this second doctorate, however, was at the time still a prerequisite for applications to professorships, the pool of potential east German applicants at this level was also lower. The decline among the number of women qualifying at second doctorate level further reduced their chances of building an academic career in the transformed system of higher education. In future years, an increase of east German professorial applicants can be expected, because the academic assistants hired since the mid-1990s will have completed their *Habilitation* before competing for positions in the top tier of the academic employment market. At the time of writing, it is impossible to predict how many women will be among them.[5]

Gender Equality Policy in Higher Education in Germany

On the eve of unification, gender equality had not constituted a special focus in East German universities, but had already recast the political agenda in the west. In addition to the system transfer with its employment restructuring, loss of tenure and unfamiliar pressures of competition, the new centrality of gender strengthened women's opportunities to succeed in building an academic career.

In the middle of the 1980s, some West German universities created the post of Equal Opportunities Officer (*Gleichstellungsbeauftragte*) in order to promote gender equality inside the institution, and agreed Gender Equality Guidelines (*Frauenförderpläne*) designed to enhance women's chances of advancement and even apply affirmative action to reduce gender inequalities. These guidelines call for positive discrimination in favour of female applicants in those areas of employment where women are under-represented. Unfortunately, the guidelines specified that candidates had to be equally qualified, a clause that was too vague and too open to interpretation to break established recruitment patterns, especially at the professorial level. On the other hand, the guidelines reduced discriminatory practices by specifying appointment procedures and by making selection processes altogether more transparent.

The University of Hamburg was the first to appoint an Equal Opportunities Officer in 1985, followed by the University of Kassel one year later. Since the late 1980s, German universities are required by the law to establish such an office and elect an office holder from among their academic members of staff. Equal Opportunities Officers are responsible for increasing awareness of discriminatory practices and for initiating and implementing anti-discrimination policies. Within their institution, they monitor compliance with the guidelines on affirmative action and also participate in search committees and appointment boards. Although they do not have voting rights, they hold a *procedural veto* which allows them to object to appointment decisions if they consider that women applicants have been judged unfairly. In this case, the selection process has to be re-run (Kriszio, 1995a: 133ff).

Equal Opportunities Officers also offer counselling to individual members of academic staff and to students. In many West German universities they have helped to improve provisions for female staff and students with children. They initiated projects to make sciences more attractive to female undergraduates. In Bremen and Wilhelmshaven, the Equal Opportunities Officers at the local *Fachhochschule* promoted special study programs for women, and supported the establishment of professorships for gender studies. When unification redefined the meaning of gender in the east German university landscape, research centres for women's studies existed in Bielefeld, Bremen, Dortmund, Essen, Flensburg, Frankfurt/Main, Freiburg, Hildesheim, Kassel, Kiel, Marburg, and Oldenburg as well as Berlin, and had forged an effective network of research, teaching and advancing women's professional opportunities in academic life.

In east Germany, women in higher education readily adopted the institution of Equal Opportunities Officer. In the closing months of the GDR, such an office had begun to take shape when a *Gleichstellungsbeauftragte* was elected at the Humboldt University in May 1990. Yet many female academics in the east were rather reluctant at that time to endorse equal opportunities guidelines. One reason may have been the ubiquitous employment uncertainty which made issues such as gender equality appear secondary in the light of total employment loss. Another reason had its roots in GDR politics. There, programmes with similar names had existed in order to direct women into academic employment in line with pre-determined quotas. Sometimes, these programmes were responsible for promoting women whose qualifications were comparatively poor but who had effective contacts to the political elite and decision makers of the day. After unification, east German women wanted to distance themselves from all such practices. Their hesitancy to support an Office for Equal Opportunities arose from confidence in their own abilities and the belief that women of caliber did not need special support to succeed (Kriszio, 1996b: 148f).

The process of personnel restructuring after unification made more and more east German women aware of the necessity of gender equality policies. They noticed the virtual absence of women among foundation deans and cornerstone professors and feared that their jobs were at risk in an increasingly male setting. Since Equal Opportunities Officers were ex-officio members of professorial appointment boards and were consulted about offers of temporary appointment to tenured staff, female academics soon sought their support.[6]

More than a decade after unification, east German Equal Opportunities Officers approach their tasks in the same way as their west German counterparts, although their working conditions still differ. In east German educational law (passed, of course, by the various *Länder*) the position is not as well established as in west Germany. Thus, in (west) Berlin, Schleswig-Holstein and Hessen full-time positions were established and funded; in eastern Germany, this applies only at the Technical University of Dresden. Elsewhere in west Germany, Equal Opportunities Officers are entitled to a reduction of 50 per cent in their teaching hours, and to the support of an administrative assistant or student helper. In east Germany, reductions of teaching hours vary and are less generous in smaller than in larger universities. Only the University of Potsdam offers any kind of administrative support. Since taking office in the early 1990s, Equal Opportunities Officers have introduced affirmative action programmes and plans in most east German universities (Kriszio, 1999). They monitor the participation of women in all employment ranks, ensure access to childcare facilities, support the creation of chairs and centres for gender studies, and participate in activities to interest female students in science degrees.

State funding has also been channelled into enabling women to complete higher degrees at first and second doctorate level. The second Special Programme for Higher Education came into effect on 2 October 1990, one day prior to formal unification. It was confined to the old *Länder* and aimed at sponsoring female academics through a system of special grants (Kriszio, 1995a: 135f). East German women were included from 1996 onwards when the third Special Programme for Higher Education (*Hochschulsonderprogramm III*) came into effect (BLK, 2000: 4f; ETAN, 2000: 129). Funds were distributed between regions on the basis of population figures. While *Länder* were free to decide how to allocate these funds and some earmarked payments to assist with childcare cost to women in academic life, most replaced the grant system of the earlier scheme by a system of funding full-time academic posts for women at the academic assistant level. These positions enabled women to gain experiences in university employment and also complete the advanced research degrees or publications required for building future careers. These funded posts for women did, of course, not close the gender imbalance of academic staffing in Germany, but they helped to increase the number of female academics with recognised research qualifications who might apply for higher and tenured positions in the future. In Berlin, the success of special funding resulted in an increased representation of women among academic assistants at the Free University and the Technical University in the western part of the city; at the Humboldt University in the east, the special funding has compensated for the reduction in the number of women among university staff that occurred in the first years after unification (Zehn Jahre, 2001).

Conclusion

The situation of female academics in east and west Germany since 1990 has developed differently. In the west, where the share of women in faculty positions in general, and in middle ranks specifically, had been much lower at the beginning of the decade and where few women held tenured positions, progress towards equal opportunities was continuous as far as qualifications and access to lower level positions were concerned. There has also been a continuous increase in the numbers of female professors, but the official aim, proclaimed by the Federal Ministry of Higher Education, that at least 20 per cent of professors should be women, remains a long way off.

In eastern Germany, developments took the opposite course. The changes that followed the collapse of the GDR brought gains of personal and academic freedom and losses of tenure for the majority of female academics in post, and reduced opportunities for the next generation as new appointees were predominantly male and from western Germany. This especially affected the professional career of women in middle rank positions in a negative way, while former female professors who were not re-hired or who were retained for a limited number of years could normally take early retirement.

As the immediate impact of unification subsided and development became more sustained, a more ambiguous picture emerged. East German female professors with a sound research record who where not regarded as politically tarnished were re-hired at least as often as their male colleagues, and some west German women were even hired as professors at universities in the east. At the end of the 1990s, east German universities employed more female professors than had been in post in the GDR.

In middle rank positions, the share of women in east German universities decreased. Overall, the number of posts in this category declined compared with the GDR, and new recruitment has been limited. Although Equal Opportunity Officers succeeded in defending women in middle rank positions, they normally secured only a transitional arrangement of re-employment for a limited period. In the early 1990s, the number of women with new contracts for middle rank positions had fallen dramatically. Half way through the decade, women again secured appointments in middle rank posts, although these were no longer tenured as they had been in the GDR. Disregarding issues of tenure and employment security, women in academic positions in eastern Germany outnumber those in western Germany at professorial and middle ranking levels. Among professors, the share of women has been increasing in both parts of Germany, albeit from a low level and at a slow pace. In middle rank and lower positions there is clear progress in the west but near-stagnation in the east. Overall, the gender gap is narrowing between east and west and also within institutions. For Equal Opportunities Officers and the higher education system in Germany the issue of women's representation at all levels of academic employment will remain a challenge for years to come.

Notes

1 The fifth revision to the University Framework Legislation (*Hochschulrahmengesetz*) was passed on 2 October 2001 and laid down that from 23 February 2002 onwards, the *Habilitation* would no longer be required. In an attempt to bring the German university system in line with developments in other countries and to encourage international mobility, the law also introduced a new position of 'Junior Professor' equivalent to Assistant Professor or Lecturer in the Anglo-American context.

2 During the GDR era, no data were published on university employment by gender. Karin Hildebrandt was the first to collect this information in 1990 in the context of the 'Projektgruppe für Hochschulforschung' based in Berlin – Karlshorst. This research group has since been transferred to the Martin Luther University in Halle, Saxony-Anhalt.

3 In 2002, research centres for Womens' Studies existed at the universities of Potsdam, Greifswald, Berlin (Humboldt) and Leipzig.

4 These data relate to the Humboldt University and have been collected by the author in the course of her work as Equal Opportunities Officer. Marianne Kriszio was elected to the position of Equal Opportunities Officer in August 1993 and continues to hold it at the time of writing.

5 A more detailed analysis of gender and future opportunities will have to examine employment in different institutions and across disciplines. Such an analysis would be too detailed in the context of this chapter, but some information might be of interest. Data for 1996 (Table 7.7) show that women's chances were best in specialist institutions for the arts and music and worst in the vocationally orientated *Fachhochschulen*. A breakdown by academic disciplines (Table 7.8) shows that women's representation at professorial and middle rank was best in the humanities, followed by veterinary and medical sciences.

Table 7.7 Female Academic Staff in Higher Education by Type of Institution in East Germany, 1996

Type of Institution	Professors		Middle Rank Positions		Academic Staff overall	
	Absolute	%	Absolute	%	Absolute	%
University	309	8.95	5.435	32.3	5,744	28.4
Fachhochschule*	241	11.6	144	32.4	385	15.3
Academies of the Arts and Music	132	26.6	174	45.9	306	34.8

* a type of university offering shorter, more structured and often vocationally-orientated degrees
Source: Adler, 1998, Appendix: 3–4

Table 7.8 Female Academic Staff by Academic Disciplines in East Germany, 1996 (in %)

Discipline	Professors (%)	Middle ranks (%)	Overall (%)
Law and Social Sciences	8.3	35.1	25.1
Mathematics and Natural Science	7.0	22.5	19.2
Humanities	22.2	52.1	42.1
Sports	6.1	30.6	27.1
Medicine	8.1	40.5	37.2
Veterinary Medicine	12.5	41.8	36.1
Agronomy, Forestry, and Dietetics	8.6	31.1	24.8
Engineering	3.8	14.7	11.2

Source: Adler, 1998, Appendix: 7

6 It was up to the newly appointed Equal Opportunities Officers to collect data on female appointments at the lower academic ranks of assistant. (C1 and BATIIa) The intensive workload during the first phase of restructuring east German universities may account for the fact, that Equal Opportunities Officers often did not have the time and energy to fight for a fair share of women at the lower ranks. They concentrated, above all, on professorial posts and on defending those female colleagues who were in danger of losing their job.

Bibliography

Adler, Helga (1998) *Anteil von Wissenschaftlerinnen an den Hochschulen der neuen Bundesländer 1989–1996*. Bundeskonferenz der Frauen- und Gleichstellungsbeauftragten an Hochschulen. (Berlin: Frauenbeauftragte der Humboldt Universität zu Berlin)

BLK (2000) Bund-Länder-Kommission für Bildungsplanung und Forschungsförderung, *Frauen in der Wissenschaft –Entwicklung und Perspektiven auf dem Weg zur Chancengleichheit. Materialien zur Bildungsplanung und zur Forschungsförderung*. (Bonn:BLK), no. 87

Buck-Bechler, Gertraude, Schaefer, Hans-Dieter and Wagemann, Carl-Heinz (1997) (eds.), *Hochschulen in den neuen Ländern der Bundesrepublik Deutschland. Ein Handbuch zur Hochschulerneuerung*. (Weinheim: Deutscher Studienverlag)

Burkhardt, Anke (1995) 'Besser als befürchtet – schlechter als erhofft. Zum Stand des Berufungsgeschehens an ostdeutschen Hochschulen aus Frauensicht', *Hochschule Ost*, vol. 1995, no. 2, pp. 107–121

Burkhardt, Anke (1997a) *Stellen und Personalbestand an ostdeutschen Hochschulen 1995. Datenreport*. (Wittenberg: Institut für Hochschulforschung, Universität Halle-Wittenberg)

Burkhardt, Anke (1997b) 'New Professors – Old Structures: Results of Personal Replacement in East German Universities from Women's Point of View' in Grundy, A. F. *et al.* (eds.) *Women, Work and Computerization. Proceedings of the International IFIP-Conference* Bonn, Germany, May 24 to 27. (Berlin/Heidelberg/New York: Springer), pp. 31–44

Burkhardt, Anke and Scherer, Doris (1993) *Habilitierte Wissenschaftlerinnen in Ostdeutschland – Ein Berufungsreservoir?* (Berlin-Karlshorst: Projektgruppe Hochschulforschung)

Burkhardt, Anke and Scherer, Doris (1995) *Förderung des wissenschaftlichen Nachwuchses an den DDR-Hochschulen in den 80er Jahren – gesetzliche Grundlagen, hochschulpolitischer Kontext, statistischer Überblick.* (Berlin-Karlshorst: Projektgruppe Hochschulforschung)

Enders, Jürgen (1996) *Die wissenschaftlichen Mitarbeiter. Ausbildung, Beschäftigung und Karriere der Nachwuchswissenschaftler und Mittelbauangehörigen an den Universitäten.* (Frankfurt/New York: Campus)

ETAN (2000) ETAN Expert Working Group on Woman and Science, *Science Policies in the European Union. Promoting excellence through mainstreaming gender equality.* (Brussels: European Commission Research Directorate General/ Improving the Human Research Potential and Social Economic Knowledge Base)

Frauenreport '90, (1990) ed. Winkler, Gunnar im Auftrag der Beauftragten des Ministerrates für die Gleichstellung von Frauen und Männern, Dr. Marina Beyer. (Berlin: Die Wirtschaft)

Grund- und Strukturdaten 1992/93 (1992) ed. Bundesminister für Bildung und Wissenschaft. (Bonn: Karl Heinrich Bock)

Grund- und Strukturdaten 1998/99 (1998) ed. Bundesministerium für Bildung und Wissenschaft. (Bonn: Gebr. Garloff Verlag)

Grund- und Strukturdaten 1999/2000 (2000) ed. Bundesministerium für Bildung und Wissenschaft. (Bonn: Gebr. Garloff Verlag)

Hildebrandt, Karin (1990) *Wozu Forschungen über Frauen im Hochschulwesen?* (Berlin: Zentralinstitut für Hochschulbildung)

Hildebrandt, Karin (1992) 'Die berufliche Situation in der DDR – Frauen in der Wissenschaft' in Barbara Geiling-Maul *et al.* (eds.) *Frauenalltag. Weibliche Lebenskultur in beiden Teilen Deutschlands.* (Köln: Bundverlag), pp. 215–230

Kriszio, Marianne (1995a) 'Women in East and West German Universities before and after Unification', *Journal of Area Studies*, no. 6, pp. 130–142

Kriszio, Marianne (1995b) 'The situation of Women at East German University after the Unification' in Färber, Christine and Henninger, Annette (eds.), *Equal Opportunities for Women at European Universities.* (Berlin: Freie Universität Berlin), pp. 69–76

Kriszio, Marianne (1995c), 'Karriereverläufe von Wissenschaftlerinnen und Mechanismen struktureller Diskriminierung', *in: Unter Hammer und Zirkel: Frauenbiographien vor dem Hintergrund ostdeutscher Zivilisationserfahrungen*, ed. Zentrum fuer interdisziplinaere Frauenforschung der Humboldt-Universität zu Berlin. (Pfaffenweiler: Centaurus), pp.77–87

Kriszio, Marianne (1995d) 'Veränderungen der akademischen Personalstruktur in den neuen Bundesländern am Beispiel der Humboldt-Universität: Handlungsleitende Prinzipien, Ergebnisse und Nebenfolgen' in Sahner, Heinz and Schwendtner, Stephan (eds.), *Gesellschaften im Umbruch. Kongressband II: Berichte aus den Sektionen. 27. Kongress der Deutschen Gesellschaft für Soziologie.* (Opladen: Westdeutscher Verlag), pp. 35–41

Kriszio, Marianne (1996a) 'Zur Situation von Wissenschaftlerinnen an ostdeutschen Hochschulen nach der Wende am Beispiel der Humboldt-Universität zu Berlin' in Helfrich, Heide and Guegel, Jutta (eds.), *Frauenleben im Wohlfahrtsstaat. Zur Situation weiblicher Existenzbedingungen.* (Münster:Dädalus), pp. 48–67

Kriszio, Marianne (1996b) 'Frauen und Machtstrukturen an ostdeutschen Hochschulen vor und nach der Wende', in Penrose, Virginia and Rudolph, Clarissa (eds.), *Zwischen Machtkritik und Machtgewinn. Feministische Konzepte und politische Realität.* (Frankfurt/New York: Campus), pp. 143–159

Kriszio, Marianne (1999) 'Women's policy in higher education in Germany – context and strategies' in Fogelberg, Paul *et al.* (eds.), *Hard Work in the Academy: Research and Interventions on Gender Inequalities in Higher Education.* (Helsinki: University Press), pp. 251–258

Mayntz, Renate (1994a) (ed.) *Aufbruch und Reform von oben. Ostdeutsche Universitäten im Transformationsprozess.* (Frankfurt/New York:Campus)

Mayntz, Renate (1994b) 'Die Erneuerung der ostdeutschen Universitäten zwischen Selbstreform und externer Intervention' in Mayntz, Renate (ed.), *Aufbruch und Reform von oben. Ostdeutsche Universitäten im Transformationsprozess.* (Frankfurt/New York: Campus), pp. 283–312

Onnen-Iseman, Corińna and Oswald, Ursula (1991) *Aufstiegsbarrieren für Frauen im Universitätsbereich.* (Bonn: Bundesministerium für Bildung und Wissenschaft)

Pasternack, Peer (1999) *Demokratische Erneuerung. Eine universitätsgeschichtliche Untersuchung des ostdeutschen Hochschulumbaus 1989–1995. Mit zwei Fallstudien: Universität Leipzig und Humboldt-Universität zu Berlin.* (Weinheim: Deutscher Studienverlag)

Petruschka, Gisela (1993) 'Die Verdrängung von Frauen aus der Hochschule am Beispiel der Humboldt-Universität zu Berlin' in Schramm, Hilde (ed.), *Hochschule im Umbruch.* (Berlin: BasisDruck), pp. 216–217

Raiser, Thomas (1998) *Schicksalsjahre einer Universität. Die strukturelle und personelle Neuordnung der Humboldt-Universität zu Berlin 1989–1994.* (Berlin: Nomos)

Stein, Ruth Heidi (1993) 'Die Situation von Wissenschaftlerinnen an Hochschulen der DDR. Veränderungen nach der Vereinigung' in Schramm, Hilde (ed.), *Hochschule im Umbruch.* (Berlin: BasisDruck), pp. 198–205

Übernahmegesetz (1992) 'Hochschulpersonal-Übernahmegesetz: Gesetz über die Übernahme des wissenschaftlichen und künstlerischen Personals der Hochschulen im Ostteil Berlins in Rechtsverhältnisse nach dem Berliner Hochschulgesetz vom 11. 6. 1992', *Gesetzliche Verordnungen. Berlin,* vol. 48, no. 27, p. 191

Zimmer, Dieter (1994) 'Wunder im Osten', *Die Zeit,* 25 May

Zimmermann, Karin (2000) *Spiele mit der Macht in der Wissenschaft. Passfähigkeit und Geschlecht als Kriterien für Berufungen.* (Berlin: edition sigma)

Zehn Jahre (2001) *Zehn Jahre Landeskonferenz der Frauenbeauftragten an Berliner Hochschulen: erfolgreich und unverzichtbar.* (Berlin: Zentrale Frauenbeauftragte der Freien Universität Berlin)

Chapter Eight

Meanings of Migration in East Germany and the West German Model

Eva Kolinsky

One of the most unexpected challenges in the wake of unification concerned the meaning of migration. The establishment of democratic governance reinvented the political system and replaced its elite but also entailed an institutionalisation of the rule of law in society and a guarantee of rights and legal protection to all, regardless of residency status, nationality, religion, gender, race or background. Migration and the rights of migrants in the receiving country constitute a significant indicator of its democratic credentials (Panayi, 1996). Drawing on this link between democratic governance and migration, this chapter examines the place of migrants and their treatment with special reference to east Germany. For the period before 1945, the focus on migration can exemplify democracy deficits in German history and help define the legacies that faced both attempts at reinventing Germany, the FRG and GDR (Berghoff, 1996). For post-war developments until 1990, the focus on migration and the place of migrants can illuminate the hiatus that separated the two German states before they were unified. The main body of the chapter discusses the treatment of GDR contract workers, the changed meaning of migration in east Germany after unification and the contribution of Foreigners' Commissioners and east German officials to administering migration and facilitating settlement. Looking at attitudes towards 'others' among young people, the chapter argues that east Germans perpetuate the institutional exclusion of non-Germans from the GDR era in their negative views about the presence of 'others' and its impact on their private world.

Migration – German Legacies and New Beginnings

In Germany, as in other countries, migration followed economic fortunes (Bade, 1987). At times of hardship, Germans settled elsewhere or sought seasonal labour in neighbouring regions to supplement their income. At times of material well-being, migration occurred in the opposite direction. For most of its history since the late nineteenth century, Germany had been a pull-country and attracted migrants (Dohse, 1981). Yet, by linking citizenship to birth and origin (*ius sanguinis*), residency served the purposes of labour recruitment and supply without leading to immigration or permanent settlement (Brubaker, 1992; Joppke, 1999).

While Germany continues to declare that it is 'kein Einwanderungsland', not a country of immigration, modifications of policy are under way. Thus, shortages in information technology specialists persuaded the German government in 2000 to launch a 'Green Card' scheme of unrestricted rights of residency and employment to qualified applicants from outside the country. In June 2001, a special commission on immigration and citizenship recommended that up to 50,000 highly qualified personnel should be recruited annually, 20,000 as 'Green Card' immigrants, 20,000 on five-year contracts and the remainder for shorter period and temporary programmes (Williamson, 2001). The report's recommendations tried to address two issues that have challenged German policy makers for some time: a persistently low birth-rate threatens the German economy with labour shortages in the near future, while specific shortages in IT-related expertise need to be rectified to safeguard the innovative potential and economic leadership of the country. The proposed formula on immigration does not mark a new acceptance of migration as a humanitarian project, but is driven by economic and utilitarian concerns that fashioned German policy towards migration and non-German labour recruitment throughout the modern era.

The dichotomy between humanitarian and utilitarian principles has been the touchstone of labour migration in Germany. In Imperial Germany and the Weimar Republic, foreign workers were required to return home at least once a year in order to block any entitlement to permanent residency rights. In addition, social contacts with Germans were discouraged or forbidden for fear they might dilute German culture. When the introduction of military service in 1935 resulted in labour shortages, the National Socialists intensified the recruitment of foreign workers (*Fremdarbeiter*). During World War II they organised mass deportations of forced labour from occupied Europe for deployment in industry and agriculture (Homze, 1967; Herbert, 1984). Concentration camp prisoners were also exploited for work. Controlled by the SS, foreign labour was treated as slave labour without human or civil rights. National Socialist ideology and practice classified 'others' as socially and culturally inferior and applied racist doctrine to justify all forms of inhumane treatment, including murder. Given this legacy, continuity was impossible and change paramount if post-war reconstruction was to be credible as a new beginning.

German Migration into Germany: Responses in East and West

When the Second World War ended, some ten million survivors of forced labour and slave labour programmes were liberated inside Germany (Jacobmeyer, 1985). The Western Allies introduced the term 'displaced persons' to refer to civilians who found themselves in Germany against their will, and who should be repatriated after their liberation or resettled in another country if repatriation proved impossible (Wyman, 1998; Geis, 2000). Essentially, responsibility for assisting and rehabilitating former forced labourers and survivors of concentration camps rested with the Allies and Humanitarian Aid organisations, such as UNRRA, working in conjunction with the military in the Western zones of occupation. When the West German government was ordered to take charge of those who had, against all expectations, remained in the country, it replaced the term 'displaced persons' with the more neutral 'homeless foreigners' which did not appear to invite restitution claims or imply admissions of guilt (McNeill, 1995). In eastern Germany, neither the Soviet authorities nor the GDR administration recognised 'displaced persons' or made provision for their care, but considered this legacy of the Nazi past a Western and later a West German problem.

In the aftermath of World War II, a different migration dominated German agendas: the forced migration of Germans who fled from the advancing Red Army and were expelled from regions along the eastern border of the former Reich which had been reallocated to Poland or Czechoslovakia. While flight and expulsions had commenced in the closing months of 1944, numbers were agreed and transports authorised at the Potsdam Conference in August 1945. Between 1945 and 1947, an estimated twelve million German forced migrants arrived in occupied Germany, three million of these in the Soviet zone (Lemberg and Edding, 1959). All four zones of occupation were required to accommodate expellees. Since most were allocated to rural areas that had suffered less destruction of their housing stock than German cities, the arrival of these German migrants redrew the social map of rural Germany. Regions such as Schleswig Holstein, Lower Saxony and Bavaria saw their populations increase between 40 and 60 per cent (Zayas, 1986: 150). The last refugee camp for German migrants from the eastern regions closed in the mid-fifties, some ten years after the forced migration of Germans into Germany commenced.

East German Responses to German Migrants

Responses to the new arrivals among local populations were generally hostile, a fact that tends to be omitted in retrospective accounts of post-war reconstruction. More important in our context are differences at the level of policy. In the east, the new German migrants were called *Umsiedler*, resettlers, a term without an accusatory undertone, although the Nazis had coined it to camouflage deportations and obfuscate their murderous intent. In the West, the newcomers came to be known as 'expellees', *Vertriebene,* a choice of phrase intended to voice objection and castigate their forced migration as an injustice. East/West differences were not confined to terminology. In the East, *Umsiedler* were made initially welcome and allocated parcels of land – albeit no housing – since they arrived just when the big estates were broken up in preparation for full-scale socialisation (Steinert, 1995b). As soon as the GDR was founded, references to *Umsiedler* disappeared from public discourse, as if the German migrants and their special needs had never existed. Instead, the new state proclaimed a new doctrine of uniformity among its citizens. This doctrine stipulated a rejection of cultural, ethnic, social or national difference in favour of a centrally administered and ideologically defined GDR-identity. *Umsiedler*, therefore, were treated like all members of the remade Workers' and Peasants' State whose personal origins, social backgrounds or cultural orientations were now discarded as obstacles in the shared enterprise of building the GDR (Zwahr, 1994).

West German Responses to German Migrants

The West German response to the post-war challenge of German migration was altogether different. Although the term *Vertriebene* implied that they had been expelled unjustly and that this injustice should be rectified in the future, the newcomers themselves were, by and large, left to their own devices. There was no redistribution of land, no government-sponsored effort at creating employment, and not until the 1950s did special housing projects and material compensation assist with making a new start (Lemberg and Edding, 1959). Ten years after the end of the war, expellees in West Germany were still disadvantaged economically, more exposed to unemployment than other Germans and less likely to partake in the emerging economic miracle of the West. Yet, the retrospective narrative of post-war reconstruction in West Germany cites the successful integration of expellees as a defining achievement of a reinvented political and social order and a democratic state that encouraged and rewarded personal initiative and hard work (e.g., Geissler and Meyer, 1992: 285ff). Not only had West Germany offered expellees a new beginning, it had created an effective framework for all Germans to overcome the dislocations of the past and enjoy better living conditions than ever before. The reinvented private lives of post-war Germans seemed to mirror the reinvented political system and its successful replacement of anti-democratic by democratic structures and practices. Expellees and their socio-economic integration were no more – and no less – than a paradigm of this new and reinvented Germany.

The Cold War bestowed the special meaning on German migration into Germany as escape from injustice into a better, democratic setting. In the immediate post-war years, expellees from Eastern European countries had escaped communist control and found liberty in the West; indeed, people of German origin have always been entitled to reclaim their German citizenship and migrate into the FRG. If they came from the East, their journey was one of national quest as well as personal liberation. German migrants from Eastern

Europe who arrived outside the framework of the Potsdam Agreement have been called *Aussiedler*, resettlers rejoining the homeland of their German ancestors. Between 1950 and 1992, 2.8 million *Aussiedler* arrived in West Germany where they are recognised as German citizens and entitled to housing, assistance with social integration and welfare benefits (Migration und Integration, 1997: 227ff). Following the end of communist control in Eastern Europe, numbers rose to near 300,000 *per annum* until stricter regulations concerning proof of origin and claims of citizenship as well as the requirement to process application in the country of departure before entering Germany, somewhat curbed the influx. The GDR knew no such German migration. Since 1990, some of these migrants have also been directed for residency and settlement to the new *Länder*.

German Migration from East to West

While the GDR promoted itself as an ideologically new and socially homogeneous entity, it also defined itself as a state without migration in both directions: newcomers were normally forbidden to enter and East Germans forbidden to leave. Decreeing the borders closed to newcomers was easier than stopping population outflow. Restricting social integration of newcomers because they were perceived as potential harbingers of unwanted diversity proved easier than cutting East Germans off, mentally and physically, from the Germany in the West. Between 1949 and 1989, over three million East Germans migrated to the West, some legally, but most illegally as refugees who risked their lives and liberty to escape from the GDR (Garton Ash, 1993; Zwahr, 1994). Unification has modified, not halted, the flow. Since October 1990, nearly two million east Germans have settled in the west, this time moving legally from one *Bundesland* to another (Boyes, 2001). In 1989 alone, 300,000 had forced their way to the West in a determined bid to abandon a state and society that seemed to offer few rewards and hold no promise for the future (Joppke, 1995: 139ff.).

Citizenship rights and rights of belonging were never at issue. The Basic Law had included East Germans as would-be citizens, and policy throughout the post-war era included immediate financial support, housing and other integration aids to everyone who succeeded in leaving the GDR. Not unlike *Aussiedler*, refugees from East Germany, *Flüchtlinge*, enhanced the legitimacy of the FRG as the better of the two German states whose democratic political order and market-based economy produced superior living conditions for its population and a higher degree of popular acceptance than the centrally planned top-down model in the east. In receiving East Germans, West German authorities and inhabitants assumed that the two sides had remained alike, brothers and sisters divided by a border but not with regard to their values, preferences or attitudes. This belief in the shared characteristics of West and

East Germans, however, began to crack after the Berlin Wall was breached and East Germans arrived in larger numbers. Conversely, as west Germans travelled east to review the other part of the country and even trace former belongings they might reclaim after unification, east Germans began to view west Germans more negatively than they had done when the country had been divided. A study of east German women who had found employment in the west suggested that in the early 1990s most felt treated unequally and one in five regretted their decision to settle in the west (Übersiedlerinnen, 1991: 30).

In the post-war era, the influx of German migrants from eastern Europe and eastern Germany helped to reinvent the west. At least one in four West Germans arrived as an expellee or refugee or was born into a German migrant family. In the wake of this migration, German society in western Germany became more diverse as people from different regional and religious backgrounds began to live together in newly diverse communities. Traditional local elites were diluted, supplemented, or remodelled by new leaders in business, politics or education as the emergent risk society facilitated mobility and status change (Hradil, 1993; Beck, 1986).

This everyday diversification, however, hides another consequence of German migration and its successful integration: the assumption that integration of newcomers is only successful if it is flawless without obdurate traces of difference. In this perspective migration meant that the migrant adjusts to the new environment (Kolinsky, 2000a: 26ff). Migration is deemed successful when no difference remains visible. For German migrants who valued their shared nationality and were eager to demonstrate and rediscover their German identity, this emphasis on integration without difference might have been suitable. Migrants of other national or cultural backgrounds, however, were less well served by this post-war (west) German model of migration as integration. For the non-German migration that commenced in the FRG in the mid-1950s (and continues to this day), a different model was needed, a model with scope for diversity and without a prescribed dominant culture, a *Leitkultur*, regardless of whether it purports to be west German, east German or more generally German.

The East-West Divide of Labour Migration before 1990

Both Germanies endeavoured to rebuild their economies to positions of dominance in their respective political settings. The GDR opted for the obligatory integration of all adult citizens into the labour force and focussed its social policy from the early 1950s onwards on supporting working mothers. Recruitment of non-German labour did not commence until the 1970s when the GDR leadership decreed that export industries and industries unable to meet domestic demand should increase output by expanding an already unpopular shift system. Increased output was to be accomplished without new investment by pushing existing plant and outmoded technologies to their limits (Müggenberg, 1996). The additional manpower required to meet the new output targets was to come on a contract basis from outside the GDR. Originally, recruitment countries were located in the socialist bloc with Poland and Hungary strongly represented (Kolinsky, 1995: 3). After the onset of democratisation in eastern Europe, the GDR turned to similar regimes in Africa and Asia. In the late 1980s, the recruitment of foreign labour was again stepped up to meet ambitious production targets and also to compensate for population loss as more and more East Germans left for the West. The so called 'exodus' of 1989 triggered a massive recruitment drive, as some 60,000 Vietnamese workers were deployed bringing the total non-German workforce to near 100,000, while an additional 90,000 workers from Mozambique had been lined up ready for deployment in the following year. State socialism collapsed and halted recruitment before they were due to arrive in the GDR.

Migration and Settlement – the Flawed West German Model

The West German bid for economic reconstruction also generated an intensive demand for labour but this was not met by recruiting women (Helwig and Nickel, 1993; Kolinsky, 1993). West Germany subscribed to traditional gender roles, and although female participation in the labour market increased significantly, much of it remained part-time and women did not constitute half the workforce as they did in the GDR (Kolinsky and Nickel, 2003). Once the expellees had been integrated, West Germany turned, as Germany has always done, to the recruitment of foreign labour to fill the gaps. These arose first in agriculture in the early 1950s but soon spread to low skilled and low paid employment throughout the economy (Bade, 1983; Cohn-Bendit and Schmid, 1992). From the early 1960s onwards, demand for non-German labour was at its most buoyant in coal mining, steel production, the hotel business, catering and unskilled public sector employment. As the economy flourished, West Germans rose to white collar and managerial positions while the blue collar and unskilled jobs were increasingly held by labour migrants from other countries.

The recruitment of *Gastarbeiter* had followed traditional German lines: contracts were limited to one year and employers were expected to 'rotate' their non-German workforce by recruiting a new person to fill the same position. Rotation, although favoured by politicians and the relevant ministries at the time, did not appeal to employers who were keen to retain reliable workers and reap the benefits of any training they had provided (Eryilmaz and Jamin, 1998: 227ff). Contrary to initial assumptions, employers renewed contracts in order to build a long-term, loyal labour force regardless of its national origin. Moreover, the democratic fabric of the Federal Republic itself and the laws governing the employment of foreign workers permitted *Gastarbeiter* to find new employment at the end of their initial contract, move to a new locality and construct their own migration biography inside Germany (Steinert, 1995a: 305–9). The narratives of arrival and settlement show that this right to relocate played a decisive role for those labour migrants who chose to settle in Germany and who were still living there in the late 1990s, some thirty years after their original recruitment (Kolinsky, 2000b).

Clearly, *Gastarbeiter* benefited from rights of social citizenship in a democracy, including the right to move between regions, to change employers, to opt for settlement. From the outset, West German trade unions had insisted that foreign workers received the same pay as Germans in accordance with their skills and levels of seniority (Klee, 1965). Yet, matters were less straight forward. Until the mid-1960s, the Foreigners' Law in the FRG resembled Nazi regulations and favoured expulsion. The revised law of 1965 refrained from detailing rights and left it to regional authorities to determine legal practice. This approach increased status uncertainties but it also created a multitude of loopholes as regions differed in their interpretations of the legal framework while German courts tended to rule in favour of extending rights of residency and social citizenship (Joppke, 1999). Gradually, rights of residency came to be linked to duration of stay which in turn could consolidate a conditional residency permit into an unconditional entitlement. The relevant law, however, was not revised until 1990, and even then the various categories of conditional and unconditional residency permits remained confusing to applicants and were not applied evenly across the country.

With regard to families, West German recruitment of foreign labour differed significantly from past practice. From the outset, employment contracts entitled workers to live in Germany with their families although the German government initially tried to withhold the right of family reunion to labour recruits from Turkey and Morocco (Jamin, 1998: 74–75). When labour migration meant no more than gaining access to better earnings in order to support the family back home, family reunion was a comparatively rare occurrence. It became a key issue, however, when the German government halted all labour recruitment by imposing an *Anwerbestopp* in 1973, thus forcing labour migrants to choose between staying or returning. Those willing to leave were given financial incentives to do so, a formula applied again in the early 1980s in an attempt to reduce the number of non-German residents, and in 1990 when the former GDR tried to rid itself of its *Gastarbeiter*-equivalent, the contract workers (Kolinsky, 1999: 198–200). Those intending to stay had to prove that they were employed and earned enough to support their family without relying on state benefit, and also that they had secured adequate accommodation. The hostels that had been deemed sufficient until then, were in the eyes of German administrators, not acceptable to house families. The *Anwerbestopp*, therefore, forced migrant workers intending to stay to find housing they could obtain and afford. This was normally located in run-down parts of major cities, the only areas where landlords agreed to accept labour migrants and their families as tenants. On the one hand, the concentration of non-German inhabitants with low incomes turned inner city areas into something like a ghetto; on the other hand, the proximity of non-German residents of related cultural backgrounds facilitated the development of social and religious institutions to support the culture of origin and also led to the establishment of retail shops, eateries and entertainment outlets devoted to the products and produce of the various home countries (Cohn-Bendit and Schmid, 1992: 115ff).

These developments enabled labour migrants and their families to live in the German environment without being altogether separated from their own cultural and regional background. A significant body of research has evaluated the residential concentration and social segregation and their effects on educational and employment opportunities (Bade and Weiner, 1997; Milich and Peck, 1998; Seifert, 1998). There is no doubt that discriminatory practices and experiences of injustice marred the arrival and settlement of non-German labour migrants and their families in Germany. There is also no doubt that non-Germans have been exposed to greater risks of social exclusion and income poverty than Germans (Hanesch *et al.*, 1994). Yet, non-Germans have benefited from rights of social citizenship that would have been denied in the German past, and which can be regarded as the touchstone of the democratic project. These rights pertain to housing, education, training, employment, entitlement to benefit and the whole spectrum of social participation. Here, the guarantee of equality before the law has created avenues for inclusion, without, however, eliminating discriminatory practices at the level of policy and negative attitudes in society.

Since the arrival of labour migrants from outside Germany, things have changed significantly. Legislation governing residency rights and the rights of citizenship have been revised and continue to be revised to accept, *post facto*, the presence in Germany of "natives without a passport". At the same time, official policy maintains that Germany is not a country of immigration and that residency and citizenship require as preconditions familiarity with the language, immersion in the culture and something resembling assimilation to the German project. Yet, the "natives without a German passport" have become more confident than the first generation migrants. They distrust prescribed integration but regard rights of citizenship and residency as an additional facet of choice to shape their own multi-faceted migration biographies and those of their families.

Contracted to Work, Forbidden to Settle: Labour Migrants in the GDR

In December 1989, population statistics of the GDR showed that 170,000 non-Germans lived there, about two thirds of them so called *Vertragsarbeiter*, contract workers, the remainder students, trainees, diplomats and their spouses.

For the vast majority, residency in the GDR was temporary and concluded with a return to the home country. Contrary to the FRG, a longer stay did not translate into a more secure residency status, and there were no individual rights to change employment or to build a personal migration biography (Peck *et al.*, 1997: 61ff). The East-West differences can be illustrated with reference to employment and living conditions. As we have seen earlier, public policy towards *Gastarbeiter* in West Germany oscillated between inclusion and exclusion, an ambiguity that produced many injustices, but also secured rights of participation and equal treatment in society. In the GDR, public policy and social practice were designed to institutionalise social exclusion. Employment contracts were not negotiated between employer and the individual worker but between governments. Their contents remained secret. This meant that labour recruits were not informed about their entitlements, notably to language courses, minimum housing standards or rates of pay (Müggenberg, 1996: 13ff). Contracts also stipulated that trade debts of the home government to the GDR could be recouped by withholding payments from contract workers on their return. As so often in the GDR, official documents and their promises bore no relation to social practice and their application.

East German enterprises requested a certain number of contract workers for specific tasks in line with agreed central planning for the industry and region. Companies or local authorities provided dormitory-style accommodation in warden-controlled hostels that were kept locked at night (Kolinsky, 1999: 194f). If rental charges are compared with those paid by Germans for their apartments, hostels were extremely expensive (VertragsarbeitnehmerInnen, 1998: 48). Access of visitors was restricted or forbidden altogether, as was social communication between contract workers and Germans. At the workplace, contact was kept to the minimum required by the work situation, while German employees were expected to report all informal contact to the authorities. If things went wrong at work, it was common practice to blame contract workers and dock parts of their pay. Since most contract workers knew only enough German to understand the commands relevant to their work-function, they could not mount a defence. The trade union and other work-related bodies or committees did not include contract workers into their activities. Since passports were withheld until departure, mobility inside the GDR was severely restricted, not least since all interchange with the German population was deemed undesirable and subject to surveillance and punishment. Family reunion or migration with a partner had no place in this institutionalised exclusion. If a female contract worker became pregnant, she was forced to undergo an abortion or face deportation. Recruitment contracts stipulated a maximum five-year stay in the GDR, although a small number of individuals were able to extend their stay beyond the original maximum. The majority of contract workers, however, were sent back to their home country at the end of the stipulated employment period without an option to stay on or even settle.

East Germans took the segregated existence of contract workers for granted. Unease and even hostility, however, surfaced with regard to the only right contract workers were able to activate, not least since their own government viewed it as advantageous: the right to send goods to the value of 50 per cent of the annual wages back home. Since this could be done once a year only, the despatches were conspicuous. Purchases tended to concentrate on goods that were in short supply in the country of origin, such as electrical appliances, bicycles or mopeds. Although contract workers faced no restrictions as to what they were permitted to buy and send, East Germans in the GDR accused them of robbing them of essentials, of operating a black market and of exacerbating the shortages that plagued the economy at all levels (Commichau, 1990: 1434–5).

The GDR government could, of course, have clarified matters by informing the East German public of the clauses in the inter-governmental contracts concerning the purchase and export of goods. These clauses were of particular significance in the contracts with Vietnam and activated above all by Vietnamese workers. In December 1988, newspapers in Vietnam complained that their countrymen faced unfair restrictions of their rights in the GDR. In response, the Central Committee of the SED issued a declaration on 'the use of Vietnamese workers in socialist countries' (Müggenberg, 1996: 25–6). In it, it chose not to divulge information about the rights of Vietnamese workers, but implied that East Germans' fears were correct and contract workers had been overstepping the mark: 'The increased export of consumer goods by Vietnamese workers to Vietnam makes the introduction of restrictions inevitable. Our postal system cannot cope with the current rate of despatching parcels (*Paketaufkommen*) to Vietnam'. (ibid.: 61)

The collapse of state socialist control occurred in the autumn of 1989. It was succeeded by an unelected coalition government headed by Hans Modrow and a Round Table that offered opposition groups, emerging political parties and some former SED-controlled mass organisations a public forum to debate future moves towards reinventing the GDR (Thaysen, 1990). These transitory developments towards parliamentary government were superseded in March 1990 when the first free election in eastern Germany since 1932 returned as the winner the former bloc party Christian Democrats (CDU) under its new name of Alliance for Germany. The resulting coalition government was led by Lothar de Maizière. This last government of the GDR remained in office until unification on 3 October 1990 ended the existence of the state itself. Indeed, the election on 18 March 1990 had served as a plebiscite in Eastern Germany as to whether unification should be ventured or a reformed and remodelled GDR retained as a separate state.

The end of state socialist control preceded the end of the GDR by nearly one year. During this time, the post-socialist GDR included a variety of actors who might have addressed the issue of migration and focused on the plight of contract workers. This could have been undertaken by the two interim governments and the East German parliament, the *Volkskammer,* or the Round Table in its national or local versions as special institutional creations of East German system transformation. The issue of migration and social justice for contract workers could also have been articulated by political parties. More than a dozen were active in East Germany in 1990, some of which tried to reinvent themselves from former bloc parties of the SED, and others emerged as voices of opposition and innovation from September 1989 onwards when the *Neues Forum* made its first appearance (Joppke, 1995). The Central Round Table in Berlin, whose proceedings were televised to involve East Germans in their emerging democracy, was stymied by organisational rivalry and infighting, but did undertake one distinctive project: the drafting of a new constitution for a reformed and remade GDR. Completed and published after the East German electorate had already established a popular preference for unification, the constitution was a last-ditch attempt to avoid it. It missed its chance to speak out for equality and the rights of migrants. Its key phrase on this issue, 'all people owe one another recognition as equals', reads like a moral appeal, not as a policy commitment by a future state and its government (Jarausch and Gransow, 1994: 135f).

During the interim between the end of one-party government in 1989 and unification in October 1990, two measures focussed on 'foreigners' and their place in the changing GDR. In February 1990, the Round Table suggested that an office of 'Foreigners' Commissioner' should be created at the local level to address the 'foreigners' problem' that had arisen. Leipzig instituted such an office, but few other towns or cities did so until after unification (Kolinsky, 1995). The problem that had attracted the concern of the Round Table had arisen when many East German companies closed their hostels and dismissed their contract workers in order to streamline costs in preparation for a market economy. In consequence, thousands of unemployed and homeless former contract workers were stranded in the GDR. The second measure emanated from the *Volkskammer* after the election in March 1990. In June 1990, it decided that former contract workers could be permitted to stay in the GDR for the duration of their original contract, provided they had employment and adequate housing. At the same time, it offered financial incentives to anyone willing to leave. These consisted of part of the wages they would have been paid but for their dismissal, and the cost of the return ticket home. In its bid for departure, the *Volkskammer* replicated the worst of West Germany's flawed model. On the other hand, the ruling was the first in the GDR to spell out the conditions under which former contract workers could extend their stay (*Bleiberecht*) and also the conditions of leaving. To that extent, the *Bleiberecht* of June 1990 has to be seen as an improvement compared with the lack of rights that had previously prevailed in the GDR.

Workers from Vietnam, Mozambique and Angola were the least willing to return home, partly because they feared reprisals from their respective governments for allegedly failing to fulfil their contract, and partly because Germany appeared to offer better opportunities to improve their material situation than they could find in their home country. By June 1990, at least half the contract workers had already left Germany, Those determined to stay were confined to street trading as a source of income and had to provide evidence of secure housing. A former contract worker from Mozambique who had lived in the GDR since 1986 recalls how he fared between the old and the new system:

> What I did not like then (in the GDR) was that one could not have any contact with other people. Life consisted of nothing but hostel, training school and shopfloor. In my home country, people communicate and get on well together. But here, many people hated me because of the colour of my skin, although I could not change this since I was born that way. And I was really hurt by the stupid talk of some Germans who said that Africans 'bring Aids to us'. ..But in the GDR, the hatred of foreigners was not as openly expressed as it is now. I could even travel from Stralsund to Suhl. I could do this until 1990 when I was sacked from my employment. In 1990, three new problems suddenly presented themselves: where to live, where to work, and how I could stay and obtain a residency permit. All offices and administrative authorities were closed to me, there was no chance at all for people who had come as contract workers. One did not find housing without employment and did not find employment without housing and did not get a work permit without a residency permit. I was no more than a football. In the end, I was forced to retrain in order to quality for a conditional stay. I could not go back to my home country due to many catastrophic events there. I had to fight on to stay here and try to make a living. (Pedro Gidiao Abrao, in *Jahresbericht Sachsen,* 1997: 21–22)

Contract Workers between Expulsion and Residency after the GDR

Unification introduced new parameters. Attempts by former contract workers to be registered as asylum seekers fell foul of the ruling that any asylum seeker has to enter Germany directly from a hostile country. The previous sojourn in Germany, therefore, disqualified all former contract workers from seeking political asylum. By contrast, the established West German practice of basing residency status on the duration of stay in the country proved more adaptable. In 1993, the *Bundestag* agreed that former contract workers who were employed on 17 June of that year, had no criminal record and had lived in Germany without interruption since unification, were entitled to conditional residency rights (*Aufenthaltsbefugnis*) for two more years. Since a residency of at least five years normally tends to protect migrants from expulsion, the modification constituted a significant gain, although it fell short of offering unconditional residency rights that required a stay in Germany of eight years or more. In addition, migrants with conditional residency rights enjoy only limited welfare rights. Thus, they are not eligible to child benefit, benefit for long-term unemployment or income support, and risk deportation if they become unemployed (Ausländer in Thüringen, 1999: 7).

After 1993, east German demands for *Bleiberecht* for former GDR contract workers, their *'Gastarbeiter'*, intensified. As unification unleashed a 'problematic normalisation' (Segert and Zierke, 1997: 48), the fight for an unconditional *Bleiberecht* became a vehicle to castigate policy making since unification as a neglect of east German causes. The former contract workers (*'Gastarbeiter'*), constituted such a cause. The new critique of federal politics has tended to overlook the fact that a key obstacle to their residency rights originated during the *Wende* in the GDR, the interim period between 1989 and 1990 when socialist control had collapsed and unification had not yet come into force. Banned from most employment other than street trading, scores of former contract workers violated local and regional trading regulations or were accused – although rarely convicted – of black market activities. East German police, it seems, took to arresting non-German street traders, confiscating their wares, and releasing them without specifying a charge. It often took several years before charges were pressed. The matter came to a head in 1995 when the German and Vietnamese governments signed a *Rücknahmeabkommen*, an agreement on the return of the 20,000 former contract workers still in Germany. This agreement gave deportations the appearance of legality, causing charges to soar. By the criteria applied in east Germany, 80 per cent of Vietnamese living there were deemed to have a criminal record that made them ineligible for residency (John, 1997).

By the time the *Rücknahmeabkommen* with Vietnam paved the way to deport former contract workers, the consensus on forced return as the preferred option had begun to crack. The Foreigners' Commissioners had originally been appointed from 1990 onwards to tackle what was perceived as a problem with foreigners, an *Ausländerproblem*. They were to aid the departure of homeless and unemployed former contract workers from Germany. Contrary to this negative brief, Foreigners' Commissioners emerged as their most ardent and effective advocates. In Leipzig, the Commissioner's Office had tried from the outset to facilitate a *Bleiberecht* by issuing individual rental agreements for accommodation in erstwhile hostels, because such agreements would be recognised by the city administration as evidence of secure housing (Kolinsky, 1999). It therefore came as a complete shock to the well-intentioned helpers when the city unexpectedly requisitioned the former hostel whose residents should have been provided with rental agreements. Allegedly, the civic authorities had to meet other urgent needs. Homeless, the occupants were again vulnerable to forced return.

By 1993, Foreigners' Commissioners in the new *Länder* had begun to demand that former contract workers be offered residency for the duration of their original contract, a demand which soon lost its conditionality. Instead, pressure was put on the federal government to treat the former foreigner workers of the GDR as if they were *Gastarbeiter*, foreign workers who had been recruited for employment into West Germany. While the demand to place *Gastarbeiter* and *Vertragsarbeiter* on the same footing tends to play down the injustices perpetrated during the GDR years, the shift of focus opened a new, enabling perspective. Rather than accepting the parameters that had been set by the GDR for the stay of former contract workers, Foreigners' Commissioners now argued for firming up residency rights, for extending the right of family reunion to former contract workers, and in particular to calculate the duration of their stay in Germany by including the time spent in the GDR.

The *Bleiberecht* of 1993 had recognised residency only since unification, but included the right of family reunion. While contract workers in the GDR had been forced to live apart from their spouses and children, the new conditional residents of unified Germany were able to establish some kind of permanency and normality by arranging for their wives, husbands and children to join them for the duration of their stay. The right of family union, however, was restricted to former contract workers who had been married and forced to live apart from their families prior to June 1993 when the new *Bleiberecht* came into effect. Contrary to the right of family union for former *Gastarbeiter*, former contract workers who married at a later stage had no right of family reunion. Those who had married a partner from their home country or another foreign country were expected to live there. In detailing these restrictions, several reports by Foreigners' Commissioners point to a ruling by the Federal Constitutional Court which argues that the protection of marriage and the family guaranteed in the Basic Law (Para. 6/1) does not mean that for 'purely foreign marriages' the protection of the family demands a stay in Germany. Foreigners, it was implied, could establish their family in their home country (Jahresbericht Sachsen, 1997: 122).

Until 1997, residency of former contract workers in Germany was essentially temporary, based on concessions that could be revoked, not rights that had been granted. The situation of former contract workers from Vietnam living in the capital of Mecklenburg-Vorpommern, Schwerin, can illustrate the problem. In 1996, 225 remained in the city, one third of the number who had worked there in 1989. Just sixteen (7 per cent) held unconditional residency permits, normally because they were married to a German partner. For the vast majority, residency was conditional and the risk of a forced return to Vietnam was ever present. Indeed, after the *Bleiberecht* ruling of 1993, the city granted an extension of conditional residency permits by two years only for those applicants who were in full-time, permanent employment and held an employment contract to prove it (Bericht Landeshauptstadt Schwerin, 1996: 16). Since the majority of former contract workers worked as street traders or were self-employed in the restaurant trade, normally running an *Imbiss*, a food stand or market stall without secure premises or contract, they did not qualify for the new *Bleiberecht* by the relevant deadline and lived under the shadow of forcible repatriation (ibid: 17).

In May 1996, the *Land* Sachsen Anhalt reopened the debate by demanding that time spent in the GDR should not be disregarded, but counted fully in assessing residency entitlement. The region cited humanitarian reasons and in particular the detrimental effect of an uncertain residency status on employment opportunities. In the *Bundestag*, the demand for revised regulations culminated in the demand for 'equal treatment of contract workers with West German guest workers' (Jahresbericht Sachsen, 1997: 13). The *Bundestag* accepted the principle that residency in the GDR should be counted, but was prepared to recognise only half the number of years spent there. The legislation needed *Bundesrat* approval since it would have to be implemented at regional level. After the *Bundesrat* rejected the *Bundestag*'s formula, the matter was put before to the Federal Mediation Committee (*Bundesvermittlungsausschuss*) which ruled in favour of the original proposal to give equal weighting to the years spend in the FRG and the GDR when calculating overall duration of stay in Germany (Bericht der Ausländerbeauftragten Land Brandenburg, 1998: 22).

The revised legislation of 1997 strengthened the legal claim of former contract workers, and non-Germans generally, to secure unconditional residency permits in Germany on the basis of duration of stay. While the shift from *ad-hoc* toleration or institutionalised conditionality to a defined right did not mean that former contract workers could turn their precarious stay into settlement without further obstacles, it marks a significant departure from their treatment and experiences of exclusion in the GDR and the reluctance of policy makers to facilitate their transformation from labour migrants to residents in Germany, similar to the transformation of the *Gastarbeiter* population to a settled minority inside German society in the 1970s (Jahresbericht Sachsen, 1997: 16).

No less important in facilitating this transformation was a decision by the Minister of the Interior to reconsider the severity of criminal offences. On 5 September 1996, the minister at the time, Manfred Kanther, agreed to accede to a request from the east German *Länder* to declare a virtual amnesty for sentences of thirty days imprisonment or an equivalent fine for offences committed by non-Germans in the east before the *Bleiberecht* ruling in unified Germany on 30 June 1993. These sentences were to be reclassified as 'minor offences', *Bagatellstrafen,* and discounted when assessing applications for residency permits and settlement. As mentioned earlier, east German police had made extensive use of their right of arrest and were given to press charges long after the alleged incident when suspects often found it difficult to clear their name through evidence. While the new amnesty did not clear the slate altogether, it cleared it for those non-Germans whose sentences indicated that their alleged offence should not be equated to serious crimes and impede their chances of making a life in Germany.

In line with federal practice, it was then left to the *Länder* to translate the new regulations into specific measures. Brandenburg responded on 18 September 1996 by granting such 'minor offenders' conditional residency rights and protecting them from a forced return to their country of origin. This protection was particularly significant for former contract workers from Vietnam who could have been returned, following an agreement in 1995 between Germany and Vietnam (Bericht der Ausländerbeauftragten *Land* Brandenburg, 1996/7: 21). Saxony-Anhalt claimed to have been particularly lenient in issuing conditional residency permits and disregarding minor offences even before the federal government had consented to do so (Jahresbericht Sachsen-Anhalt, 1997/98: 11). Saxony was more reluctant to implement a full-scale amnesty and adopted its own, watered down version on 13 January 1997. This reading of 'minor offences' explicitly excluded infringements of German tax laws, the use of drugs and weapons, offences against the Foreigners' Law, as well as prostitution and related criminal acts (Jahresbericht Sachsen, 1996: 9).

Them and Us: Non-Germans and their East German Advisors

As liberalisation takes effect and migration gains a more permanent status, east Germany is no longer as uniform as it had been when the outgoing GDR defined former contract workers and foreigners more generally as 'others'. Legislation in June 1990 stipulated that rights of residency should, at best, be temporary and last no longer than the original labour contract between the GDR and the sending country. More than a decade on, legislative change as well as the participatory avenues and civic rights that emerged in the transformed post-communist east are enabling former contract workers to articulate choices, consolidate rights and ultimately define their migration biographies. Forced migration as labour recruits destined to be removed at the will of governments is beginning to turn into intended migration with a view to settlement. The restrictive practices and inbuilt enmity to immigration of German legislators that blighted the experiences of non-Germans in the past have not disappeared. Like the former West Germany, unified Germany continues to oscillate between integration and rejection, between inclusion and forced return. On balance, however, the constitutional pledge of equal treatment and social citizenship has moderated tendencies towards exclusion and has facilitated diversity and the emergence of plurality. Assisted by regional and district courts, some political parties and policy makers, and agencies such as the Foreigners' Commissioners at federal, regional and local level, contribute to removing barriers and creating new avenues of inclusion that may soften the illiberal intentions of legislative frameworks, officials or public opinion (Joppke, 1999; Benz, 1993).

The challenge of unification was far greater than redefining the status and rights of former contract workers, as their numbers dwindled from around 100,000 in 1989 to below 15,000 ten years later. The Unification Treaty required the new *Länder* in the east to operate federal administrations. This included receiving and accommodating asylum seekers in line with population numbers. Accordingly, one in five asylum seekers were to be directed to the east from December 1990 onwards. During the first year of unification, this quota amounted to about 40,000 individuals rising to over 80,000 in 1992/3 when the total influx peaked at well over 400,000 before restrictive legislation in 1993 reduced entry rights and curtailed numbers. Taking all categories of refugees together who were resident awaiting permission to settle or who had been accepted for settlement, numbers have been significant, totalling 1.8 million in 1992 and 1.9 million in 1993 for Germany as a whole. Despite the introduction of restrictive legislation in 1993, numbers still stood at 1.4 million four years later (Bundesausländerbeauftragte, 2000). Nearly half these refugees were only permitted to stay for a transitional period until their application for asylum had been turned down or until a war situation in their home country had abated. The remainder, however, held unconditional or conditional residency permits.

On paper, one in five of these newcomers were expected to proceed to eastern Germany. Despite the stipulation that the new *Länder* should take their fair share of all categoies of newcomers, i.e., asylum seekers, refugees fleeing the wars in the former Yugoslavia, Jewish refugees from eastern Europe and German-origin resettlers from the same regions, movement to and settlement in the east has been slower than anticipated. On 31 December 1998, a total of 241,471 non-German residents lived in the new *Länder* and a further 72,000 in east Berlin, at least one third of these European Union citizens or foreign nationals on employment contracts with companies in Germany (Bundesausländerbeauftragte, 2000: Table 11; Statistisches Jahrbuch Berlin, 2000: 56). Of the 7.3 million non-German residents in united Germany at the end of 1998, just 3 per cent lived in the eastern regions where non-Germans constituted about 2 per cent of the inhabitants.

Despite the quota instructions, the new *Länder* were slow to comply (Kolinsky, 2000a: 148ff). It took several months before the required legislative framework was in place and a further year or more until the administrative rules had been agreed as to how the legislation should be implemented. While regional governments created the post of *Ausländerbeauftragte* (Foreigners' Commissioner) to oversee the new policy domain, local authorities were less directly modelled on western practices, slower to replace personnel and less willing to devote efforts or funds to tackle the new tasks. Most took recourse to familiar practices and utilised former hostels for contract workers to house non-German newcomers. Since numbers soon overtook the available places, they commissioned private operators to offer and run accommodation on a pay-as-you-go basis (Kolinsky, 1995; 1999). Most of these facilities were not suitable for regular east German residents and consisted of caravan sites, decommissioned army barracks or similar out-of-town installations.

Each *Land* was required to provide facilities for the reception of newcomers where applications of asylum seekers and refugees were prepared prior to submission. In addition, each *Land* had to ensure that newcomers whose case had been processed and who were waiting for a decision which could entail appeals and might take months or even years, were housed adequately for the duration of their provisional stay. This would end either in acceptance of their application and the onset of integration into German society with regard to housing, employment and benefit provision, or it would end in a rejection of the original application. Although some 90 per cent or more of applications tend to be rejected, rejection does not necessarily result in a return to the home country, since the law frequently forbids expulsion, or personal circumstances make it possible for a failed applicant to receive a toleration, *Duldung*, for a specified or unspecified period, a status with fewer rights of benefit but with defined, albeit conditional, residency rights (Migration und Integration: 291).

East Germans were unprepared for the new tasks of managing migration and responding to the complexity of migrants' rights. The regions and their local authorities considered it more than sufficient to provide hostel-style mass accommodation for non-German newcomers. Statistical records from the early 1990s also show that east German *Länder* were much more forceful in administering deportations than west German *Länder* and voiced complaints when they discovered that unsuccessful asylum seekers who had been earmarked for a forcible return to their home country had absconded without permission and surfaced in another region beyond their administrative or punitive reach (Migration und Integration, 292–3). Furthermore, the provision of accommodation itself threw up unexpected challenges. Used to the compliance of former contract workers with hostel conditions and assuming that state decrees could create and control social conditions, regions were caught out on two counts. Firstly, the rapid rise of migration figures after 1991 from 200,000 to well over 400,000 nationally, persuaded local authorities in east Germany to commission further hostel accommodation from private companies and sign long-term contracts in order to ensure that referral from reception centres to other accommodation would be smooth, and no demands arose for accommodation inside eastern German communities. After the legislative restrictions of 1993, however, numbers fell sharply, leaving local authorities with unfilled places and large debts arising from their contractual commitments to private operators of these hostels (Kolinsky, 1999: 201).

While this kind of over-provision could be corrected when contracts came up for renewal, another unexpected development posed different challenges. East German administrations had anticipated that hostel accommodation would be used in the interim between arrival and departure or integration, a process which might take months, although it has been known to take years. In reality, however, some 60 per cent of those whose application for political asylum in the FRG has been turned down are eligible for toleration and are thus able to stay. Given their uncertain residency status, permanent employment and housing are normally unobtainable, forcing most to remain in hostel accommodation that had not been designed for long-term residency. Multi-occupancy rooms, shared kitchens, shared bathrooms, a severe shortage of trained personnel to help with adjustments and facilitate integration resulted in a high degree of dissatisfaction among residents and among the Foreigners' Commissioners at the local level (Bericht der Ausländerbeauftragen Land Brandenburg, 1998: 29–30).

No less significant were the financial drawbacks for local authorities for this kind of mass accommodation. Asylum seekers receive funding from central government while their applications are being processed. Former asylum seekers or other refugees whose application for a residency permit has been unsuccessful but who have escaped forcible repatriation or deportation for humanitarian or other reasons, remain eligible for more than two years for financial support from central government funds. After this period, they become the responsibility of local authorities as recipients of *Sozialhilfe*, income support and other benefits. Contrary to the funding for newcomers, benefits for residents, even if they do not hold unconditional residency permits, have to be paid from local budgets.

The problem is by no means marginal. In 1998 for instance, Saxony-Anhalt offered accommodation in seven hostels, one with 1,700 places for new arrivals and six with a total of 5,400 places for bona-fide screened applicants for residency. In 1996, however, 5000 of these places were taken up by residents who had failed to secure recognition but had secured a *Duldung* (Jahresbericht Sachsen-Anhalt, 1997/98: 23–25). When east German legislation was framed in 1991 on how to accommodate and process newcomers and their residency applications, the problem that some might stay despite having been turned down did not even come into the frame. Of course, east German legislators could have looked west and taken lessons from there. They chose not to. Consequently, east German regional legislation did not include provisions as to how to deal with 'toleration' and its beneficiaries. Nothing was specified with regard to financial support or housing provisions. Moreover, the small number of communities with hostel accommodation received relatively large numbers of non-German newcomers, while most other east German communities included virtually none (see also Bericht des Landes Mecklenburg-Vorpommern, 1998: 14–15).

When Saxony-Anhalt revised its *Landesaufnahmegesetz* – its regional law for the reception of asylum seekers and other newcomers from outside Germany – in January 1998, it tried to accomplish several aims. Instead of the concentration of newcomers in mass accommodation, it now advocated dispersal across the region and its communities in accordance with population figures. Dispersal, it was argued, would prevent ghettoisation and facilitate 'understanding' between Germans and foreigners (Jahresbericht Sachsen-Anhalt, 1997/98: 26). In order to meet these new objectives, new housing projects had to be developed which had not only to be smaller than before, but also include counselling facilities and regular access to social workers and advisors (ibid.: 24). No such provisions had been envisaged in 1991 and had therefore not been instituted. Implementation of the new law, however, rests on the region's communities who are expected to come forward with offers of suitable housing for both asylum seekers and German-origin resettlers from eastern Europe. At the time of the report, a handful of communities had made such offers, usually involving disused barrack-style buildings in out-of-town locations. Most communities had not made any offers. The revised legislation permitted communities to decide for themselves whether to participate in the scheme. As a form of carrot, they were told that the new influx of residents might enable them to keep child-care facilities open which might otherwise have to close in the wake of the low birth-rate. As a form of stick, none seemed to be earmarked. To hurry the change along, the *Land* proposed to cancel its contracts with private providers of accommodation facilities and only continue its commitment to the reception centre for new arrivals (ibid.: 25; see also Jahresbericht Sachsen, 1998: 64ff).

Legislative intent may differ significantly from implementation and output. In his analysis of public policy in Germany, Katzenstein argues that consensus building has been institutionalised at all levels in German politics and ensures that change is never more than 'incremental', as all interested parties have an input and modify innovation (Katzenstein, 1987: 45f). Furthermore, while legislation and parliamentary decision making define future directions, they remain ineffective until administrative procedures have been worked out and instructions published on how to implement them (Paterson and Southern, 1991; Pulzer, 1995). This translation of legislation into practical measures and action usually takes several months and may take years. Nor is it standardised across the Federal Republic. Since legislation tends to be implemented at regional and local level, regional administrations ultimately interpret legislative intent by incorporating it into administrative procedures and provisions. At the interface of the public and the private spheres, officials determine the entitlement of clients or citizens to services and state support by communicating and executing interpretations and applications of legislation passed by parliament at the national or regional level.

Here, developments in east Germany generated additional problems. While the system transfer in 1990 extended the institutional structures and the laws of West Germany to the east, it could not instantly reinvent how these institutions and laws were perceived by citizens as well as officials. The authoritarian set-up of the GDR was, of course, riddled with injustices, personal favours and networks to bypass official channels, but it did not incorporate the right to diversity and individuality in its top-down collectivism (Dennis, 2000). The democratic framework that took its place lacked the certainties of decrees that are issued by the state. It also did not lay down exactly how an individual was to be treated. Rules, although defined, had to be activated by matching them to individual cases with a view to optimising the rights of individuals, not curtailing them. While GDR administrative practice implied that each case allowed only one, politically correct, answer, the administrative practice in the FRG had emerged by exploiting legal ambiguities for regional purposes or individual beneficiaries.

This contrast between clear-cut regulations and legal flexibility has been particularly stark with regard to non-Germans and migrants where East German practice decreed exclusion while West German practice utilised an ill-defined legislative framework to enhance or curtail support. When the asylum seekers and other unexpected newcomers arrived in east Germany while former contract workers had to be treated as citizens-in-waiting, east German administrations were challenged not just to tackle a new policy field but do so with legislation that was not prescriptive enough to offer state-formulated recipes for individual cases (Diewald, 1999). Moreover, local administrations were the last to be reformed and restaffed following unification, and were more likely than *Land* administrations to provide continuity for GDR officials and public employees (Glässner, 1996). This continuity of personnel even applied to the office of Foreigners' Commissioner which was normally constituted within the housing department. Only in Leipzig did it emerge as a separate unit with its own distinctive identity and accountable directly to the city's mayor (Kolinsky, 1995). The administrators charged with implementing the new policy towards *Ausländer* faced several unfamiliar challenges: the changed function of administration and the new relationship between state authorities and private citizens; the unexpected uncertainty of legal regulations and the discrepancy between laws and their implementation; the unexpected policy field of supporting non-Germans and other migrants, rather than administering their segregation and, of course, the ubiquitous uncertainties after unification about the new competitive climate, employment security, the new link between personal achievement and professional advancement, and the demise of ideology as a shared consensus about the priority of the state and the gist of public policy (Flockton *et al.*, 2000). In addition to specifically East German constellations, the West German approach to the migration and settlement of non-Germans has been a flawed model of rejecting immigration without preventing it altogether, and of engaging in repeated bouts of exclusionary activity including financial incentives for repatriation.

In 1998, a research team from the *Fachhochschule* Erfurt conducted an empirical study of questionnaires and interviews to ascertain how east German officials coped with the multiple adjustments and compounded uncertainties of administering migration and settlement of non-Germans in Thuringia (Riehe and Zeng, 1998). The study focussed on those sectors of local administration where direct contact with non-Germans would normally occur: housing, employment, benefit offices and the *Ausländeramt*, the office designated to deal with non-German clients. Just 3 per cent of responses originated from the Labour Exchange, compared to 46 per cent from the *Ausländeramt*, 30 per cent from the benefit offices and 21 per cent from the housing department (ibid.: 5). The low participation of the Labour Exchange suggests that its officials did not perceive unemployment among non-German migrants or contact with them as salient everyday tasks. Only 3 per cent of respondents stated that they had never experienced problems when communicating with non-Germans while 32 per cent had encountered frequent and 65 per cent occasional problems. Half the respondents working in an *Ausländeramt* reported frequent problems in their dealings with their non-German clientele (ibid.: 6). The authors interpret these findings as evidence for 'Problemdruck', the special pressures over and above those inherent in ordinary administrative duties and a day at the office. Asked to identify the source of these pressures, respondents pointed mainly to language barriers (59 per cent), ignorance among migrants about the law and administrative processes in Germany (53 per cent), unexpected or unsuitable behaviour patterns among their non-German clients (47 per cent), while a minority (23 per cent) thought that the regulations pertaining to foreigners were too complicated (ibid.: 6–7).

One of the characteristics of legislation pertaining to foreigners in Germany has been that it defined possibilities and options without specifying clear entitlements. From the point of view of migrants seeking advice or orientation, this kind of legislation allows officials to make actual decisions and exercise more power than merely carrying out pre-defined instructions (ibid.: 18–19). East German officials, however, did not share these perceptions. They did not regard their function as giving advice, but rather as abiding by the letter of the law. The head of an *Ausländeramt* explained the function of his officials as follows: 'We ensure that the law is followed. If someone asks me what he could apply for, I can enumerate what is available. I present information, I do not give advice. For dictatorial (sic) and principal reasons, I give plain information. I will not point anyone in one direction or another by suggesting what he might do. Here, I and my colleagues hold back, and we must hold back'. (ibid.: 22).

Repeatedly, interviewees voiced doubts that their clients could be trusted to tell the truth and suspected them of seeking unfair advantages beyond their entitlement while hiding behind a poor command of German. Some, it was alleged, used different cultural reference points and behaviour traits to pretend that they did not understand their legal position or the information provided. The consensus among east German officials appeared clear cut that the *Amtssprache* – the official language – was German: ' I, as the authority, see no need to make provisions of any kind so that people may express themselves only in their native language. If we did this, who knows where it would end. Finance itself would be disproportionate' (ibid.: 38). When confronted with an east German official in an east German office, the foreigner was viewed as being on German turf and therefore obligated to abide by German rules. There did not appear to be scope for diversity of approach or cultures:

I see it this way. When a foreigner comes here, he has to fit into German culture. This is also required by the law. Nobody can demand that I should somehow empathize with his situation. I think it is up to him to adhere to his traditions while he is here. I don't care if he dances under a tree or whatever. But he also has to bow to the rules and fit in. (ibid.: 39–40)

Some respondents even argued that the law did not make different provisions for different cultural or national groups but treated everyone alike: 'Before the Foreigners' Law all are equal, and I therefore do not need to know about intercultural differences. ' (ibid.: 40) When clients vented their anger about failed applications or withheld provisions, east German officials felt that they were overstepping the mark by demanding material and other provisions. This 'Anspruchsdenken', the assumption by non-German applicants that they had a right to certain provisions, emerged as a major irritant for east German officials who assumed that their charges should have what Riehe and his team call 'Gasttugenden', the virtues of a guest:

> Migrants are expected to show gratitude and modesty. The accusations of being over-demanding arise not because respondents believe that migrants do not have a legal claim to provisions but because they believe that they are not entitled to anything because they are foreigners. They come and want something from us without serving a useful purpose for us in return. (ibid.: 54f).

East German officials, even those employed specifically to advise non-German migrants and newcomers, felt stressed by their task, resentful of the problems with communication and unwilling to accommodate the special needs of their clients by employing interpreters or seeking to understand their personal and cultural determinants. They regard themselves as purveyors of information, not as advisors, as announcers of the law, not as guides through its intricacies. In particular, they cling to German as their *Amtssprache,* the language of authority and therefore communication and to established rules of German administrative culture. Non-German clients are expected to conform to these rules and, above all, to appear backward, helpless, submissive in their approach towards the German authorities and officials.

These expectations appear to persist in east Germany despite changes in German culture that have reduced the helplessness of non-German newcomers and created new avenues of assertiveness. Of prime importance here has been independent access to legal advice both in the old and the new *Länder.* The fact that clients whom east German officials tend to regard as essentially fraudulent and without entitlement can employ legal help and challenge the approach of the public authorities and their application of the law, has been an altogether new and unwelcome experience. East German officials feel stressed by the unfamiliar tasks of mediating between German law and the non-Germans at whom it is aimed. Department heads complain about staff shortages, about the impossibility of accommodating special needs by giving extra time or unscheduled understanding. Their reluctance to engage in inter-cultural communication with their clients may also reflect their unease at serving as a 'buffer' between public policy obligated at least to accommodate non-Germans and public opinion that remains unwilling to embrace migration and settlement in east German society (ibid: 47; also Ausländer und Asylbewerber, 1996).

From Institutionalised to Personal Exclusion

In the GDR, non-Germans were kept apart socially while their presence was defined through their function as workers, diplomats and students, in accordance with state policy. Unification removed these state agendas. Public policy, as shown in this chapter, now required the reconstituted east German authorities to accommodate migrants while east Germans encountered non-Germans in their environment without the protective shield of institutionalised exclusion that had existed in the past. With non-Germans at liberty to seek housing, employment, participate in everyday life and claim social citizenship, provided their residency status allowed them to do so, east Germans were confronted with the challenge of relating to 'others' (Peck *et al.*, 1997; Hajek, 1998). The democratic principle that everyone regardless of colour, creed, nationality or background, should enjoy equal civil and personal rights held few attractions in an environment where east Germans themselves thought they were treated as second class citizens, and where post-communist transformation had left them dislocated, uncertain and unwilling to embrace even more diversity (Falter *et al.*, 2000). Maaz argues that the emotional turbulence caused by the collapse of the GDR traumatised east Germans into blaming 'others' and especially foreigners, for their plight (Maaz, 1998: 26). Farin and Seidel-Pielen locate xenophobia in the uncertainties arising from post-communist transformation (Farin and Seidel-Pielen, 1992). Others point to strong currents of xenophobia in the GDR, hidden under a mantle of secrecy that left violence against foreigners unreported (e.g., Stoess, 1999). The GDR gave rise to neo-Nazi youth gangs that were disillusioned with socialist state ideology. It appears to have encouraged authoritarian styles of socialisation and applied a double speak of international friendship in official proclamations and institutionalised exclusion in actual policy. In public opinion, a right-wing consensus persisted beneath a veneer of left-wing statecraft (Schröder, 1997; Butterwege, 1996; Farin and Seidel-Pielen, 1992).

The exclusion of non-Germans from normal social life compounded by the determination of the state to prevent migration and deny rights of settlement confirmed east Germans in their assumptions that institutionalised exclusion was benign and 'others' had no claim to a regular, legally protected place in their society. Moreover, migration in the 1990s had lost its link with work, as arrivals, even those with residency rights, did not have contracts in their pockets and found it all but impossible to secure employment and to earn a living (Marshall, 2000). The *Gastarbeiter* migration could not be repeated.

Despite their different residency status and experiences of uncertainty, asylum seekers, German resettlers, Jewish refugees and former contract workers constitute a new challenge as migrants without employment. In the east German setting, this new migration cannot build on established cultural diversity or an acceptance of difference. Rather, it conflicts with a tendency to define identity through employment and reject all employment change as uncertainty. Persistently high unemployment has also shifted the risk of social and material exclusion from 'others' to Germans. Opinion polls taken in the early 1990s arrived at conflicting results, as east Germans seemed to be more positively inclined towards foreigners than west Germans. In December 1990, for instance, 61 per cent of east Germans, compared to 37 per cent of west Germans, stated that benefits for asylum seekers who were entitled to stay in the country should be identical to those given to Germans (Kürsat-Ahlers, 1995: 66–67). At the time of the survey, new-style asylum seekers had yet to arrive in east Germany, and it appears that the positive view of 1990 related to the handful of approved political refugees who had been taken in by the GDR and whose equal status to East Germans was accepted without reservations. Once actual asylum seekers began to arrive, most east Germans regarded them as bogus without legitimate claims to residency or support. A comparative study of young people in East and West Berlin in 1990 showed that easterners were more inclined to advocate the use of violence and hold right-extremist views than their peers in the west, although, of course, east Germans did not classify their views as right-extremist at the time (Minkenberg, 2001). A survey of attitudes towards foreigners in Leipzig revealed, in 1996, that the city's inhabitants regarded themselves as 'friendly towards foreigners' although most had never met one in their life. Those who had contacts to report were predominantly negative in their evaluation and especially so where asylum seekers were concerned (Ausländer und Asylbewerber, 1996).

Statistics on the development of right-wing activities in east Germany and the undisputed lead of the region in the league table of xenophobic assaults and acts of violence do not suggest that the onset of migration together with the onset of democracy, have fostered an acceptance of diversity and dispelled xenophobia in its institutional or personalised forms (Verfassungsschutzbericht, 1999). A more specific measure of attitudes towards non-Germans in eastern Germany can be derived from two east/west comparisons of young people conducted in 1992 and in 1999 under the auspices of the Deutsche Shell. The first survey focused on young people in the immediate aftermath of unification, when residues of GDR orientations would still have been in place. Respondents in the second survey grew up in post-unification Germany and their voice may be taken as indicative of attitudes shaped in the course of post-communist transformation, and thus likely to impact, within this cohort at least, on behaviour and preferences in the future (Jugend, 1992; Jugend, 2000).

Between January and April 1990, attitudes towards foreigners among young East Germans became more hostile. Since employment was no longer decreed, their uses were in doubt. Referring to contract workers, one respondent noted: 'We no not need them any more. And in any case, they buy mopeds and bicycles in such huge quantities' (Jugend, 1992: 58). Negative classifications at the time seemed confined to nationalities or cultures with a presence in the GDR – Russians, Blacks, Vietnamese – but they also included Turks whom young East Germans would not have encountered (ibid.: 59). A handful of respondents argued that foreign workers took the menial jobs nobody wanted, and for this reason they should be allowed to stay. The majority held the view that the employment of Germans had priority and left no room for others after the GDR. In interpreting these findings, the 1992 study concluded that young east Germans had never lived in 'a personal environment of solidarity and friendship among peoples' (ibid.: 59). Time would heal these deficits and change attitudes towards the better.

This optimism was not borne out. In 1999, xenophobia remained more widespread in the east than in the west of Germany (Jugend, 2000: 256) and significantly stronger among young men than young women (ibid.: 260). In the east, more young people than in the west believed that there were too many foreigners in the country. With 93 per cent in east Germany and 88 per cent in west Germany, this view prevailed among young people who held xenophobic attitudes.

The study also showed that young east Germans were given to exaggerate the number of asylum seekers entering the country and estimated the number of non-Germans living in the new *Länder* at more than ten times the actual population (ibid.: 259). In the new *Länder*, as in the old, xenophobic attitudes were more pronounced among young people with low or intermediate levels of education and among those in blue collar employment. There was no evidence that unemployment itself boosted xenophobic orientations (ibid.: 258).

The most significant finding of the Shell study concerns the frequency of contacts between Germans and non-Germans. The pivotal role of personal contact has already been highlighted in research on the impact of integration in education and at work, although for west Germany it emerged that few of these institutionalised contacts continued at the personal level or in the private sphere (e.g. Waldhoff *et al.* 1997). Contacts of young east Germans with non-Germans constitute an exception. Ten years after the collapse of the GDR, over 90 per cent of young people in the east still reported that they had never, or virtually never, had such contacts (Jugend, 2000.: 223). In east Germany, boys were less likely to have met non-Germans than girls, in west Germany the reverse was true (ibid.: 224). In west Germany, 50 per cent of young people spent their leisure time exclusively with other Germans. In contrast, more than half of the young non-Germans spent their leisure time in mixed groups. For east Germans, contacts have been too infrequent and numbers too minute to make comparisons. The west German case, however, suggests, that young Germans tend to regard non-German peers as marginal to their lives, while young non-Germans define their social environment and circle of friends as including members of their own culture and Germans. Similarly, 81 per cent of young west Germans lived in exclusively German neighbourhoods; in east Germany most neighbourhoods and most communities are nearly 100 per cent German.

Given the key role of personal contacts in breaking down assumptions and pre-determined views about non-German migrants and residents, eastern Germany remains problem territory. Where contacts through education, employment, neighbourhoods and social activities remain so sparse and where they are experienced as essentially negative, where policy agendas mix benevolence with restrictive and punitive approaches, where institutionalised exclusion has been replaced by expressions of personal dislike that are no less segregating in their effect, the present has little to offer for migrants and new residents from other countries and cultures, while the future has much to deliver.

Bibliography

Ausländer in Thüringen (1999) *Ausländer in Thüringen. Daten und Fakten.* (Erfurt: Der Ausländerbeauftragte)

Ausländer und Asylbewerber (1996) *Ausländer und Asylbewerber in Leipzig. Ihre reale Präsenz sowie Erfahrungen und Einstellungen aus der Sicht der Deutschen.* (Leipzig: Amt für Statistik und Wahlen)

Bade, Klaus J. (1983) *Vom Auswanderungsland zum Einwanderungsland? Deutschland 1880–1980.* (Berlin Colloquium)

Bade, Klaus J. (ed.) (1987), *Population, Labour and Migration in 19th and 20th Century Germany.* (Oxford: Berg)

Bade, Klaus J. and Weiner, Myron (eds.) (1997) *Migration Past, Migration Future. Germany and the United States.* (Oxford: Berghahn; vol. 1 of Weiner, Myron (ed.), *Migration and Refugees*)

Benz, Wolfgang (ed.) (1993) *Integration ist machbar. Ausländer in Deutschland.* (Munich: Beck)

Berghoff, Hartmut (1996) 'Population Change and its Repercussion on the Social History of the Federal Republic' in Larres, Klaus and Panayi, Panikos (eds.), *The Federal Republic of Germany since 1949. Politics, Society and Economy before and after Unification.* (London: Longman), pp. 35–73

Bericht der Ausländerbeauftragten Land Brandenburg (1998) *Zwischen Ankunft und Ankommen. Die Situation von Zugewanderten im Land Brandenburg 1995–1997.* (Potsdam: Die Ausländerbeauftragte des Landes)

Bericht des Landes Mecklenburg-Vorpommern (1998) *Vierter Bericht des Bürgerbeauftragten des Landes Mecklenburg-Vorpommern für das Jahr 1998.* (Schwerin: Der Bürgerbeauftragte des Landes)

Bericht Landeshauptstadt Schwerin (1996) *Lebenssituation "ausländischer* Bürger" *in der Landeshauptstadt Schwerin.* (Schwerin: Büro der Ausländerbeauftragten)

Boyes, Roger (2001) 'German exodus turns old East into ghost town', *The Times,* 28 April 2001

Beck, Ulrich (1986) *Risikogesellschaft. Auf dem Weg in eine andere Moderne.* (Frankfurt/Main: Suhrkamp)

Brubaker, Rogers (1992) *Citizenship and Nationhood in France and Germany.* (Cambridge: Harvard UP)

Bundesausländerbeauftragte (2000) 'Die Entwicklung der Zahl der ausländischen Flüchtlinge' in www. bundesauslaenderbeauftragte/de/fakten (Table 8)

Butterwege, Christoph (1996) *Rechtsextremismus, Rassismus und Gewalt.* (Darmstadt: Wissenschaftliche Buchgesellschaft)

Cohn-Bendit, Daniel and Schmid, Thomas (1992) *Heimat Babylon. Das Wagnis der multikulturellen Demokratie.* (Hamburg: Hoffmann+Campe)

Commichau, Imke (1990), 'Ausländer in der DDR – die ungeliebte Minderheit', *Deutschland Archiv* vol. 24, no. 9, 1432–1439

Dennis, Mike (2000), *The Rise and Fall of the German Democratic Republic 1945–1990.* (London: Longman)

Diewald, Martin (1999) 'Aufbruch oder Entmutigung? Kompetenzentfaltung, Kompetenzentwertung und subjektive Kontrolle in den neuen Bundesländern' in Schmitt, Manfred and Montada, Leo (eds.), *Gerechtigkeitserleben im wiedervereinigten Deutschland.* (Opladen: Leske+Budrich), pp. 99–132

Dohse, Klaus (1981) *Ausländische Arbeiter und bürgerlicher Staat. Genese und Funktion staatlicher Ausländerpolitik und Ausländerrecht. Vom Kaiserreich bis zur Bundesrepublik.* (Königstein: Hain)

Eryilmaz, Aytac and Jamin, Mathilde (eds.) (1998) *Fremde Heimat. Eine Geschichte der Einwanderung aus der Türkei.* (Essen: Klartext)

Falter, Jürgen, Gabriel, Oscar W. and Rattinger, Hans (eds.) (2000) *Wirklich ein Volk? Die politischen Orientierungen von Ost- und Westdeutschen im Vergleich.* (Opladen: Leske+Budrich

Farin, Klaus and Seidel-Pielen, Eberhard (1992) *Rechtsruck. Rassissmus im neuen Deutschland.* (Berlin: Rotbuch Verlag)

Garton Ash, Timothy (1993) *In Europe's Name: Germany and the Divided Continent.* (London: Cape)

Geis, Jael (2000) *Übrig sein – Leben 'danach'. Juden deutscher Herkunft in der britischen und amerikanischen Zone Deutschlands 1945–1949.* (Berlin: Philo)

Geissler, Rainer and Meyer, Thomas (1992) 'Struktur und Entwicklung der Bevölkerung' in Rainer Geissler, *Die Sozialstruktur Deutschlands.* (Opladen: Westdeutscher Verlag, pp. 284–304

Glässner, Gert-Joachim (1996) 'Regime Change and Public Administration in East Germany', *German Politics* vol.5 no. 2. pp. 185–200

Hanesch, Walter, *et al.* (1994) *Armut in Deutschland.* (Reinbek: Rowohlt)

Hajek, Friederike (1998) 'Multiculturality in the German Democratic Republic and the Reception of African-American Literature' in Milich, Klaus J.and Peck, Jeffrey M. (eds.), *Multiculturalism in Transit.* (Oxford: Berghahn), pp. 111–118

Helwig, Gisela and Nickel, Hildegard Maria (eds.) (1993) *Frauen in Deutschland 1945–1992.* (Berlin: Akademie Verlag)

Herbert, Ulrich (1984) *Fremdarbeiter: Politik und Praxis des 'Ausländer-Einsatzes' in der Kriegswirtschaft des Dritten Reiches.* (Berlin: Colloquium)

Homze, E.L. (1967) *Foreign Labour in Nazi Germany.* (Princeton: Princeton UP)

Hradil, Stefan (1993) *Socialstrukturanalyse in einer fortgeschrittenen Gesellschaft.* (Opladen: Leske+Budrich)

Jacobmeyer, Wolfgang (1985) *Vom Zwangsarbeiter zum Heimatlosen Ausländer: Die Displaced Persons in Westdeutschland.* (Göttingen: Vandenhoeck and Ruprecht)

Jahresbericht Sachsen (1996) *'Am farbigen Abglanz haben wir das Leben'. Vierter Jahresbericht des Sächsichen Ausländerbeauftragten, 1.1.–31.12 1996.* (Dresden: Sächsischer Landtag, Drucksache 2/5065)

Jahresbericht Sachsen (1997) *'Unsere Heimat ist der Mensch'. Fünfter Jahresbericht des Sächsichen Ausländerbeauftragten, 1.1.–31.12 1997.* (Dresden: Sächsischer Landtag, Drucksache 2/8620)

Jahresbericht Sachsen (1998) *'Wer ist denn mein Nächster?' Sechster Jahresbericht des Sächsichen Ausländerbeauftragten, 1.1.–31.12.1998.* (Dresden: Sächsischer Landtag, Drucksache 2/12033)

Jahresbericht Sachsen-Anhalt 1997/98 (1998) *Mittendrin. Gestaltung von Zuwanderung und Integration als Zukunftsaufgaben.* (Magdeburg: Der Ausländerbeauftragte der Landesregierung)

Jamin, Mathilde (1998) 'Die deutsch-türkische Anwerbevereinbarung von 1961 und 1964' in Eryilmaz, Aytac und Jamin, Mathilde (eds.), *Fremde Heimat.* (Essen: Klartext), pp. 69–83

Jarausch, Konrad H. and Gransow, Volker (1994) *Uniting Germany. Documents and Debates, 1944–1993.* (Oxford: Berghahn)

John, Barbara (1997) 'Migration and Multiculturality in Germany', paper delivered at the conference *Migration and Multiculturality in Europe.* (Keele University, 22 May)

Joppke, Christian (1995) *East German Dissidents and the Revolution of 1989.* (Basingstoke: Macmillan)

Joppke, Christian (1999) *Immigration and the Nation State. The United States, Germany and Great Britain.* (Oxford: OUP)

Jugend 1992: Die Neuen Länder. Rückblick und Perspektiven (1992) ed. Jugendwerk der Deutschen Shell, 3 vols. (Opladen: Leske+Budrich)

Jugend 2000. 13. Shell Jugendstudie (2000) ed. Deutsche Shell, 2 vols. (Opladen: Leske+Budrich)

Katzenstein, Peter J. (1987) *Policy and Politics in West Germany. The Growth of a Semisovereign State.* (Philadelphia: Temple UP)

Klee, Ernst (ed.) (1965) *Gastarbeiter.* (Frankfurt/Main: Suhrkamp)

Kolinsky, Eva (1993) *Women in Contemporary Germany. Life, Work and Politics.* (Oxford: Berg)

Kolinsky, Eva (1995) 'Foreigners in the New Germany: Attitudes, Expectations, Perceptions', *Keele German Papers Research Series* no 1

Kolinsky, Eva (1999) 'Multiculturalism in the Making? Non-Germans and Civil Society in the New Länder' in Flockton, Chris and Kolinsky, Eva (eds.) *Recasting East Germany. Social Transformation after the GDR.* (London: Cass), pp. 192–214

Kolinsky, Eva (2000a), 'Unexpected Newcomers' Asylum Seekers and other non-Germans in the New Länder' in Flockton, Chris, Kolinsky, Eva and Pritchard, Rosalind (eds.), *The New Germany in the East. Policy Agendas and Social Developments since Unification.* (London: Cass), pp. 148–164

Kolinsky, Eva (2000b) *Deutsch und türkisch leben. Bild und Selbstbild der türkischen Minderheit in Deutschland.* (Berne: Lang)

Kolinsky, Eva and Nickel, Hildegard Maria (eds.) (2003) *Reinventing Gender. Women in East Germany since 1990.* (London: Cass)

Kürsat-Ahlers, Elçin (1995) *Die multikulturelle Gesellschaft: Der Weg zur Gleichstellung?* (Frankfurt/Main: Suhrkamp)

Lemberg, Eugen and Edding, Friedrich (1959) *Die Vertriebenen in Westdeutschland. Ihre Eingliederung und ihr Einfluss auf Gesellschaft, Wirtschaft, Politik und Geistesleben.* (Kiel: Hirt)

Maaz, Hans-Joachim (1998) 'Du bist schuld, dass es mir schlecht geht'. Psychosoziale Ursachen von Ausländerfeindlichkeit und Rechtsextremismus' in *Ausländerfeindlichkeit und Rechtsextremismus in den neuen Bundesländern. Dokumentation einer Fachtagung.* (Magdeburg: Der Ausländerbeauftragte der Landesregierung Sachsen-Anhalt), pp. 25–28

Marshall, Barbara (2000) *The New Germany and Migration in Europe.* (Manchester: MUP)

McNeill, Margaret (1995) *An den Wassern von Babylon. Erfahrungen mit Displaced Persons in Goslar zwischen 1945 und 1948.* (Bielefeld: Verlag für Regionalgeschichte; English original, 1949)

Migration und Integration in Zahlen. Ein Handbuch (1997). (Berlin: Mitteilungen der Beauftragten der Bundesregierung für Ausländerfragen)

Milich, Klaus J. and Peck, Jeffrey M. (eds.) (1998) *Multiculturalism in Transit. A German-American Exchange.* (Oxford: Berghahn)

Minkenberg, Michael (2001) 'The Radical Right in Unified Germany: Dividing the Nation in the Name of the People', *Politik. Newsletter of the Conference Group on German Politics,* no. 16, pp. 5–7

Müggenberg, Andreas (1996) *Die ausländischen Vertragsarbeitnehmer in der ehemaligen DDR. Darstellung und Dokumentation.* (Berlin: Mitteilungen der Beauftragten der Bundesregierung für die Belange der Ausländer)

Panayi, Panikos (1996) 'Race in the Federal Republic of Germany: Immigration, Ethnicity and Racism since the Second World War' in Larres, Klaus and Panayi, Panikos (eds.), *The Federal Republic of Germany since 1949.* (London: Longman), pp. 191–208

Paterson, William E. and Southern, David (1991) *Governing Germany.* (Oxford: OUP)

Peck, Jeffrey M., Ash, Mitchell and Lemke, Christiane (1997) 'Natives, Strangers and Foreigners: Constituting Germans by Constructing Others' in Jarausch, Konrad H. (ed.), *After Unity. Reconfiguring German Identities.* (Oxford: Berghahn), pp. 61–102

Pulzer, Peter (1995) *German Politics 1945–1995.* (Oxford: OUP)

Riehe, Eckart and Zeng, Matthias (1998) *Kommunikation und Kommunikationsprobleme zwischen Migranten und Verwaltung in Thüringen*. (Erfurt: Der Ausländerbeauftrage der Thüringer Landesregierung)

Schröder, Burkhard (1997) *Im Griff der rechten Szene. Ostdeutsche Städte in Angst.* (Reinbek: Rowohlt)

Segert, Astrid and Zierke, Irene (1997) *Sozialstruktur und Milieuerfahrungen. Aspekte des alltagskulturellen Wandels in Ostdeutschland.* (Opladen: Westdeutscher Verlag)

Seifert, Wolfgang (1998) 'Social and Economic Integration of Foreigners in Germany' in Schuck, Peter H. and Münz, Rainer (eds.), *Paths to Inclusion. the Integration of Migrants in the United States and Germany.* (Oxford: Berghahn), pp. 83–114

Smith, Gordon (1989) 'Structures of Government' in Smith, Gordon *et al.* (eds.), *Developments in West German Politics.* (Basingstoke: Macmillan)

Statistisches Jahrbuch Berlin (2000) (ed.), Statistisches Landesamt, Berlin

Steinert, Johannes Dieter (1995a) *Migration und Politik. Westdeutschland – Europa – Übersee 1945–1961.* (Osnabrück: Secolo)

Steinert, Johannes Dieter (1995b) 'Die grosse Flucht und die Jahre danach: Flüchtlinge und Vertriebene in den vier Besatzungszonen' in Volkmann, Hans-Erich (ed.), *Ende des Dritten Reiches – Ende des Zweiten Weltkrieges.* (Munich: Hanser), pp. 557–579

Stoess, Richard (1999) *Rechtsextremismus im vereinten Deutschland.* (Bonn: Bundeszentrale für politische Bildung)

Thaysen, Uwe (1990) *Der Runde Tisch. Oder: Wo blieb das Volk? Der Weg der DDR in die Demokratie.* (Opladen: Westdeutscher Verlag)

Übersiedlerinnen: Perspektiven, Erfahrungen, Strategien (1991) ed. Bundesministerium für Frauen und Jugend, *Materialien zur Frauenpolitik*, no. 12, Bonn, June 1991

Verfassungsschutzbericht 1999. (Bonn: Bundesminister des Inneren)

VertragsarbeitnehmerInnen (1998) *Vietnamesische VertragsarbeitnehmerInnen in Schwerin gestern und heute.* Eds. Jelen, Frieder and Köppinger, Annette (Schwerin: Der Ausländerbeauftragte).

Waldhoff, Hans-Peter, Tan, Dursun and Kürsat-Ahlers, Elçin (eds.) (1997) *Brücken zwischen Zivilisationen. Zur Zivilisierung ethnisch-kultureller Differenzen und Machtungleichheiten. Das türkisch-deutsche Beispiel.* (Frankfurt/Main: Iko)

Williamson, Hugh (2001) 'Berlin urges to break with the past over immigration', *Financial Times*, 4 July 2001

Wyman, Mark (1998) *DPs. Europe's Displaced Persons, 1945–1951.* (2nd. ed. Ithaka: Cornell UP)

Zayas, Alfred-Maurice de (1986) *The German Expellees. Victims in War and Peace.* (Basingstoke: Macmillan)

Zwahr, Hartmut (1994) 'Umbruch durch Ausbruch und Aufbruch: Die DDR auf dem Höhepunkt der Staatskrise 1989' in Kaeble, Hartmut, Kocka, Jürgen and Zwahr, Hartmut (eds.), *Sozialgeschichte der DDR.* (Stuttgart: Klett Cotta), pp. 426–468

Chapter Nine

Between Integration and Exclusion: Jewish Immigrants from the Former Soviet Union in Germany

Karin Weiss

Immigrants from the Soviet Union

The immigration of Jews from the former Soviet Union has radically changed the size and composition of the Jewish population in Germany. The collapse of the socialist states and the unification of Germany in 1990 marked the start of a new chapter in the history of Jews in Germany. With the opening of the borders to western Europe, a massive exodus of Jews from the Soviet Union began; most of them went to Israel (more than 800,000) and the United States, but many also went to Germany. Almost overnight Germany became the third most popular destination for Jewish immigration. With an estimated 30,000 Jews living in West Germany before unification, the emigration of about 25,000 Jews to Germany by 1993 meant the number of Jews in the country had almost doubled. By the end of 1998, the number of Jewish immigrants from the former Soviet Union had risen to 100,000. One year later, the German embassies in the successor states of the Soviet Union had received a total of 175,000 applications by would-be immigrants[1] and the influx appears set to continue in the years ahead. The annual rate has stabilised at between 15,000 and 20,000. Thus it is not surprising that the resources of Germany's once small Jewish communities are being stretched to capacity as they try to integrate the enormous numbers of new arrivals.

Jewish immigration from the former Soviet Union is a direct consequence of German unification. West Germany had no special regulations governing the immigration of Jews. Those who came before the fall of the Berlin Wall did so in accordance with the regulations that covered all foreigners seeking entry. It was the last – and first freely elected – government of the German Democratic Republic of Lothar de Maizière that opened its borders to immigrants from the former Soviet Union. Since the end of the Second World War, socialist East Germany always insisted that it bore no special responsibility for the Holocaust and the fate of the Jews because, in contrast to West Germany, it was not the successor of the Nazi state. At the same time, the East German government's relationship to its Jewish population was far from straightforward, veering between support and anti-Semitism, the latter barely disguised behind a facade of anti-Zionism.[2] The de Maizière government wanted to make a clear gesture of good will and in early 1990, in response to a sudden upsurge in racist persecution in the Soviet Union, granted two thousand Jews from there the status of refugees and, with it, the right to reside in East Germany. The Unification Treaty of 1990 did not provide any special right for Jews from the Soviet Union to come to Germany. In December 1991, however, in response to pressure from the Jewish communities and also to growing anti-Semitism in the Soviet Union's successor states, it was agreed that Jews from there would, as a group, be accorded the status of refugees under the law governing the admission of migrants in the context of humanitarian aid measures. The German term for their legal status is *Kontingentflüchtling*, that is, 'refugee as a member of a contingent'. It is almost equivalent to the status of a refugee who has endured political persecution in his/her home country, and accords all the rights set out in the Geneva Convention. One difference, however, from the status of refugee as defined by the latter is that persecution does not have to be demonstrated in each individual case. Germany treats all Jews from the former Soviet Union as if they had suffered persecution.

This agreement of 1991 was motivated both by the wish to provide humanitarian aid and also by the wish to strengthen the Jewish communities and Jewish life in the new unified Germany. Applicants for immigration under this programme only have to prove their Jewish descent in order to obtain permission to come to Germany. Such immigrants enjoy all the rights guaranteed to refugees by articles 2 to 34 of the Geneva Convention: the right of sojourn, the right to work, the right to assistance with assimilation. Although they do not have a right to German citizenship on arrival, they may apply for it later.

These immigrants are spread out across Germany: each federal state is assigned a number in proportion to its population, as set out in the 'Königsstein key'. The immigrants do not have the right to choose where they live and are obliged to remain in the town to which they are sent for as long as they receive welfare benefits; no consideration is given to their wishes or family connections once the authorities have decided where to send them. Groups of immigrants are deliberately sent to towns without a Jewish community in order that they might establish new ones. The declared aim is the revival of Jewish life in Germany. Is that, however, possible?

Preconditions and Problems of Integration

Before addressing the question of whether a revival of Jewish life in Germany is possible, one must first analyse the situation of these recent Jewish immigrants from the former Soviet Union – the *Kontingentflüchtlinge* – and what the basis might be for their integration into German society. The findings below derive in part from two studies which the author conducted in the state of Brandenburg designed to further the integration of Jewish immigrants (see also Ausländer-beauftragte, 1998 and 1999). One study was an evaluation of the effectiveness of these projects; the other was a research project with students at the *Fach-hochschule* in Potsdam (Weiss and Geisler, 2000; Projektbericht, 2001). Quanti-tative methods were complemented by group discussions and structured interviews.[3] The chapter also draws on the findings of a nationwide survey of *Kontingentflüchtlinge* conducted by Julius Schoeps (Schoeps *et al.*, 1999b) and on several regional studies (see Urania-Schulhaus, 1998a and 1998b).

Most *Kontingentflüchtlinge* do not have any clearly defined Jewish identity when they arrive in Germany. They often lack even a basic familiarity with Jewish history, traditions or culture. In the Soviet Union, it was often impossi-ble to live a Jewish life: there were no Jewish organisational structures and no religious services. As a consequence, there was no Jewish group identity. In the Soviet Union, 'Jew' denoted a nationality, which was entered in an individual's passport, whether or not that individual had a Jewish identity.[4] To be classified as a Jew brought with it disadvantages and discrimination; it restricted access to education, training and work, and was therefore something one tried to hide. Repeated waves of anti-Semitism in the Soviet Union left their mark on the way Jews there felt about their Jewish heritage: to be a Jew meant suffering discrimination; more and more restrictions made living as a Jew a risky busi-ness. One of the people interviewed in the Brandenburg project put it this way: 'For a long time it was forbidden to practice our faith. It was absolutely forbid-den and very dangerous. There were times when people were arrested because they were learning Hebrew; it was a crime...' (Projektbericht, 2001: 53)[5] Only a minority of the immigrants from the former Soviet Union had developed a Jew-ish identity or had maintained Jewish traditions or Jewish culture. In addition, many of the immigrants have only one parent classified as being of Jewish nationality and often arrived with a non-Jewish spouse. Under these circum-stances, Jewish traditions and any Jewish connections that may have existed were often abandoned. An experience common to these immigrants was that of discrimination and social exclusion, not that of shared Jewish traditions or culture (Schoeps *et al.*, 1999b: 41ff; Polnauer, 1996; Petschauer, 1999). Another interviewee had this to say: 'I was a Jew because that is what it said in my pass-port. ... It had absolutely nothing to do with faith ... most of us were atheists....' (Projektbericht, 2001: 58).

Few emigrated to Germany for religious reasons. Most came because they felt that staying put was too dangerous given the upsurge in anti-Semitic vio-lence following the collapse of the Soviet Union, the desperate economic situ-ation and the general insecurity. Many decided to face the upheaval and stress of emigration less out of a desire for a better life for themselves than out of the hope that their children might have a better, and above all, safer, future

(Schoeps *et al.*, 1999b: 41ff; Urania-Schulhaus, 1998b: 16; Weiss and Geisler, 2000: 8). Very few of these immigrants had any clear idea of what awaited them in Germany. A care worker in one of the Brandenburg integration projects stated: 'Most of these Jewish immigrants don't even have the basic information they need to live in Germany. As a rule, they came without knowing the language, without any concrete or realistic notion of what German society is like, without any familiarity with the law, without any knowledge of the political and economic situation' (see Berlin-Brandenburg Auslandsgesellschaft, 1999).

Quite apart from the challenge of crafting a new Jewish life in Germany, the process of integration in a new country and a new culture always involves a plethora of problems and difficulties. These Jewish immigrants not only face the 'normal' immigration-related problems; they also have other quite specific problems: they are for the most part relatively old, highly educated, and hardly speak German.

As in all other European countries, the average age of the Jewish population in the former Soviet Union was higher than that of other nationalities. The Holocaust had devastated entire generations, and of the few people who returned after the war most were elderly. On the other hand, many of the younger people – who were not very numerous to start with – had already emigrated to Israel in the years preceding German unification. It was the elderly who stayed behind in the Soviet Union. It is always harder for older immigrants to assimilate in a new culture and environment.

A major problem is that these Jewish immigrants know virtually no German. Hardly any knew the language before arriving in the country. While they are all entitled to attend a language course, the quality of the available courses is very uneven; and since the classes are made up almost entirely of Russian-speaking immigrants, there is little immediate pressure to make use of what they learn. The upshot is that they never attain a high level of competency. More than 50 per cent of the immigrants evaluate their knowledge of German as poor, even those who have lived in Germany for five years or longer (Schoeps *et al.*, 1999b). The author's research on Brandenburg ascertained that only a minority knew enough German to get by in everyday life, although it should be noted that the sample only included immigrants who had been in Germany for at least three years. The prospects for integration are minimal for anyone who does not know the local language.

The level of education among the immigrants is high: more than three quarters have at least a first degree from a polytechnic university (Schoeps *et al.*, 1999b: 44). What might appear to be a significant advantage often proves to be a drawback: it is hard for the immigrants to find appropriate employment. Because of disparities in academic standards and curricula between Germany and the then Soviet Union, hardly any of the unversity graduates among the immigrants find a job in their profession (see also Urania-Schulhaus, 1998a). Given difficulties with the language as well, many end up taking unskilled jobs

– or competing for such jobs with other immigrant groups. After a professional career in the Soviet Union, many Jewish immigrants in Germany find themselves unemployed or having to accept a menial job. Although many find it hard to come to terms with such a fall in social status, the harsh alternative is unemployment and dependence on the social welfare system. The psychological consequences are enormous. This is how one woman interviewed, a former headmistress, put it: 'This situation made me very sick. ... They (the immigrants) are doctors or engineers or teachers, and of course they have a different mentality, they have had a different upbringing and education. And when they come here, they are nothing ....' (Projektbericht, 2001: 49). The unemployment rate among the Jewish immigrants is extremely high. Even two and three years after their arrival, between 60 per cent and 70 per cent do not have work. In Germany's new *Länder*, the problem is likely to be more acute, since unemployment there is above that in the old *Länder*. More than 75 per cent of Jewish immigrants live on social welfare, even years after they had settled in Germany (Schoeps *et al.*, 1999b: 66ff).

These three problems – advanced age, poor knowledge of German, poor prospects in the labour market – are clearly of enormous significance with regard to the integration of the Jewish immigrants. Without financial independence, they are not in a position to choose where to live, a mobility which is never likely to be achieved by the vast majority of these immigrants. The issue, however, of choosing where they want to live is of great importance to the many who have been sent to small towns all over the country. Most of them want to live in big cities with large Jewish communities where they could find help, establish contacts, and pursue their own cultural interests, based on their old – Russian – traditions. Most lived in large cities back home, and small-town life is alien to them. Highly educated individuals, accustomed to a rich cultural life in a big city, in close contact with their family and friends, find themselves in an unfamiliar small town milieu, without work, without the support of their former social networks, and without the money or language skills needed to take part in the cultural or social life around them. Frustration and isolation in such an environment are unavoidable. The consequence is withdrawal and the creation of tiny ethnic colonies. Social workers report that people from a single town in the former Soviet Union settled in the same neighbourhood because they feel the need to remain together. This sometimes involves moving from one town to another without the authorisation to do so. The immigrants try to recreate their old way of life, cling to old values, traditions and customs, and in their cultural associations lead a life that has no future in Germany. Both social support and social control within these small communities are strong. To live almost entirely within such a group precludes integration: these immigrants have no contact with Germans, a factor which does nothing to help them overcome their language difficulties. This is underlined in an interview with one of the women: '(We) live in our own world with Russian television, Russian language, with Russian friends, without contact to German people...a very closed circle... a small former Soviet Union...' (Projektbericht, 2001: 58). The quantitative study of immigrants who had all been in Germany for at least three years and were attending integration courses found, for example, that over 90 per cent had 'never' or 'almost never' been engaged in political life in Germany (Weiss und Geisler, 2000: 19).

At the same time, however, the German environment is not always friendly or welcoming; increasing right-wing extremism makes the process of integration even more difficult. More than half the Jewish immigrants have had negative experiences with Germans. The experiences have a racist or anti-Semitic background and include verbal attacks, occasional physical violence as well as discrimination at government offices or social welfare organizations (Schoeps *et al.*, 1999b: 83). Thirty per cent of the participants in the author's study said they did not feel accepted in Germany. Of those who had been in the country for between three and five years, no fewer than 70 per cent said they were frightened of being attacked by racists. Of those who had been there at least five years, 30 per cent expressed the same fear. In all, more than 55 per cent of the participants in the integration courses offered in Brandenburg said they had had confrontations with Germans which they said were linked to xenophobia (Weiss und Geisler, 2000: 20). Their reports ranged from negative remarks, or being spat at in the street by far-right youths, to physical attacks. Negative experiences appear to be part of their everyday life. Although most immigrants differentiate between sporadic incidents and the basic attitudes of Germans as a whole, they nonetheless withdraw ever more into their own social group.

According to Schoeps *et al.* (1999b: 81), problems with the language, unemployment, cultural differences, and encounters with anti-Semitism and racism have led two thirds of the immigrants to give up any ambition of being involved in the politics or culture of their new society. They withdraw into their family and social group – into a 'small former Soviet Union', as one woman put it. The bitter conclusion is that integration is not taking place.

The Immigration of Soviet Jews and their Impact on the Jewish Communities in Germany

Although one can scarcely speak of integration into German society, the immigration of Jews from the former Soviet Union has radically transformed the country's Jewish communities. The extent of the processes of transformation initiated by the immigrants can only be appreciated in the context of the history of the Jewish communities in Germany before unification.

The Holocaust destroyed Jewish life in Germany. By the end of the Second World War, fascism had wiped out the Jews in Germany, along with their rich culture, their buildings, their symbols and the traces of their existence. The little that was left was in ruins. Nonetheless, shortly after the end of the war, a small number of Jews returned to Germany; and a far larger number of Jewish 'displaced persons', survivors from eastern Europe, who were in transit camps in Germany waiting to go to other countries in the West decided to stay. Some Jews – those with a non-Jewish spouse and a number of individuals with a part-Jewish family background – had survived the fascist era in Germany and now sought contact with other survivors. The first post-war Jewish communities (*Gemeinden*) were established as early as 1945. In 1950, five years after the end of the war, the Jewish communities in West Germany had a total membership of 15,000. Whereas Schoeps *et al.* estimate that the communities in East Germany had 8,000 members (1999a: 24 ff.), Gay puts the figure at 3,800 (2001: 212–213). The numbers were tiny compared to those of the period before the Nazis took power in 1933, but it nevertheless represented a new beginning.

This new beginning was accompanied by profound debates among the Jews in Germany – and elsewhere – about whether, after the Holocaust, it was morally acceptable for Jews to live in Germany at all and what role the newly founded – or re-established – Jewish communities should play. On the one hand, it was argued that the presence of Jews in Germany would contribute to the covering-up and forgetting of the Nazis' crimes and that the Jewish communities would function as a kind of figleaf for the new Germany, in effect hindering an authentic confrontation with what had happened. On the other hand, it was argued that re-establishing Jewish communities was necessary and right, proof of the Jewish people's resilience and will to survive; the presence of Jews in a new Germany would always remind it of its terrible fascist legacy and help ensure that the Holocaust would never be forgotten. From the very start, the shadows of history loomed over the small Jewish communities of post-war Germany: their very existence was bound up with – and their development influenced by – both the highest of hopes and expectations and the deepest of fears.

Just as the two post-war German states developed along very different political paths, so too did the Jewish communities of West and East Germany. As a consequence of the mounting tensions between the Western allies and the Soviet Union, the Central Council of Jews in Germany, which was established in 1950, excluded the communities of East Germany from the start. The membership of the communities of East Germany soon began to fall. The reasons for the decline were the anti-Semitic stance of East Germany in the early 1950s, the state's economic problems, and a socialist ideology which was hostile to all religion. In 1961 there were just 1,500 members, and by the 1980s a mere 350 in all the Jewish communities of socialist East Germany, with a population of some 17 million.[6] According to Gay, in 1974, over 90 per cent of the members of East Germany's Jewish communities were more than fifty-five years of age, and almost all of them lived in East Berlin. The community's basic function was to provide religious services; to have taken a political stand would have endangered its existence. Due to the paucity of members and their advanced age, Gay likens the East German communities to 'museums' rather than to living entities (Gay, 2001: 225). They were barely visible from the outside; there was in effect no organised Jewish life with any public presence in East Germany.

In West Germany, it was quite a different story. Soon after the Second World War and despite the horrors of the Holocaust, Jews began to migrate from other European countries to West Germany. It became a main destination, as Germany had been before the Nazi era. The first Jews to come after the war had lived in Germany before the Holocaust and were relatively few in number. In the early 1950s, most Jewish immigrants to West Germany came from eastern Europe. In the aftermath of the Holocaust, all West German governments adopted a relatively liberal approach towards granting residency to foreign Jews, but there were no special regulations governing the immigration of Jews until after German unification. By the 1970s, the immigrants from eastern European had swelled the ranks of the West German Jewish communities to between 27,000 and 28,000; it is estimated that a further 20,000 Jews lived in the country without being registered as members of a community. While Jewish life in East Germany was barely discernible, Jewish communities in West Germany took an active part in political life, saw themselves as the heirs of pre-war German Jewry and acted as a warning and admonishing voice. Jews hardly played a significant role in everyday life in West Germany, numbering as they did well below 50,000 out of a total population of some 65 million. At the political level, however, the Jewish communities had an important role to play, as a "moral authority" (Dillmann, 2001: 58), concerned primarily with reminding the nation of the past, and recalling the Holocaust. The Jewish communities were visible in the political realm, but not in everyday life, as Jews were too few in number to be a distinct presence.

In public, while the Jewish communities presented a united front, in reality they were very heterogeneous. While the overall number of Jews remained relatively stable – and low – until German unification, the composition of the communities fluctuated. The German Jews who returned after the war tended to be old. As they died, the numerical loss was offset by a continuous flow of immigrants from eastern Europe. The proportion of German Jews declined as that of eastern European Jews rose. Between 1955 and 1985, more than 40,000 Jews came to West Germany from Hungary, Poland, Romania, Czechoslovakia and even the Soviet Union. It was a small group of mainly elderly German Jews that led the communities and represented them in public; they regularly made statements – often laced with references to the Holocaust – about West German political events. The bulk of the membership, however, consisted of eastern Europeans. This constellation changed fundamentally with the collapse of the Soviet Union and the start of Jewish immigration from its successor states. Even though not all immigrants joined Jewish communities, this wave of immigration had dramatic effects on the communities, as can be seen from Figure 9.1, which charts the number of members of the Jewish communities in Germany since the end of the Second World War.[7]

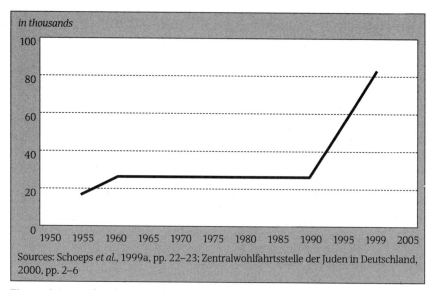

in thousands

Sources: Schoeps *et al.*, 1999a, pp. 22–23; Zentralwohlfahrtsstelle der Juden in Deutschland, 2000, pp. 2–6

Figure 9.1 Membership of Jewish Communities in the Federal Republic of Germany since 1950

The new wave of Jewish immigration that began in 1990 attracted the attention of the media, which praised it as heralding the renaissance of Jewish life in Germany and as a turning point in German-Jewish relations. Rarely did the media reflect on that very term, 'German-Jewish relations', which obfuscates the complex relationship between non-Jews and Jews in Germany by confusing the level of ethnic-religious classification and the level of citizenship or nationality. The German public was led to believe that the immigrants would bring about the rebirth of German Jewry and the normalisation of the relationship between Germans and Jews. The immigrants were thus expected to fulfil a specific mission: they had been assigned the task of helping to create a new, relaxed and normal relationship between Germans and Jews. Before anything of that order could be achieved, however, a necessary precondition would first have to be fulfilled: they would have to have a Jewish identity, on the basis of which a new relationship to Germany could be forged. A Jewish identity, however, is precisely what the immigrants from the former Soviet Union did not have (see also Schoeps *et al.*, 1999b: 109ff; Polnauer, 1996; Petschauer, 1999). The German public ignored this problem, and viewed the immigration of Jews from the former Soviet Union as immigration into and for the Jewish communities. The fact that many of these immigrants did not see any connection between having a Jewish background and having a Jewish identity – which would seek fulfilment in a Jewish community – was virtually ignored by the German public, administration and institutions. They did not appreciate the difference or consider the relationship between Jewish nationality as defined by the Soviet Union, Jewish religion and Jewish identity. Yet, since it was only the leaders of the communities and their representative bodies that made public appearances, these leaders were taken by many to be at one with – or to represent – the Jewish population as a whole. The German public may have associated the Jewish immigrants with the Jewish communities, but many of the immigrants themselves did not make any such connection, and did not join a community – either because they did not want to or because they were not allowed to. A comparison of the number of immigrants from the Soviet Union who received a residency permit in Germany because of their Jewish descent or as family members and the number of members in the Jewish communities shows that only about 40 per cent of the immigrants actually joined a community; the majority has remained outside.

In order to join a Jewish community in Germany, the applicant has to be Jewish as defined by *halakhah* or (traditional) Jewish law: that means s/he is either born of a Jewish mother or has converted to orthodox Judaism. For the German immigration authorities, however, Jewish nationality (as defined or determined by the Soviet authorities) is what counts here, irrespective of whether it is an individual's father or mother who is Jewish. The authorities also allow members of the family of a Jewish *Kontingentflüchtling* to settle in Germany, without regard to whether they are Jewish or of Jewish descent. On the basis of *halakhah*, however, the Jewish communities do not recognise the children of a Jewish father and a non-Jewish mother as a Jew, even if they consider themselves Jewish by tradition and culture. The communities do not admit non-Jewish family members. So membership in a community is not open to non-Jewish partners, relatives or children.

The Jewish immigrants can be divided into three groups: those who may join Jewish communities and want to do so; those who are Jews as defined by Jewish law but do not want to join a Jewish community; and those who regard themselves as Jewish, have a Jewish spouse and would like to join a community but are not admitted. Even individual families can be fractured along these lines, comprising members who belong to the different groups. These divisions cause deep conflicts – within families, within the Jewish communities, and also in the outside world. In one interview, a woman described her problems after unification as follows: 'My mother is German, my father is Jewish. I am in Germany as a Jewish immigrant, but for our Jewish community I am not a Jew. They say, stop, you are German, your mother is German, you aren't a Jew ... but in my heart ... I have always been and am now a Jew, I am a Jew and have always been a Jew....' (Projektbericht, 2001: 56) The assessment of the two integration courses in Brandenburg revealed that immigrants and community can relate to each other in a variety of ways (see Figure 9.2 and Weiss and Geisler, 2000). The *Zentralwohlfahrtsstelle*, the central Jewish welfare agency in Germany, estimated in 2000 that of the 5,500 Jewish immigrants who were assigned to Brandenburg about 3,500 still lived there, and only about 850 of them, or 25 per cent, belonged to a Jewish community.[8] Thus, there are two forms of Jewish life in Germany: one, organised through the Jewish communities, is visible in the public realm, while the other is diffuse and private and invisible to the German public.

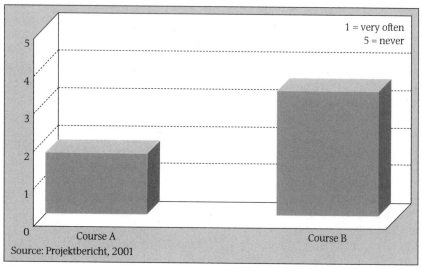

Figure 9.2 Contacts with Jewish Communities by Participants in Integration Courses in Brandenburg

Development of the Communities in the East and the West

In order to discuss immigration and its impact on the development of the Jewish communities in Germany, one must differentiate between the communities in eastern and western Germany. The communities in the two German states had developed in very different ways, and continued to do so following unification and under the impact of the new wave of immigrants. While the communities in western Germany face the problem of dealing with soaring numbers of members and integrating them into existing communal structures, in eastern Germany most of the Jewish communities are entirely new and very small, often established in small towns, as a direct and intended consequence of the federal states' policy of spreading immigrants across the country. The members of these new communities are almost all immigrants who have neither a stable Jewish identity nor the social and cultural knowledge they would need to deal with their new and alien environment. As recent arrivals, they have not formed a relationship with the local authorities in the towns where they were expected to set up new Jewish communities. So the post-unification history of Germany's Jewish communities has continued to be a double history: in the west, existing communities struggle to cope with an unmanageable surge in membership; in the east, immigrants have established small new communities. Table 9.1 shows how membership of the Jewish communities in western and eastern Germany grew between 1989 and 1999 in numerical and percentage terms. It also makes clear the differences in scale between the east and the west.

Table 9.1 Membership of Jewish Communities, 1989 and 1999 (by region)

West:	1989*	1999	Increase	Percentage Increase
Baden	1.259	3.303	2.044	162.4
Bavaria	1.434	6.945	5.511	384.3
Berlin	6.411	11.190	4.779	75.5
Bremen	132	976	844	639.4
Frankfurt am Main		6.602		
Hamburg	1.344	4.270	2.926	217.7
Hessen	1.598	4.105	2.507	156.9
Cologne		3.654		
Munich & Upper Bavaria		7.219		
Lower Saxony	501	6.165	5.664	1130.4
North Rhineland	2.679	12.687	10.008	373.6
Rhineland-Palatinate	352	1.587	1.235	350.8
Saar		931		
Westphalia	745	5.570	4.825	647.7
Württemberg		2.207		
Total		*77.393*		
Average		*5.159.5*		

East:	1989	1999		
Brandenburg	–	663		
Mecklenburg-Vorpommern	–	931		
Saxony-Anhalt	–	1.015		
Saxony	–	1.213		
Thuringia	–	525		
Total		*4.347*		
Average	–	*869.4*		

Sources: Zentralwohlfahrtsstelle der Juden in Deutschland, 2000, p. 2 ff; Schoeps *et al.*, 1999b, p. 100
* not available for all communities

The communities of eastern and western Germany are fundamentally different in their structure and composition. While the 77,000 members of communities in the western *Länder* make up just a tiny fraction of the overall population, the communities there are nonetheless functioning institutions. The communities in eastern Germany have just 4,000 members, spread across all five eastern states, and one can hardly speak of Jewish life there at all. In the east Jews are scarcely visible in the public sphere and the communities are too small to develop effective organisational structures of their own. They are almost all immigrants, steeped in Russian culture, and, as mentioned earlier, with little knowledge of German and with a very low income, and many are unemployed, without any connection to the German world around them. They are all strangers in Germany, scattered across the country in small towns that are entirely strange to them. In Brandenburg, of the 850 members of Jewish communities, about 350 live in Potsdam. The other 500 belong to six other communities, each with an average membership of eighty-five. All these members come from the former Soviet Union. The creation of an integrated German-Jewish culture does not appear feasible.

Often their religious leaders are not from Germany either. The rabbis who serve these small-town communities originate from elsewhere and usually perform religious duties while on visits from their own larger communities. The small, poor, new communities do not have the money to employ their own rabbis, who might otherwise function as an integrative and cohesive force. Almost all the rabbis who have been engaged come from abroad; in post-war Germany there was nowhere to study to become a rabbi. This means that the rabbis are also strangers in an unfamiliar environment, who have not, over time, developed a social network. Small Russian Jewish ethnic enclaves have emerged; they have minimal social and financial resources, are inward-looking and focus predominantly on their old – Russian – culture. This focus may serve to foster a new Jewish identity, but it will do little to promote the integration of these groups into German society.

These developments impact on the function and position of the new communities with regard to the legacy of the Holocaust. The history of the communities in western Germany is closely bound up with the Holocaust. As mentioned earlier, they felt bound to address that past; they saw themselves as heirs to pre-war German Jewry and sought to preserve its memory. This self-image and agenda played an important role in post-war German Jewish history. The new eastern German communities have an entirely different relationship to these problems. Most of their members are newcomers to Germany; they do not see themselves as part of their new host culture and do not feel that they belong there. Nor are they the heirs of pre-war German Jewry. In the old Soviet Union they did not develop a special focus on the Holocaust nor any stable or clear relationship to Judaism or being Jewish. They are not in a position to, and do not want to, assume the role that had been played by the Jewish communities of West Germany before unification.

The old western German communities themselves have, however, had to change. Before unification, the Jews of West Germany formed a single block; its relationship with the outside world was clearly structured; its role was to warn and admonish; a central theme was the very presence of Jews in Germany and what that meant. The various Jewish communities were represented at the political level and in the media by a single entity, the Central Council of Jews in Germany. It was the only Jewish representative body which the federal government recognized and with which it dealt. As the Jews living in the former Federal Republic were so few in number, it was impossible for them to develop different movements or political groupings. A relatively small and closely knit group of elderly individuals, deeply marked by the Holocaust, represented the entire West German Jewish community. Their authority and direction was accepted by the large contingent of Jews who had come in the early post-war years from all over eastern Europe and who had become integrated into the existing Jewish communities.

The situation changed dramatically with the massive influx of Russian Jews. Different political groups soon emerged within the Jewish communities. These groups took a variety of positions on two main issues concerning the nature of Judaism and of Jewish observance. The first issue was the relationship between orthodox and liberal Judaism. The second was whether Jewish communities are to be considered purely religious institutions which only represent individuals who are members and who cultivate religious traditions, or whether the communities are primarily social institutions which are open to everyone – including people who regard themselves as Jews without being religious and people who are not Jews according to traditional Jewish law but who consider themselves to be so. New groups and movements emerged which have widely differing world views and political agendas. The chasidic Lubavitch movement began in Germany, for example, and Jewish feminists started to develop their own organisations. However, the wide range of groups and currents did not fit into the traditional community structures and were not recognised by the official communities.

The dispute about pluralism and unity in the Jewish community reached a climax in 1997, when for the first time the German state acknowledged an independent Jewish group outside the official Jewish communal structures as a religious body in its own right – the neo-orthodox Adass Jisroel community in Berlin. This recognition was a blow to the very foundations of the *Einheitsgemeinde*, the unitary Jewish representative and communal organisations that had existed – in West Germany – before unification.

The old German *Einheitsgemeinde* not only faces challenges and uncertainties at the political and religious levels; its very organisational structure is set to be turned on its head; furthermore, its financial resources are stretched to breaking point. The ratio of Jews who have lived in Germany for many years to recent arrivals has changed so dramatically that now it is a minority of German Jews who are supposed to undertake the integration of a majority of Russian immigrants. It is a task that would seem bound to fail. Figure 9.3 compares the overall membership figures for Germany's Jewish communities to the numbers of members who are immigrants.

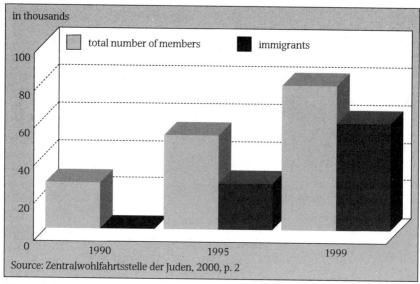

Figure 9.3 Membership of Jewish Communities since 1990

In 1999, 81,739 individuals were members of a Jewish community. Of these, 62,488 – or more than 76 per cent – were immigrants from the former Soviet Union. The old German members have dwindled to a small minority. As the national Jewish weekly, *Allgemeine Jüdische Wochenzeitung*, put it: 'The question now is, who should be integrated into which group?'.[9] Many old members have the feeling that it is not the immigrants who have to adapt to the community, but the 'old guard' that has to adapt to the new situation. Russian has become a *lingua franca* in many communities and German a minority language. Even in the long-established western German communities Russian culture is as much an influence on social life as German culture. German is often spoken in the communities as a second language: in 2000, for example, only one of the people working in the library of the Berlin community – the biggest in Germany – was a native German speaker (Gay, 2001: 268). The older members no longer feel at home in their community and community social workers report that they are withdrawing from communal life. Kessler (1999), for example, writes that alongside caring for immigrants and helping them integrate, social workers in the communities are just as concerned with trying to prevent older German members from retreating from social functions and even leaving the communities altogether. Some communities have even split into two, riven not only by religious and political differences but also by social conflicts between immigrants and old-established members. In many communities there are autonomous Russian cultural organisations and circles, alongside German groups and circles; the latter now explicitly describe themselves as a counter-culture. All in all, integration is not taking place. On the contrary, the differences and divisions between German and Russian Jews are becoming greater.

All the communities, whether in the east or the west, are threatened by financial collapse. Their main source of income is membership fees, as laid down by law. The fees each member pays depend on her/his taxable earnings. Since a majority of the immigrants live on welfare, the revenue of the communities is correspondingly small. At the same time, the cost of specially designed integration programmes is enormous. While the communities in the eastern states have neither money nor any choice in the matter, since almost all their members are immigrants, the communities in the west are debating – with ever greater urgency – whether it is their job to finance the social services the immigrants need out of the contributions of the old-established members, or whether they should restrict their activities to religious matters in order to ward off imminent bankruptcy. Such discussions often involve criticism of the immigrants, who are not interested in religious life but who wish to benefit from the community's social services.[10] In the meantime, calls have been made for limiting immigration to individuals who are Jews as defined by traditional Jewish law. Some communities are considering capping the number of new members and only allowing people to join who define themselves as practising Jews. For the first time in post-war Germany, the questions of who is a Jew and what Jewish life should be have become burning issues, as has the question of whether and under what circumstances a Jew may be barred from joining a Jewish community.

Prospects for the Future

The immigration of Jews from the former Soviet Union has transformed the Jewish communities of Germany. Massive new challenges and problems demand a swift solution. The immigrants have made the German Jews a minority in their own communities. This minority has the almost insurmountable task of organising the integration of the recent arrivals, who constitute the majority. The German Jews will not be able to achieve that goal unless they too change.

More than half a century after the Second World War, the Jewish community in Germany faces the challenge of pluralism as it is called upon to deal with a new multicultural mix and developments in its midst. This new plurality calls into question the very structures of the unitary communities. They will have to change. The *Einheitsgemeinden* will not be able to survive in their present form.

The new, post-unification Jewish community in Germany faces the task of bridging the great social and structural differences between its old and its new members, and between the communities in the east and in the west. These differences derive not only from differences in financial and social resources but also from differences of history, tradition and identity and from differences in their relations with the surrounding culture.

The rapid growth of the Jewish communities poses new questions about how and where to recruit or train religious personnel. The few rabbis who serve in Germany have not been trained and ordained there. In any case, there is a dearth of foreign-educated rabbis willing or able to serve in German communities. For many decades the issue of establishing a religious seminary in Germany was avoided, because it was so closely bound up with the question of Jewish identity in Germany in the aftermath of the Holocaust. The discussion has now begun. It is a discussion that calls into question the role of the German Jewish community as a moral authority and as a living reminder of the past. It is no longer enough to play this one role. In autumn 2000, the first post-Holocaust rabbinical seminary since 1948 opened in Potsdam. The debate about whether it is right and proper for such an institution to exist has been an emotional one. It is not only within Germany that Jewish organisations have been rethinking their roles and functions. Until well into the 1990s, international Jewish bodies avoided holding official events in Germany. In March 2001, the Conference of European Rabbis met in Germany for the first time since the Holocaust. This event launched a related debate about what kind of relationship exists and should exist between the Jewish community in Germany and Jewish organisations at the European level and about how international Jewish bodies should view the Jewish community of Germany.

At the same time, a new debate began about Jewish identity in Germany in the light of a resurgence of anti-Semitism and xenophobia and of the emergence of a new generation of communal leaders. This new generation – which for the first time also represents the immigrants from the Soviet Union – is having to find its way and create its own identity as a generation that grew up in post-war Germany and in response to the new situation following German unification.

It is not, however, only among the Jews that change is needed. The German public must also consider new issues regarding the Jewish community. The German authorities delegate to the Jewish communities the responsibility for integrating the Jewish immigrants. It is only slowly dawning on German institutions that most of these immigrants either do not consider themselves to be part of the Jewish community or are not accepted as such, and that as a consequence there is some kind of Jewish life outside of the established Jewish community.

German society must rethink its position and acknowledge that it also bears responsibility for its Jewish immigrants – not just its Jewish population. The relationship of the post-Holocaust German state and the German nation to its

Jewish community needs to be re-thought and redefined. This will also involve discussion of the function of Jewish immigration to Germany. If the Jewish immigrants from the former Soviet Union are supposed to create a new integrated Jewish community in that country, how can these immigrants be denied German citizenship? Without it, real integration and participation in the political life of the country are impossible. The immigrants are considered to be foreigners and are not even allowed to vote at the local government level in the very towns in which they are supposed to create new Jewish communities. Unless Jewish immigration is complemented by the political, financial and social resources that are needed to make integration possible – within and outside the Jewish communities – then calls for a new German Jewish community are merely hollow words. Allowing Russian Jews to settle in Germany is only a first step as this has to be followed by a process of integration. Responsibility for integration cannot lie only with the Jewish communities, but has to be accepted by German society and German institutions.

The old-established Jews, the immigrants, and German society at large are all called upon to redefine the relationship between Jews and non-Jews in Germany. They can only do so together. No single group alone can force that process of redefinition. Without a joint effort, the integration of Jewish immigrants will simply not occur. It is an entirely open question whether, in years to come, there will merely be communities of Jews living in Germany or a new German Jewish community.

Notes

1 Figures from Germany's Federal Commissioner for Foreigners' Affairs.
2 On the relationship of East Germany to its Jews, see Gay, 2001: 194 ff
3 The quantitative study evaluated two integration courses with twenty participants each. The courses were run by the *Berlin-Brandenburgische Auslandsgesellschaft* in Brandenburg and Potsdam. In the qualitative study, in-depth thematically structured interviews were held with six participants of the course in Potsdam. Two four-hour group discussions were also held with members of the course in Brandenburg (Weiss und Geisler, 2000; Projektbericht, Fachhochschule Potsdam, 2001). All the data were gathered between early 1998 and early 1999.
4 The basic question of the relationship between Jewishness as a religious and as an ethnic identity is not addressed in this chapter.
5 The interviews were conducted in German.
6 On the history of the East German communities, see also Gay, 2001; Dillmann, 2001.
7 The figures until 1990 refer only to communities in the former Federal Republic. Membership of the GDR's Jewish communities had fallen so low, to around 350 by 1990, that the numbers would not have much impact on the overall picture.
8 Interview with Matthias Jahr, Zentalwohlfahrtsstelle der Juden in Deutschland, Berlin.
9 Allgemeine Jüdische Wochenzeitung, 2 April 1998.
10 Schoeps *et al.* (1999b: 113ff.) found that only 20 per cent of the immigrants attend religious services and that 40 per cent say they have never attended a service. Projektbericht 2001 reported similar findings.

Bibliography

Ausländerbeauftragte des Landes Brandenburg (1998) *Zwischen Ankunft und Ankommen. Die Situation von Zugewanderten im Land Brandenburg 1995–1997. Bericht der Ausländerbeauftragten.* (Potsdam: Landesregierung Brandenburg)

Beauftragte der Bundesregierung für Ausländerfragen (1999) *Migrationsbericht 1999. Zu- und Abwanderung nach und aus Deutschland.* (Bamberg: Europäisches Forum für Migrationsstudien)

Berlin-Brandenburgische Auslandsgesellschaft (1999) *Petrus Migrans für ENEB.* Projektbeschreibung. (Potsdam: BBAG)

Dillmann, Hans Ulrich (2001) *Jüdisches Leben nach 1945.* (Hamburg: Europäische Verlagsanstalt)

Gay, Ruth (2001) *Das Undenkbare tun – Juden in Deutschland nach 1945.* (Munich: Beck)

Kessler, Judith (1999) 'Identitätssuche und Subkultur. Erfahrungen der Sozialarbeit in der Jüdischen Gemeinde zu Berlin' in Schoeps, Julius H, Jasper, Willi and Vogt, Bernhard (eds.), *Ein neues Judentum in Deutschland? Fremd- und Eigenbilder der russisch-jüdischen Einwanderer.* (Potsdam: Verlag für Berlin-Brandenburg), pp. 140–162

Petschauer, Hanna (1999) 'Für die Alten ein Zufluchtsort. Eine Befragung unter russisch-jüdischen Zuwanderern in Leipzig' in Schoeps, Julius H, Jasper, Willi and Vogt, Bernhard (eds.), *Ein neues Judentum in Deutschland? Fremd- und Eigenbilder der russisch-jüdischen Einwanderer.* (Potsdam: Verlag für Berlin-Brandenburg), pp. 140–162

Polnauer, David (1999) 'Jüdische Gemeinden im Wandel' in Schoeps, Julius H; Jasper, Willi and Vogt, Bernhard (eds.), *Russische Juden in Deutschland. Integration und Selbstbehauptung in einem fremden Land.* (Weinheim: Beltz), pp. 269–279

Projektbericht (2001) *Projektbericht Soziale Arbeit mit Zuwanderern.* Unpublished report, Fachhochschule Potsdam

Schoeps, Julius H, Jasper, Willi and Vogt, Bernhard (eds.) (1999a) *Russische Juden in Deutschland. Integration und Selbstbehauptung in einem fremden Land.* (Weinheim: Beltz)

Schoeps, Julius H, Jasper, Willi and Vogt, Bernhard (1999b) 'Jüdische Zuwanderer aus der GUS – zur Problematik von sozio-kultureller und generationsspezifischer Integration. Eine empirische Studie des Moses-Mendelsohn-Zentrum 1997–1999' in Schoeps, Julius H, Jasper, Willi and Vogt, Bernhard (eds.), *Ein neues Judentum in Deutschland? Fremd- und Eigenbilder der russisch-jüdischen Einwanderer.* (Potsdam: Verlag für Berlin-Brandenburg), pp. 13–128

Urania-Schulhaus-Potsdam (1998a) *Empirische Erkundungsstudie zu Bedürfnissen, Interessen und Konflikten im Verlauf der sozialen und beruflichen Integration von Spätaussiedlern und Kontigentflüchtlingen im Land Brandenburg,* study conducted by Frenk, Margarete and Liublina, Natalja. Potsdam. (unpublished material of the Urania-Schulhaus-Potsdam)

Urania-Schulhaus-Potsdam (1998b) *Zweite empirische Erkundungsstudie zu Bedürfnissen, Interessen und Konfliktlagen im Prozeß der sozialen und beruflichen Integration von Spätaussiedlern, jüdischen Emigranten und Ausländern im Raum Potsdam,* study conducted by Frenk, Tatjana and Peterhänsel, Peter. (Potsdam: unpublished material of the Urania-Schulhaus-Potsdam)

Weiss, Karin and Geisler, Wally (2000) *Das Projekt ENEB – Evaluationsbericht.* (Potsdam: unpublished material of the Institut für Forschung und Entwicklung, Fachhochschule Potsdam)

Select Bibliography

Benz, Wolfgang (ed.) (1993) *Integration ist machbar. Ausländer in Deutschland.* (Munich: Beck)

Brussig, Martin *et al.* (eds.) (1997) *Kleinbetriebe in den Neuen Bundesländern.* (Opladen: Leske+Budrich)

Buck-Bechler, Gertraude, Schaefer, Hans-Dieter and Wagemann, Carl-Heinz (eds.) (1997) *Hochschulen in den neuen Ländern der Bundesrepublik.* (Weinheim: Deutscher Studienverlag)

Dennis, Mike (1993) *Economic and Social Modernization in Eastern Germany from Honecker to Kohl.* (Basingstoke: Macmillan)

Dennis, Mike (2000) *The Rise and Fall of the German Democratic Republic 1945–1990.* (London: Longman)

Engler, Wolfgang (1999) *Die Ostdeutschen. Kunde von einem verlorenen Land.* (Berlin: Aufbau-Verlag)

Falter, Jürgen, Gabriel, Oskar W. and Rattinger, Hans (eds.) (2000) *Wirklich ein Volk? Die politischen Orientierungen von Ost- und Westdeutschland im Vergleich.* (Opladen: Leske+Budrich)

Farin, Klaus and Seidel-Pielen, Eberhard (1992) *Rechtsruck. Rassismus im neuen Deutschland.* (Berlin: Rotbuch Verlag)

Flockton, Christopher (1998), 'Germany's long-running fiscal strains: unification costs or unsustainability of welfare state arrangements?' *Debatte*, vol. 6, no. 1, pp. 79–93

Gay, Ruth (2001) *Das Undenkbare tun – Juden in Deutschland nach 1945.* (Munich: Beck)

Geissler, Rainer (1996) *Die Sozialstruktur Deutschlands.* (Opladen: Westdeutscher Verlag), 2nd edition

Glees, Anthony (1996) *Reinventing Germany: German Political Development since 1945.* (Oxford and Washington DC: Berg)

Hanesch, Walter et al. (1994) *Armut in Deutschland.* (Reinbek: Rowohlt)

Hajek, Friederike (1998) 'Multicuturality in the German Democratic Republic and the Reception of African-American Literature' in Milich, Klaus J. and Peck, Jeffrey M. (eds.), *Multiculturalism in Transit.* (Oxford: Berghahn), pp. 111–118

Herzog, Marc (1998) 'Determinants of entrepreneurial success in east Germany', in Hölscher, Jens and Hochberg, Anja (eds.), *East Germany's Economic Development since Unification: Domestic and Global Aspects.* (London: Macmillan), pp. 79–91

Hough, Daniel (2002) *The Fall and Rise of the PDS: 1989–2000.* (Birmingham: Birmingham University Press)

Hradil, Stefan (1993) *Sozialstrukturanalyse in einer fortgeschrittenen Gesellschaft.* (Opladen: Leske+Budrich)

Jarausch, Konrad H. (ed.) (1999) *Dictatorship as Experience. Towards a Socio-Cultural History of the GDR.* (New York and Oxford: Berghahn)

Joppke, Christian (1999) *Immigration and the Nation State. The United States, Germany and Great Britain.* (Oxford: OUP)

Knabe, Hubertus (1999) *Die unterwanderte Republik. Stasi im Westen.* (Berlin: Propyläen)

Kolinsky, Eva (ed.) (1995) *Between Hope and Fear. Everyday Life in Post-Unification East Germany.* (Keele: Keele University Press)

Kolinsky, Eva (2000) 'Unexpected Newcomers: Asylum Seekers and other non-Germans in the New Länder' in Flockton, Chris, Kolinsky, Eva and Pritchard, Rosalind (eds.) *The New Germany in the East. Policy Agendas and Social Developments since Unification.* (London: Cass), pp. 148–164

Kriszio, Marianne (1996) 'Frauen und Machtstrukturen an ostdeutschen Universitäten vor und nach der Wende' in Penrose, Virginia and Rudolph, Clarissa (eds.), *Zwischen Machtkritik und Machtgewinn. Feministische Konzepte und politische Realität.* (Frankfurt am Main and New York: Campus), pp. 143–159

Lange, Thomas and Shackleton, J. R. (1998) *The Political Economy of German Unification.* (Oxford: Berghahn)

Larres, Klaus and Panikos, Panayi (eds.) (1996) *The Federal Republic of Germany since 1949. Politics, Society and Economy before and after Unification.* (London: Longman)

McAdams, A. James (1996) 'The Honecker Trial: the East German past and the German future', *The Review of Politics,* vol. 58, no. 1, pp. 53–80

Mayntz, Renate (ed.) (1994) *Aufbruch und Reform von oben. Ostdeutsche Universitäten im Transformationsprozess.* (Frankfurt am Main and New York: Campus)

Milich, Klaus J. and Peck, Jeffrey M. (eds.) (1998) *Multiculturism in Transit. A German-American Exchange.* (Oxford: Berghahn)

OECD (2001), *Economic Survey of Germany.* (London: OECD)

Padgett, Stephen and Poguntke, Thomas (2001) *Party Government and Political Culture in Germany.* (London: Cass)

Patton, David (1998) 'Germany's Party of Democratic Socialism in Comparative Perspective', *East European Politics and Societies,* vol. 12, no. 3, pp. 500–526

Pritchard, Rosalind M. O. (1999) *Reconstructing Education: East German Schools and Universities After Unification.* (Oxford and New York: Berghahn)

Sa'adah, Anne (1998) *Germany's Second Chance. Trust, Justice and Democratization.* (Cambridge, Massachusetts, and London: Harvard University Press)

Schoeps, Julius H., Jasper, Willi and Vogt, Bernhard (eds.) (1999) *Russische Juden in Deutschland. Integration und Selbstbehauptung in einem fremden Land.* (Weinheim: Beltz)

Schröder, Burkhard (1997) *Im Griff der rechten Szene. Ostdeutsche Städte in Angst.* (Reinbek: Rowohlt)

Segert, Astrid and Zierke, Irene (1997) *Sozialstruktur und Milieuerfahrungen. Aspekte des alltagskulturellen Wandels in Ostdeutschland.* (Opladen: Westdeutscher Verlag)

Siebert, Horst (1992) *Das Wagnis der Einheit.* (Stuttgart: DVA)

Winkler, Gunnar (1997) *Sozialreport 1997: Daten und Fakten zur sozialen Lage in den neuen Bundesländern.* (Berlin: Verlag am Turm)

Yoder, Jennifer (1999) *From East Germans to Germans? The New Postcommunist Elites.* (Durham and London: Duke University Press)

Glossary

Abitur: A-level equivalent examination in Germany
Abwicklung: winding up of institutions of higher education
Altersübergangsgeld: benefit between employment and onset of pension
BaföG (Bundesausbildungsförderungsgesetz): federal student loan system
Basic Law: Constitution of West Germany, and since 1990, of Germany
Bleiberecht: right of residence for non-German nationals
BStU (Bundesbeauftragte für die Unterlagen des Staatssicherheitsdienstes der
    ehemaligen DDR): Federal Authority for the Records of the State Security of
    the former GDR
Bundesgerichtshof: Federal Court
Bundesländer, see Länder
Bundesrat: Second Chamber of Parliament, representing the Länder
Bundesrechnungshof: Federal Court of Auditors
Bundestag: German parliament; until 1990: West German parliament
CDU: Christian Democratic Union
Christlich Soziale Union, see CSU
Christliche Demokatische Union, see CDU
CSU: Christian Social Union (based only in Bavaria)
DM: Deutschmark, currency in West Germany and united Germany
Dozent: university teacher below the level of professor in the GDR
east Germany, territory of the former GDR since unification
East Germany: territory of the former GDR, i.e. prior to unification
Eigensinn: self-determination
EU: European Union
Fachhochschule: university with vocational focus
FDP: Free Democratic Party
Fraktion: parliamentary party
Freie Demokratische Partei, see FDP
FRG: Federal Republic of Germany
Gastarbeiter: guest worker
GDR: German Democratic Republic
Gemeinschaftsaufgabe: Joint Task promoting development in eastern Germany
Gleichestellungsbeauftragte: Equal Opportunities Officer
Habilitation: second doctorate required for professorship
Hochschule: university
Hochschulrahmengesetz: University Framework Legislation
HV A (Hauptverwaltung Aufklärung): Main Administration for Reconnaissance
Kombinate: large monopolistic state concerns; combines
Kontingentsflüchtlinge: refugee contingent from eastern Europe
Land: German region with its own parliament and government
Länder: German regions, each with its own parliament and government

Landrat: district council
Lebensraum: living space
Mittelbau: middle rank positions in universities
Mittelstand: middle class, especially owners of small- and medium-sized busi-
    nesses
NSDAP: National Socialist German Workers' Party
OECD: Organisation for European Co-operation and Development
Ostmark: currency of the GDR
Ostpolitik: FRG policy towards Eastern Europe, including East Germany
Partei des Demokratischen Sozialismus, see PDS
PDS: Party of Democratic Socialism
R&D: Research and Development
Rechtsstaat: state based in the rule of law
Rechtsstaatlichkeit: rule of law
Rücknahmeabkommen: agreement regulating the return of foreign workers to
    country of origin
SED: Socialist Unity Party
SME: small- and medium-sized enterprises
Sozialdemokratische Partei, see SPD
Sozialistische Einheitspartei, see SED
SPD: Social Democratic Party
Stasi: GDR Ministry of State Security
Technische Hochschule: Technical University
Treuhandanstalt: trustee agency
Umsiedler: GDR-term for German expellees
Unrechtsstaat: state without rule of law
Vertragsarbeiter: contract workers (GDR)
Vertriebene: FRG-term for German expellees
Volkskammer: parliament of the GDR
Volksparteien: people's parties
Vorruhestandsgeld: early retirement benefit
West Germany: former FRG, prior to unification
west Germany: territory of the former FRG since unification
Wissenschaftsrat: Council for the Humanities and Sciences
Zentralwohlfahrtsstelle: central welfare agency (Jewish)

Index